$35   1/28/88

Public Administration

PUBLIC ADMINISTRATION AND PUBLIC POLICY

A Comprehensive Publication Program

Executive Editor

JACK RABIN
Graduate Program in
Public Affairs and
Human Services
Administration
Rider College
Lawrenceville, New Jersey

Other volumes in preparation

Public Administration
*A Bibliographic Guide
to the Literature*

Howard E. McCurdy

College of Public and
International Affairs
The American University
Washington, D.C.

MARCEL DEKKER, INC.   New York and Basel

Library of Congress Cataloging in Publication Data

McCurdy, Howard E.
    Public Administration

    (Public administration and public policy ; 29)
    Includes index.
    1. Public administration--Bibliography.   I. Title
II. Series.
Z7164.A2M29 1985   (JF1351) 016.35 85-25436
ISBN 0-8247-7518-X

MARCEL DEKKER, INC.
279 Madison Avenue, New York, New York 10016

Current printing (last digit):
10 9 8 7 6 5 4 3 2 1

PRINTED IN THE UNITED STATES OF AMERICA

Preface

To the practitioner seeking a bit of advice or the student trying to understand the operation of government, a journey into
the literature of public administration can be a bewildering
experience. The collective wisdom of public administration
emerges from at least six separate fields and disciplines; bits
of knowledge sought by one set of experts may be hidden
behind another's disciplinary boundary; principles drawn from
one field have a tendency to contradict lessons drawn from
additional sources; no unifying theory exists to help guide the
investigator. Experts frequently cannot agree upon a definition
of public administration. Some view the subject broadly so as
to include the entire process of running a modern government,
while others view it as narrowly confined to the administrative
policies that governments formulate, such as laws regulating
the hiring and firing of personnel. The field comes from so
many places -- and leads to so many subjects -- that even
people who make a profession out of studying the subject have
trouble keeping up with it all.

This bibliography seeks to provide students, practitioners, and
scholars with an orientation guide to the body of knowledge

that supports the study and practice of public administration. The bulk of that knowledge is to be found in books. Practically all of the important discoveries to emerge since the formal study of public administration began have been recorded in books. Findings which were first put forward as journal articles have found their way into books, expanded into book-length works or published within anthologies. This bibliography identifies the most frequently cited books in public administration, 181 in all. Through short reviews, the bibliography identifies the principal findings of each work and the contribution that it has made. These reviews form the basis for two essays which outline the development of public administration as a formal field of study, an enterprise that is hardly one hundred years old. The first essay, which opens this volume, examines recent developments. The second essay provides a historic overview. Finally, the bibliography identifies thirty-three specialized areas of study within public administration and lists some 1200 books within them. These thirty-three areas represent the field of study broadly defined, from the grand questions of political philosophy to the practical problems of supervising public employees.

In 1972, I prepared a similar guide to the field which was published by the College of Public and International Affairs at the American University. This is a new work. It has a new publisher, the essays and reviews have been rewritten, it contains new books, and the field has changed in important ways. It reports on the refocusing of the field which took place in the 1970s and the opening of a fourth "era" of public administration in 1980. The structure of the two books remains the same, but readers will find the contents to be quite different.

All of the books in this bibliography were identified by cross referencing a series of reading lists, textbook citations, and specialized bibliographies prepared by experts in the field. For a book to climb into this bibliography, it had to be cited by a number of people working in the field of public administration and the disciplines associated with it. In all, eighty-one lists were cross referenced to create the ranking scheme used in this guide. The books that emerge are the ones that people working in the field consider to be significant; this is not in any way the personal collection of a single individual.

The cross referencing scheme requires a book to prove its staying power before it moves into the "most frequently cited" category. This is accomplished, in part, by cross referencing lists of books from different periods of time. After much experimentation, I decided to adopt this procedure rather than use lists of books strictly from the most recent set of years. Under this procedure, people must continue to use and cite a book in order for it to stand high in the rankings. Just because a book is a best seller one year, or addresses a hot new management reform in another, does not guarantee that the work will have a sustained influence on the field of study. It may be very popular for a year or so, but make no long-term contribution to the development of the field. An important book, on the other hand, will be cited continuously for a number of years as proof of its value. It takes time for important books to climb up in the ranking. This bibliography deliberately errs on the side of caution in recognizing important new titles, just as it is slow to push an important book off of the ranking once its contribution is established.

This method of construction means that recently published books (those which have been issued in the last five years) tend to be underemphasized in the ranking. Since it is slow to recognize new titles, readers will find it useful to use this bibliography in conjunction with an up-to-date textbook on public administration. As a reference work, the bibliography records the established judgement of people in the field concerning the books that support our long-term understanding of public administration. A good textbook will complement this with an assessment of new developments in research and practice that may turn into established contributions.

I hope that this bibliography assists students and practitioners in acquiring a sense of orientation, helping them to find their bearings among all of the works that have made a contribution to the study and practice of public administration. I still remember the disconcerted feeling I had when my own professors handed me what seemed like an endless list of books and urged me to read the most important ones in order to earn my degree. This bibliography is dedicated to all students of public administration, especially those who encounter the field for the first time and must read and understand that literature. It is also directed to all of those legislators and administrators who support the schools that educate those students. They are to be complimented for their insight in recognizing the need to educate students in administration as a means for improving the performance of the public service. Not only does this bibliography provide a list of some of the books that ought to be in their libraries, I hope that it promotes a deeper understanding of a field of study that does not always fit into the traditional mold of academic disciplines.

I am indebted to Wanda Baez, Barbara Schwemle, Vincent Cipriani and Michael Bindner, my research assistants, who did much of the basic work involved in the construction of this bibliography. Many persons helped with the task of designing a computer program that could be used to organize and typeset the book: Sherry Joy, Linda Thurston, Thomas Southall, and Jim Roberts of the Quantitative Research Lab in the College of Public and International Affairs. My research assistants and I wish to express our appreciation to all of the authors and teachers who responded to our calls for advice and lists of books. In particular, I want to thank the persons who provided special assistance, encouragement, or allowed me a forum in which to test my findings: Guy Adams, Gerald Caiden, Robert Cleary, Jean Courturier, Larry Keller, Joe Robertson, and Jay Shafritz. All errors, of course, are mine.

Howard E. McCurdy

Contents

Contents

Public Administration

I Back to the Mainstream: Recent Trends in the Development of Public Administration

Public administration can be viewed as a political process, one of the methods of governing a large and diverse nation. Public administration can be viewed as a matter of good management, the principle means for carrying out the various functions of the state. Many people view it as consisting of both politics and administration. Since public servants who manage public programs work in small groups, improving the performance of government agencies can be viewed as a problem in the social psychology of group dynamics. Since big governments operate on the basis of big bureaus, public administration can be viewed as part of the sociological development of a bureaucratic society.

Public administration can be approached as a problem in economics, not only because the science of economics underlies taxing and spending, but because economics contains theories about the incentives that prod large institutions to improve their performance or go out of business. In a constitutional system, public administration must operate within the precepts of law, making it a matter of administrative due process. In an age of science and technology, public administration

1

responds to new developments in computer technology and automated information systems.

Public administration as a field of study can be viewed as all of these things: good government, business-like management, group dynamics, bureaucratic sociology, economic science, legal due process, computer technology and a host of smaller but also important processes. At the end of the 1960s, when the field had just gone through a period of transition, it tried to be all of these things. In trying to be all of these things, specialists in public administration reached out to other fields and disciplines that contained these different perspectives, borrowing books and ideas from them. The borrowing became so frantic, in fact, that most of the top-ranked books used by people in the field never specifically addressed problems of public administration. They dealt with organizations in general, business management, or human behavior, and were often written by people who did not have an extensive knowledge of the challenges posed by administrative operations in the public sector. Worried that this flood of imported knowledge would contribute little to the improvement of governmental administration, scholars devoted to the study of public administration began to complain that people promoting the use of these types of books had lost their bearings, forgetting the original reason for going off in search of all this knowledge in the first place. In the words of Professor Dwight Waldo, public administration was in danger of becoming a field without "a unifying center."

As public administration moved into the 1980s, the field of study returned to its central concerns. Although the borrowing from other fields and disciplines continues, creating a most eclectic base of knowledge, that base is now organized around a core of books that translate knowledge from diverse sources into lessons for public servants. Public administration has returned to the mainstream, and with it to the recognition that administration in the public sector ultimately must be viewed as part of the governing process.

This essay reveals these developments by comparing books from two sets of rankings -- one produced as the field made the transition from the 1960s to 1970s, the second as the field moved from the 1970s into the 1980s. The two sets of rankings, which form the basis for this reference guide, show in a remarkable way the effect of recent trends on the development of public administration. Both rankings were created by cross referencing a representative cross-section of reading lists, textbook citations, and bibliographies covering particular areas of study which were prepared by experts in the field. Forty lists were merged to create the first ranking; forty-one lists were combined to produce the second ranking. The first ranking was used to produce the bibliography I published in 1972.

The two rankings produce what might be called the "top twenty" books in public administration (Tables 1 and 2). Each of these tables captures a picture of public administration as specialists viewed it in the years around 1970 and again in the 1980s.

The first table is dominated by books from the behavioral revolution, which at that time had just completed its sweep through the social and managerial sciences. These books did not treat administration in government as intrinsically different from administration in general. Books such as March and Simon's Organizations and Douglas McGregor's Human Side of Enterprise were applied as easily to business administration as to public administration. In fact, business administration is strongly represented on the first ranking -- both traditional texts such as Koontz and O'Donnell's Principles of Management and books from the then-emerging field of management science. In the first ranking, only three books specifically address issues of governmental administration, and one of those was written by a sociologist. Scholars at that time were correct when they explained that public administration was undergoing a crisis of identity, uncertain of its subject matter, as its builders searched through different fields and disciplines for knowledge they could use.

Look at how much that situation changes in the second ranking, the list of books based on more recent sources of citations (Table 2). Fully one-half of the books on the new "top twenty" are center, mainstream public administration. They deal with the following subjects: the politics of the budgetary process, the politics of bureaucratic power, the politics of government organization, democracy and the civil service, the problems of implementing public programs, and the relationship of public administration to political theory. Twelve books --

Table 1.   The Most Frequently Cited Books
From the First Ranking (1972)

Abbreviated Author & Title	No. of Citations
1. Cartwright & Zander, Group Dynamics	16
2. Wildavsky, Politics of the Budgetary Process	15
3. March & Simon, Organizations	14
3. March, Handbook of Organizations	14
3. Simon, Administrative Behavior	14
6. Barnard, Functions of the Executive	13
7. McGregor, Human Side of Enterprise	12
7. Rubenstein & Haberstroh, Theories of Organization	12
9. Gulick & Urwick, Papers on the Science of Administration	11
9. Merton, Reader in Bureaucracy	11
11. Bennis, Changing Organizations	10
11. Haire, Modern Organization Theory	10
11. Homans, The Human Group	10
11. Koontz & O'Donnell, Principles of Management	10
11. Leavitt, Managerial Psychology	10
11. Likert, New Patterns of Management	10
11. Selznick, TVA and the Grass Roots	10
11. Selznick, Leadership in Administration	10
11. Truman, The Governmental Process	10

or sixty percent of the titles on the new "top twenty" -- are addressed specifically to issues of governmental administration, as compared to only three books on the first table.

It is hard to imagine how public administration could center itself around studies that did not deal with government, yet this was the case in the years leading up to 1972. Among the most frequently cited books from that ranking (over 150 books in all), sixty percent came from fields of study that held no particular distinction between between business administration, public administration, or any other type of administration. The largest single bloc of books came from organization theory -- twenty-six percent in all. To the extent that the the field of public administration emerged from the 1960s with any focus at all, as reflected in the first set of rankings, it would have to be the politically neutered area of organization theory and behavior.

Table 2.   The Most Frequently Cited Books
From the Second Ranking (1985)

Abbreviated Author & Title	No. of Citations
1. Wildavsky, Politics of the Budgetary Process	21
2. Barnard, Functions of the Executive	17
2. March & Simon, Organizations	17
3. Rourke, Bureaucracy, Politics & Public Policy	16
3. Simon, Administrative Behavior	16
6. Gulick & Urwick, Papers on the Science of Administration	15
6. Mosher, Democracy and the Public Service	15
8. Pressman & Wildavsky, Implementation	14
8. Seidman, Politics, Position & Power	14
10. Crozier, Bureaucratic Phenomenon	13
10. Katz & Kahn, Social Psychology of Organizations	13
10. Lyden & Miller, Public Budgeting	13
13. Downs, Inside Bureaucracy	12
13. McGregor, Human Side of Enterprise	12
13. Marini, Toward a New Public Administration	12
13. Weiss, Evaluation Research	12
17. Haveman & Margolis, Public Expenditures & Policy Analysis	11
17. Schick, Budget Innovation in the States	11
17. Stahl, Public Personnel Administration	11
17. Waldo, Administrative State	11

The new ranking clearly displays a reversal of that trend. Seventy percent of the top 150 books based on recent citations deal with issues of governmental administration, as compared to only forty percent of the top 150 books from the old ranking. In the new ranking, the largest single bloc of books deal with politics, policy making and political theory. Holding onto one-fourth of the new top 150, they dominate the field of study today in the same way that the behavioral revolution dominated it in the 1950s and 1960s. The influence of these politically sensitive books is complemented in the new ranking by works that deal with public policy analysis, public finance and budgeting, public personnel administration, and state and local administration -- all areas of study rooted in the study of government and all of which increased their share in the new top 150.

As these governmentally sensitive areas gained in importance
in the new ranking, others areas less oriented toward the
public service lost ground. The behavioral revolution, remembered in classics such as Chester Barnard's Functions of the
Executive, remains a powerful influence in the memory of
public administration. As a proportion of the whole, however,
books on organization theory dropped from a quarter of the
whole to less than ten percent of the new top 150. The
applied behavioral sciences, which go by the title of organization development and are represented by books such as Rensis
Likert's New Patterns of Management, are the only exception
to the diminution of the behavioral trend. They hold onto a
ten percent share of the top-cited titles in both the old and
the new set of rankings.

The citing of business management and management science
texts, which is quite pronounced in the first ranking, drops off
significantly in the new top 150. This fact reflects the
refound confidence among public administrators in using their
own approaches to solving problems of governmental administration. The study of comparative public administration,
launched by the attempt to export modern public management
to the less developed countries, placed well in the first ranking, then practically disappeared in the second. The books
from the first fifty years of public administration dwindled in
importance as the memory of the era of orthodoxy grew dim.
The study of bureaucracy, launched by Max Weber's famous
essay on the subject, generated enough new titles on the agony
of operating governments with bureaucratic organizations to
maintain a modest share of the new top 150.

In shifting its attention toward administrative problems in the
public service, especially those where politics plays a role, the
field of public administration recommitted itself to practical
problem-solving. Public administration remains an applied field
of study, significantly oriented toward practice. This orientation reveals itself particularly well if one concentrates on a
special set of books in the second ranking -- books that not
only placed high in the second ranking but also were newly
published or recognized (Table 3).

Practical guides to public administration are very well represented. The titles dealing with policy analysis are how-to-do-it
books: how to do program evaluation, how to do economic

analysis, and how to engage in "systematic thinking." The book by Richard Nathan is an evaluation report. Among the titles on finance and budgeting, one is a textbook, one explains how to do PPBS, and a third explains how to do zero-base budgeting. Proceeding further into this bibliography, one can find books on how to do personnel administration, operations research, organization development, organization structure, how to motivate employees and how to manage change. Roughly forty percent of the most important titles in public administration are practical instruction manuals.

No science can exist on applications alone. Someone must do the descriptive work upon which the applications are based. Among the most frequently cited books that appear in this

Table 3. The Most Frequently Cited Books From the Second Ranking (Newly Published Titles Only)

Abbreviated Author & Title	No. of Citations
1. Pressman & Wildavsky, Implementation	14
1. Seidman, Politics, Position & Power	14
3. Marini, Toward a New Public Administration	12
3. Weiss, Evaluation Research	12
5. Haveman & Margolis, Public Expenditures & Policy Analysis	11
5. Schick, Budget Innovation in the States	11
7. Dvorin & Simmons, Amoral to Humane Bureaucracy	10
7. Merewitz & Sosnick, The Budget's New Clothes	10
9. Pyhrr, Zero-Base Budgeting	9
10. Allison, Essence of Decision	8
10. Hoos, Systems Analysis in Public Policy	8
10. Mainzer, Political Bureaucracy	8
10. Ostrom, Intellectual Crisis in American PA	8
10. Reagan, New Federalism	8
10. Rivlin, Systematic Thinking for Social Action	8
10. Waldo, Public Administration in a Time of Turbulence	8
17. Benveniste, The Politics of Expertise	7
17. Heclo, A Government of Strangers	7
17. Kaufman, Administrative Feedback	7
17. Krislov, Representative Bureaucracy	7
17. Lee & Johnson, Public Budgeting Systems	7
17. Nathan, Monitoring Revenue Sharing	7
17. Perrow, Complex Organizations	7

bibliography, roughly as many books are descriptive or scholarly as applied. Those descriptive titles are also well represented on Table 3. Harold Seidman describes how politics shapes government organizations, Lewis Mainzer describes the politics of accountability, Guy Benveniste describes the politics of planning, Pressman and Wildavksy describe the politics of implementation, Hugh Heclo describes the politics of personnel, and Graham Allison explains bureaucratic politics. Michael Reagan reports on new developments in federalism and Herbert Kaufman explains how government executives find out what their subordinates are doing. Descriptive, scholarly studies such as these are the foundation of the field. As more and more of them are done on governmental administration -- as opposed to administration in general -- the applications that grow out of them become more sensitive to the particular issues involved in managing government organizations.

Public administration is only in part a problem of management technology. Public administration is also part of the governing process, of deciding what is to be done and who shall carry the burden. In the last decade, public administration has moved closer to issues of governance. In the process, administrative theory has drawn more frequently on history, ethics and political philosophy. This trend is exceptionally well represented on Table 3.

One third of the titles on Table 3 advocate new approaches to governmental administration or challenge tenants that underlie the field. The books by Marini and Waldo call for a new public administration. The book by Dvorin and Simmons advocates a more humane, proactive bureaucracy. Krislov's study explains why governments must represent minorities and women within the civil service in order to promote political stability. Ostrom's book advances the case for abandoning the Wilson-Weberian view of public administration and turning instead to what is known as the "public choice" approach. Ida Hoos attacks the efforts of systems analysts to make public administration more "objective." Even Perrow's book on organization theory, where one would expect to find a purely descriptive tome, turns out to be a polemic on behalf of bureaucratic organization.

These books represent the degree to which public administration has been forced, for a variety of reasons, to reconsider many of the assumptions that support government in the modern administrative state. Often these books proceed from a fairly high philosophic, political or social plane; generally they wind up making recommendations about how to change our approaches to governmental administration. Though growing in importance, such "outward looking" books by no means dominate the field. They hold onto less than twenty percent of the top-cited books in this bibliography. Nonetheless, their importance in shaping basic approaches to the study and practice of public administration make them an important influence in the field.

All of these trends appear in the bibliography and are discussed in more detail in the essay that follows. The older trends and the newer directions are represented with equal force. Newer trends are not overrepresented simply because they are new; mature trends are not discarded because they are old. As a field of study, public administration has a half-life approaching twenty years. This means that roughly half of the most frequently cited books in this bibliography are less than twenty years old; the other half predate the mid-1960s. In practical terms, someone who graduated from a public affairs program twenty years ago would be unfamiliar with about half of the most important books in the field if that person had not gone back to school or kept up with their reading.

Twenty years is a fairly long half-life as sciences and disciplines go. Some branches of medicine, for example, have a half-life of four years. Public administration, by contrast, contains books with important lessons that first appeared more than twenty years ago. It is worth noting that the top three books on Table 2 were all published prior to 1965, even though this is a table based on recent citation frequencies. When asked to list their favorite books, modern experts rank old books highly. Any bibliographic guide to the literature of public administration must represent both the old and the new. This guide is constructed in such a way as to do this. It is a bibliography with a memory.

II Knowledge Supports Practice: The Development of Public Administration

KNOWLEDGE SUPPORTS PRACTICE

No modern farmer would attempt to practice agriculture without a knowledge of the sciences upon which it is based. Neither a doctor nor an engineer could be caught unaware of the scientific findings that support their professions. Increasingly, the same can be said for public administration. It is becoming a field of practice based upon applied sciences.

This was not always so. The systematic study of public administration is hardly one hundred years old, yet people have been practicing public administration ever since governments arose. We know something about ancient public administration and how it was employed to raise temples, construct public works, regulate water rights, manage cities, organize armies, administer empires, keep records and collect taxes. We know that the Egyptians had a large bureaucracy centered at Thebes and that some blame the fall of the Roman empire in part on a bloated civil service that grew too large for the resources of the empire to support it.*

In those days public managers were not trained in administration per se. Many received training in the policy being administered, as the manager of a public works project might study engineering. Some received an education in the liberal arts, as in ancient China and the modern British empire, where generalists were expected to rule. Others simply relied upon personal experience acquired on one job after another.

This approach, as one early administrative scientist pointed out, led to a wild assortment of methods and opinions. There is no "lack of methods," wrote Henri Fayol, "but good and bad are to be found side by side at the same time in the home, workshop and State. . . . Each one thinks that he has the best methods and everywhere there may be observed . . . the most contradictory practices under the aegis of the same principle" (Fayol, 1916, p. 10). The assorted methods proved unreliable, sporadic in their successes and inescapable in their failure.

Public administration was practiced like this for thousands of years. One hundred years ago a significant event occurred. People who were familiar with cases of successful administration began to record their insights, extract the lessons contained therein, and offer the lessons to novices as training in administration. The movement began with more resolve in the realm of business administration, where aspiring capitalists discovered that the success stories of industrialization could be explained not so much by good luck or hard work as by the application of right principles. The notion penetrated public administration slowly, but eventually the effect was the same. Executives came to realize that good administration could be studied and taught.

As a scholarly field of study, public administration possesses many of the characteristics of an academic discipline, especially as that term is applied in the twentieth century. As a

---

* The Roman thesis can be found in J. H. Hofmeyr, "Civil Service in Ancient Times," in Nimrod Raphaeli, ed., Readings in Comparative Public Administration, Boston: Allyn and Bacon, 1976, pp. 69-91. One of the best histories of administrative practice is E. N. Gladden, A History of Public Administration, 2 vols. London: Frank Cass, 1972.

field of practice, public administration is becoming increasingly professionalized. Yet public administration is not exactly a profession nor precisely a discipline if one applies the historic standards defining such terms. Public administration is a distinctly modern field of study, often difficult to define except on its own terms.

Public Administration Is Like a Profession

Public administration exists to be practiced. The lessons of public administration, like law or medicine, are directed at people who would be practitioners. In the realm of practice, public administration resembles a profession. Strictly speaking, it is not a profession in the tradition of law or medicine, where entrance to practice is regulated through special examinations, boards, or licensing procedures. Nevertheless, public administration shares with law, medicine and other professions a number of common elements. One is especially important. The practice of public administration rests upon a body of knowledge which the practitioner is expected to comprehend.

Professions, by definition, are based upon bodies of "specialized knowledge (requiring) intensive preparation including instruction in skills and methods as well as the scientific, historical, or scholarly principles underlying such skills and methods" (Webster's, 1976, p. 1811). Increasingly this is true for public administration as education and training programs flourish and executive development becomes a prerequisite for higher level service. Additionally, a profession is expected to have for "its prime purpose the rendering of a public service" and generally organizes itself into professional associations so as to maintain "high standards of achievement and conduct" (Webster's, 1976, p. 1811).

The professional character of public administration means that the practitioner of administration, like the practitioner of law or medicine, is obliged to become proficient in the elements of the field through study and practice. It is not enough to rely upon personal experience, a liberal education, or training in a technical field. The practitioner must understand the sciences that underlie management and administration. The political executive to whom the practitioner reports and the public that the practitioner serves have a right to expect this, just as they have a right to expect that their personal physician has finished medical school.

Most professions are still practiced as arts, and public administration is no exception. Even medicine, based upon sciences as hard as they get, remains in practice much a matter of art. In the realm of public administration, principles remain imprecise and the underlying sciences are still incomplete. In diagnosing and resolving administrative problems, practitioners must combine the underlying bodies of knowledge with judgement, intuition, and experience. The element of art, however, does not mean that public administration is all intuition. The practitioner practicing an art still has to master the underlying bodies of knowledge.

What then is that body of knowledge that the practitioner must master? In a phrase, it is the knowledge base of public administration: the field of study. Assembled largely within professional schools of public administration, the field of study has taken on many of the characteristics of a modern academic discipline.

A Modern Discipline

In the dictionary, an academic discipline is defined simply as "a field of study" (Webster's, 1976, p. 644). Public administration has developed into a field of study, never simply. As a field of study, public administration lacks the simplicity of the older, more traditional academic disciplines to which it is often compared.

To begin its loss of simplicity, the field of study evolved in such a way as not to be based upon a single science. It is based upon many. Dwight Waldo, in his discussion of education for public administration, observes:

> Administration has as its purpose preparation for careers. . . . No single discipline, as these are now constituted and named, provides the knowledge base for preparation for such careers. No single discipline even comes close; instead, many disciplines and foci now contribute and should contribute. (Waldo, 1975, p. 233)

Waldo likens the situation to that of medicine, which is based upon a number of sciences, from anatomy to biochemistry. Like medicine, public administration lacks a "single, unified theory of illness and health, theories and the technologies based on them constantly change, there are vast unknowns, there is bitter controversy over . . . questions of vital importance, (and) the element of 'art' remains large and important" (Waldo, 1975, pp. 223-4).

Public administration rests upon a foundation of primary and secondary sciences. It draws significantly on economics, sociology, psychology, political science, and one field of study which is just as diverse as public administration: business administration. In Europe, the study of law must be added to this list, as public and administrative law provide an important foundation for administrative practice. Public administration draws with less force, but still importantly, from mathematics, philosophy and ethics, history, the computer sciences, education, industrial and labor relations, and even architecture, from which comes urban planning. Students of public administration will borrow a good idea from any place that they can find it. They will even borrow books from authors who were not really thinking about public administration when they drafted their books. In preparing this bibliography, I found that roughly half of the most frequently cited books in the field were written by authors writing for other fields of study and not -- at least not primarily -- for public administration.

The presence of so much borrowing creates one of the most difficult aspects of public administration. It creates the illusion that public administration consists of nothing but material borrowed from other fields. It encourages the idea that public administration does not itself constitute a field of study.

Nothing could be further from the truth. Among the most frequently cited books listed in this bibliography, some forty-six percent were written by persons who view public administration as their primary field of study, who are practitioners of public administration, or who -- even though they may reside in departments of political science or schools of management -- have made direct contributions to the subject through writing textbooks or publishing articles in leading journals in the field. Two points of comparison may prove helpful here. The discipline from which public administration most frequently borrows is economics; the discipline from which public administration emerged is political science. Among the most frequently cited books in this bibliography, thirteen percent were contributed by persons whose primary field of study is economics. Seven percent were contributed by persons specializing in political science. The forty-six percent contributed by specialists in public administration, therefore, is by contrast a sizeable number.

Most certainly, public administration relies upon the contributing disciplines of economics, political science, sociology, psychology, philosophy, history, mathematics, and fields such as computer science, architecture, law, business administration, education and industrial relations. It relies upon them, it draws books from them, yet at the same time it consists of more than them. In effect, there is a field of public administration within the field of public administration. This idea is difficult to grasp, no doubt, but public administration does not promise to be a simple thing.

To comprehend this relationship, it is useful to see the shape of the entire field of study. This is portrayed on the adjoining page. At the base of the field of study are the disciplines and fields that support public administration: social sciences like economics and amorphous fields like business administration. Rising above them are the various schools of thought within which authors and scholars tend to collect. People in the behavioral school, for example, have a much different view of administration than specialists from the orthodox school. It would be simpler if the specialists would agree upon a single school or approach, but that would be uncharacteristic of the field.

Building upon the fields, disciplines and schools of thought are special areas of application, such as policy analysis or personnel administration. It is here that the core knowledge is translated into applied science for consumption by practitioners. Occasionally, an area of application grows up that is not directed at practice, but provides an area where scholars gather to study a particular phenomenon such as the growth of bureaucracy.

Into this structure flow the books, ideas, and research findings that comprise the knowledge base of public administration.

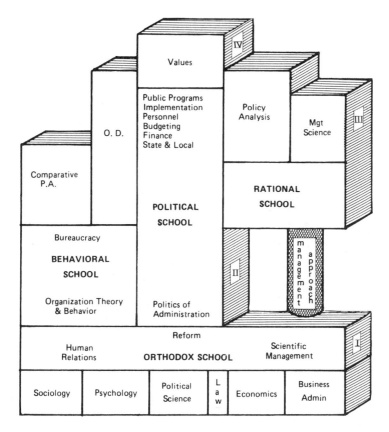

Figure 1. The Knowledge Base of Public Administration

This figure represents the development of public administration, beginning with the contributing fields and disciplines at the base of the structure, moving up through the major schools of thought (in capital letters), and on to the areas of application where research findings are translated into practice. The figure also records the four major periods through which the field has progressed (the roman numerals on the side).

I.   The Orthodox Era (1880-1945)
II.   The Period of Description (1945-1965)
III.   The Era of Applications (1965-1980)
IV.   A Period of Reconsideration (Present)

Much is borrowed from other fields; much is contributed by persons specializing in public administration.

If one insists on locating a core that is closest to the center of public administration, then look to the political school of thought. This is the central pillar in the field of study, the dominant school of thought, assuredly in the United States and frequently abroad. Here one finds the greatest number of authors for whom public administration is their primary field of study. Here one finds very little borrowing.

At the other extreme one finds areas of application where the propensity to borrow is most pronounced. The best books in these areas have been collected from authors writing from points of view well removed from the realm of governmental administration. Books written by people specializing in public administration appear less often. The organization development field, an outgrowth of the behavioral school, illustrates this trend. While frequently cited by both practitioners and scholars of public administration, the leading books in organization development have been authored almost entirely by people from other fields and disciplines. Moreover, people in many other fields and disciplines use these books, from business administration to social psychology.*

----

* People who write from the perspective of public administration tend to dominate the political school, the study of comparative public administration, public personnel administration, and state and local administration. They dominate the study of values, although books by political scientists and economists are well represented among the most frequently cited titles there. Specialists in public administration share almost equally with economists the study of finance and budgeting. They share the most frequently cited books in organization theory and behavior with sociologists, psychologists, and people from the field of business administration. The two fields of public administration and business administration contribute most of the books still cited from the orthodox era and the management approach. When one enters the realm of policy analysis, the number of specialists in public administration falls off. A majority of the leading books from the policy approach used in public administration are authored by economists and political

As a field of study, then, public administration is two things. It is first of all the total body of knowledge that is brought to bear on the practice of administering public programs, a structure of understanding drawn from a variety of sources. It is second of all those people who specialize in public administration. They radiate out from the center to the ends of the field of study. It would be nice, for the sake of simplicity, if they would stay put in one place. They do not, however. They spread themselves throughout the entire structure, like the nails holding together a house. It would be as difficult to draw a simple diagram around them as it would be for an architect to draw a blueprint for a house that showed only the positions of the nails.

Clearly, this is not an edifice that resembles the more unified social sciences that support public administration: political science, economics, sociology, or psychology. When political scientists look at public administration, they shudder. They do not see a conventional academic discipline -- certainly not one that fits the criteria of political science.

Public administration, however, cannot be defined strictly in the same manner as political science and the "older" social sciences. As a field of study, public administration emerged under vastly different conditions than political science. The older social sciences emerged and were defined in response to conditions set up by nineteenth century academe. They emerged from a period in which many academics hoped to build a single, unifying social science. To prove their right to secede from this dream, newly emerging disciplines such as political science had to confine themselves "to a single area of social reality" (Nisbet, 1976, p. 988). To enhance their claim to separate social science status, they were expected to

---

scientists. Although specialists in public administration are represented among the people studying bureaucracy, most of the important books are authored by sociologists. Public administration defers to social psychology, psychology, and business administration for the best books on organization development (OD). It turns to a number of fields, from mathematics and computer sciences to business administration for the leading books on management science and the systems approach.

possess clear boundaries, address specific objects of study, and utilize scientific methods of inquiry.

Areas of study which could not meet these stiff tests were forced to remain as subfields within larger disciplines. Those which could meet the tests were allowed to construct themselves as separate academic departments within universities, the ultimate test of whether or not a field of study had achieved disciplinary status. (Public administration, given that criterion, has not done badly. A recent survey by the National Association of Schools of Public Affairs and Administration revealed that fifty percent of its members had achieved separate institutional status, compared to thirty-eight percent still caught within departments of political science.)

By the time that public administration was ready to blossom as a field of study, the defining characteristics of the social science disciplines had started to change. What was started in the nineteenth century was altered by developments in the twentieth.

As the social sciences moved through the twentieth century, the best of the disciplines increased their base of knowledge to the point where experts had to specialize in particular areas of study in order to maintain their standing as masters of their fields. As understanding of social phenomena grew, social science disciplines were increasingly used as instruments for making policy. Their popularity spread out into society and across national boundaries. Once adopted as policy making instruments, the disciplines began to take on the characteristics of professions. At the turn of the century, members of the social sciences worked largely within academic institutions, preoccupied with teaching and research. Sixty years later, many had ventured out into positions of power. In the most successful social sciences today, such as economics, there are easily as many members of the discipline working outside of academic institutions (in government agencies and business enterprises) as within them.

The old social sciences emerged against a backdrop of unification and academic justification. Members of the new social sciences confronted demands for differentiation, diffusion, and professionalization. This created a different set of problems. People studying the new social sciences encountered a bewildering array of specializations, some jumping across disciplinary boundaries, others growing narrower within them. To be relevant, a code word for professional success, new social sciences had to reach out across the artificial boundaries of the older disciplines and the new fields of study that were emerging from them.

American public administration emerged in concert with these forces. It began as a specialization within political science. It took on a professional orientation by focusing on practical applications and the needs of practitioners. In seeking to be relevant, it discovered that it needed blocs of knowledge from fields beyond the mother discipline. Transcendence became a greater challenge than differentiation. To specialize was to languish; to reach across boundaries was to survive.

Had the framing ground of the nineteenth century never existed, public administration would find itself as one of the premier social science disciplines of the twentieth century. It embraces many specializations, yet transcends them all. It possesses a solid professional orientation and has spread worldwide as an area of practice and study. By the defining criteria of the late twentieth century, it looks like an academic discipline. It is as characteristic of the criteria defining social science disciplines today as the older disciplines are of the times in which they emerged.

The Field of Study

Like a profession, like a discipline, based on science but still retaining art, public administration rests upon a body of knowledge that continues to grow in richness and complexity. What follows is a guide to that knowledge base, to the schools of thought and areas of application and the most frequently cited books in the field. It is a journey through the knowledge accumulated from the past that is used in the present. This is the knowledge base that must be mastered for modern times.

THE SHADOW OF ORTHODOXY

The knowledge base of public administration can be viewed as a series of building blocks laid alongside and on top of one another, all resting upon a foundation of supporting fields and disciplines. The established blocks have been laid down in three distinct periods: an era of orthodoxy, a period of description, and an era of applications. A fourth period, an era of reconsideration, tops off the structure. This essay goes back to the beginning when the first blocks were laid down in order to inspect each of the blocks and reveal how it was put in place.

The formative era of public administration lasted nearly sixty years, from the 1880s to the 1940s, and left an impression on the field of study that even the most radically modern scholars have not been able to escape. It was a period shaped by persons who promoted sound opinion and conventional principles, the traditional definition of an orthodox point of view. The orthodox era emphasized good administration, more efficiency, better productivity, and practical applications, making it one of the primary schools of thought in public administration. Although not much is being written from the orthodox point of view any more, the orthodox writers left three strong imprints on the field: reform, science, and human relations. These are the shadows that the orthodox period casts into the modern era.

The Reform Movement

American public administration was a child of the progressive reform movement, born of a marriage that joined civic leaders with university professors. The civic leaders sought to destroy the patronage or spoils system under which victorious candidates for office installed members of their own political party in administrative offices without regard, it was said, for the technical requirements of the job. The professors were anxious to write about the movement and work within it. This was a lengthy union. It saw the passage of the U.S. Civil Service Reform Act (1883), the establishment of the National Municipal League (1894), the formation of the New York Bureau of Municipal Research (1906), and the creation of the Public Administration Clearing House in Chicago in the late 1920s. It firmly established the orientation of public administration toward practical applications and the creation of a common language that both practitioners and scholars still speak when they gather together in professional associations: words like merit system, legislative oversight, government corporation, and executive budget.

The reformers discovered, as they won and lost elections, that they knew little more about running government than the bosses they replaced. Early reformers possessed grievances and doctrine, but few administrative principles. One of the first reformers credited with calling attention to the paucity of knowledge about good administration was a young political science professor at Bryn Mawr College. Writing in the June, 1887 issue of the Political Science Quarterly, in an article titled "The Study of Administration," he called upon fellow scholars to spend less time debating great constitutional issues and more time studying governmental management. "It is getting harder to run a constitution," he wrote, "than to frame one" (Wilson, 1887, p. 484). The author was Woodrow Wilson, who would become President of the United States one quarter century later. The essay is generally taken to be the symbolic beginning of the formal study of American public administration.

Thirteen years later, in 1900, a reformer and scholar at Columbia University published an analysis of municipal administration and the spoils system titled Politics and Administration. The author, Frank Goodnow, made many contributions to American public administration, including his work on administrative law and his proposals for a centralized system of executive management, yet he is remembered most for the doctrine embodied in the title of that book: the doctrine that politics should be separate from administration.

The politics-administration dichotomy that he helped to promote operated on a number of levels. First, there was the reformers' doctrine that political bosses had no business interfering in practical public administration, whether through patronage, favoritism, or meddling in the execution of law. Reformers expressed this through the observation that "there is no Republican way to build a road." Let the politicians define the job to be done, then leave the administrative experts alone to do it professionally.

This point of view implied that administrators would engage solely in administration and not involve themselves in the creation of public policy. The separation of policy making from administration was the second major intellectual heritage of the reform movement. The idea that the job to be done can be clearly defined before administration begins still underlies many reforms that are promoted in the modern public service, from management by objectives to program evaluation.

Finally, the politics-administration dichotomy implies that good administration can be isolated from the political regime under which it is practiced. Good administration is presumed to be good administration, no matter where one finds it. A totalitarian state, no matter what one thinks of its policies, can be well administered if its civil service is guided by the right principles. Woodrow Wilson was one of the first to articulate this idea. "If I see a murderous fellow sharpening a knife cleverly," said Wilson, "I can borrow his way of sharpening the knife without borrowing his probable intention" (Wilson, 1887, p. 504).

The politics-administration dichotomy, for all of its apparent simplicity, has proved to be terribly controversial. Administrative realists thought that they had stamped it out and closed the orthodox era, but the doctrine has simply reappeared in different forms. The politics-administration dichotomy has been debated, discredited, revived and disowned every few years since the end of the orthodox era, proving again and again how attractive the doctrine really is when politicians start to interfere in the business of administering public programs.

Slowly at first, the reformers began to recognize the need to train public servants in the newly-articulated elements of public administration. In 1912, the American Political Science Association created a Committee on Practical Training for Public Service, and in 1914 university programs in municipal and public administration began to appear. In 1926 the first textbook on public administration was published, the author a professor from the University of Chicago named Leonard D. White. By 1939 the Committee on Practical Training had evolved into the American Society for Public Administration (ASPA), still the premier association in the field. With the creation of ASPA, extended by events to follow, public administration was ready to begin its slow departure from the realm of political science and establish itself as a separate field of study.

The Search for a Science of Administration

What were the scholars going to teach that was not already known to practitioners with a little experience? Schools were in place, elections won, and officials appointed, but what knowledge did the reformers possess that would better prepare them to manage government?

Political science was of little use here. Despite Wilson's call for a political science of administration, political scientists showed little interest in studying the nuts and bolts of public management. So administrative scholars did what they have been doing ever since. They did their best by borrowing the best from other fields of study, in particular, from business administration.

Scientists in general possess a peculiar faith, and administrative scientists are no exception. Consider aerodynamics as an example. For centuries people had dreamed of flying, from Icarus to Leonardo, but they had not known how. The laws of aerodynamics have always existed in the fabric of nature, present yet hidden, waiting to be discovered. Scientific inquiry and experimentation unlocked those secrets.

Could not a similar situation exist in administration? Suppose for a moment that there were laws of administration, as inviolate as the laws of aerodynamics, waiting to be discovered. Luther Gulick, an early reformer, wondered:

> At the present time (he wrote in 1937), administration is more an art than a science; in fact there are those who assert dogmatically that it can never be anything else. They draw no hope from the fact that metallurgy, for example, was completely an art several centuries before it became primarily a science and commenced its great forward strides after generations of intermittent advance and decline. (Gulick, 1937, p. 191)

Early administrative scientists embraced the faith that laws of administration must exist. They discovered what they thought to be such laws in the work of a French industrialist by the name of Henri Fayol. Fayol suggested that certain basic principles, such as the principle of unity of command or division of work, guided the operation of all successful organizations. The principles could be ignored only if one was willing to suffer the severest consequence, a loss of efficiency. In a highly competitive, rapidly industrializing economy, efficiency was "axiom number one in the value scale of administration" (Gulick, 1937, p. 192). Gulick and James Mooney modified and adopted these principles, with Mooney even suggesting that they had been operating since the dawn of civilization, though never "discovered" and written down until modern times.

The orthodox theorists truly believed that they had revealed laws of administration. They believed that the laws could be tested scientifically, measuring the presence of efficiency (or its absence) as the laws were applied and violated. Critics accused the orthodox theorists of jumping to conclusions and enshrining common sense under the mantle of science. Some critics even argued that the principles were lousy common sense, that certain of them were as likely to produce disorganization as efficiency.

In spite of their deficiencies, the logic and simplicity of principles like unity of command assured their acceptance. These principles remain among practicing administrators today the most widely known lessons on administration.

As to the use of scientific methods for testing procedures and principles, that fell to Frederick Taylor and his disciples. Taylor, the "Father of Scientific Management," began applying his methods in the 1880s at the Midvale Steel Works in Philadelphia. Imagine the research scientist, formulating hypotheses, designing experiments, measuring the relationship between independent and dependent variables. That was Taylor. He measured the relationship between the size of the scoop on a shovel and the amount of ore, ash and coal a "first class" steel worker could move. There were experiments on monotony and fatigue where, it is said, one of Taylor's disciples discovered the coffee break (the finding that a mid-morning break raised overall productivity for the day in spite of the absence of workers from the assembly line for the duration of the break.) Productivity and efficiency, as always, were the dependent variables.

Taylor had a revolutionary effect on the field of business administration and -- through borrowing -- public administration as well. Taylor established the principle that operations could be planned in advance and controlled by experts, working out of a central office, using scientific methods to discover the "one best way" of performing each job. Such principles are still at work in public administration today, in techniques such as work load measurement, wherein experts on the headquarters staff calculate the amount of time allotted to subordinates in the field to perform particular jobs (in person years, to the fourth decimal point).

A purely scientific approach, as Taylor had envisioned, never took hold in public administration during the orthodox period. Perhaps it was the enthusiasm for applications and reform that made the orthodox theorists so anxious to promote half-formed principles and findings. Perhaps it was due to the nature of government work and the opposition of labor unions to Taylor's "time and motion" studies on public projects. Either way, when the first textbook on public administration was published in 1926, its author, Leonard White, bowed in the direction of scientific study, then went on to discuss the matters that were of real interest to practitioners. White spent most of his time discussing the application of simple principles of administration to everyday governmental affairs in areas such as the creation of departments, personnel, morale, and retirement systems.

As more textbooks were written, attention moved further away from scientific analysis and closer to a discussion of the common functions of administration. Two functions in particular were emphasized: budgeting and personnel administration, of which more will be said toward the end of this essay. A third function -- generally known as organization and management (O & M) and incorporating the planning function and the process of reorganization -- received significant but relatively less attention. These functions circumscribed the three major reforms that made public administration practical: the drive for a public personnel system based on merit, efforts to consolidate the budgetary process under the direction of a strong chief executive, and attempts at governmental reorganization. The interest in practical applications and administrative functions was solidified in 1937 when Luther Gulick issued his famous definition of the work of the chief executive. Administration, said Gulick, consisted of POSDCORB: planning, organizing, staffing, directing, coordinating, reporting, and budgeting.

Human Relations

The lights had already begun to dim on the movement toward an orthodox administrative science by the time that Gulick published his Papers on the Science Administration in 1937. At the Western Electric Company's Hawthorne Works near Chicago, in a telephone relay assembly room that ought to be reconstructed in the Smithsonian Institution, the administrative scientists discovered the informal organization.

Disciples of Frederick Taylor had gone to the Chicago area in 1924 to continue earlier experiments measuring the effect of monotony, fatigue, and other working conditions on worker productivity. The scientists stuck to their standard methods of scientific inquiry: isolating variables, establishing test and control groups, and creating experiments that could be replicated with similar results. The resulting increases in productivity among the workers in the experiment dumfounded the research scientists, since the increases bore no relationship at all to the factors being studied. The results of the experiments only made sense when the administrative scientists realized that the workers were responding directly to the presence of the research team and not to the changes in working conditions under study. That phenomenon today is famously known as the Hawthorne Effect.

The particular effect that the research team produced on the workers has been much analyzed. (The complete report can be found in the book by F. J. Roethlisberger and William J. Dickson.) Modern opinion holds that the work groups at the Hawthorne Plant felt more comfortable working with the research scientists, whose collegial style of supervision and willingness to let the workers develop as a group contrasted favorably with the methods employed by company supervisors. This finding came as quite a shock to the administrative scientists who were trying to improve productivity by tinkering with rest breaks and illumination. It soon became apparent that one could improve productivity much more effectively by working on the human side of administration rather than altering the formal side of work. Managers, recognizing the possiblities implicit in this idea, promptly set out to manipulate the informal groups to which the workers belonged through a "friendly" style of supervision in the hope of maximizing productivity.

Once converted to the human relations perspective, the leading scholars went considerably beyond this coarse approach. Elton Mayo and Mary Parker Follett, among others, sought to improve the quality of life in modern organizations by explaining human needs and worker motivation. Mayo in particular worried about the problem of anomie that blighted industrial civilization, and dreamed of recreating through effective human relations the communal village of simplier times within the work groups of the modern factory. The fact that effective human relations also seemed to improve productivity simply made the program easier to sell. That humanistic orientation, and the interest in human behavior, would profoundly influence public administration in the decades to follow.

The Heritage

The wisdom of the particular contributions of orthodox theorists is still debated. Administrative reforms, simple principles and old remedies are discredited, then resurrected. We know today that reorganization rarely saves money, but it is hard to propose one without promising that. We know that alternatives to the principle of unity of command work, but it is hard to get executives to adopt them.

The orthodox era still throws its shadow onto modern practice. Taylor's scientific management provides a good example. Even during the orthodox period, it never achieved the dominance dreamed of by its founders. Yet its legacy is substantial. Today one of the major approaches to public administration is a full-blown scientific rationality that Taylor would not recognize in its details, but would be proud of in its intent.

The emphasis upon application and reform, the search for a science of administration, and the interest in human behavior are the three great legacies of the orthodox · period. They have continued to shape the search for knowledge about public administration since they were first laid down.

THE PERIOD OF DESCRIPTION

Criticism of the orthodox approach began in earnest shortly
after the publication of Gulick's Papers on the Science of
Administration in 1937. The following year the President of
New Jersey Bell, influenced by the early human relations
movement, published a book titled The Functions of the Executive. The author, Chester Barnard, attacked existing works
on administration as "superficial" and "lacking much recognition
of formal organization." He proposed in their place an
interpretation of organizational life based upon communication
and human cooperation. Seven years later an executive with
the U.S. Department of Agriculture, Paul Appleby, laid down
an assault on the politics-administration dichotomy. Public
executives, based on his experience, were not political eunuchs.
They made policy, interpreted policy, lived in a "goldfish bowl"
of public scrutiny, and were as subject to the constraints of
politics as other actors in the governmental system.

The chorus of dissent was harmonized by a new wave of graduate students emerging from doctoral programs during and
after World War II. Herbert Simon, the only public administration scholar ever to win a Nobel Prize for his theories,
published a devastating criticism of the principles of administration in 1945, exposing their inconsistencies and labeling
them nothing more than proverbs. In 1948 a young political
scientist, Dwight Waldo, published an attack on the "gospel of
efficiency" underlying the orthodox period, pointing out that
many values other than efficiency had guided governmental
activity in the past with satisfactory results.

Out of these critiques emerged two broad schools of thought:
the political approach and the behavioral revolution. These
two schools of thought guided public administration through its
middle period, the two decades beginning around 1945. Unlike
the orthodox period, which was famous for its prescriptions,
the middle period was noteworthy for its descriptions of
administrative life. It was a period during which writers on
administration pulled back to discover what they knew about
administration, respectful of the fact that before one gives
advice on how to fix something, one ought understand how it
works.

The Political Approach

The influence of the political school of thought in public administration cannot be underestimated. It was then, and remains today, the mainstream of public administration. It is the central pillar of public administration, the approach that holds the other contributions in place and gives coherence to the entire field of study. It has encouraged the popularity of the most frequently cited book in the field, Aaron Wildavsky's Politics of the Budgetary Process. It is the school of though that reminds us that public administration is primarily a matter of governing, not management.

The distinction between governing and management is absolutely crucial to an understanding of public administration. From Wilson to Gulick, orthodox theorists advanced the proposition that public administrators were essentially managers, hired to carry out the will of the state, separated from the job of making policy and freed from involvement in the political process. Appleby fought to refute this notion, reaching the widest audience in his second book, Policy and Administration.

Governing is the act of exercising the authority of the state on behalf of persons within the political community. It implies that the governors exercise discretion in deciding how that authority shall be applied, just as it implies that the political community has methods for holding the governors accountable. From declaring war to controlling urban growth, governing is a political process. The methods for making political decisions are wholly different from those used to make decisions in a modern corporation, a fact of life that is never lost upon business executives who take assignments in government.

Public administration is an extension of the governing process, according to the disciples of the political school of thought. This is an universal truth, confined not just to the government of the United States, but to European, socialist and developing regimes as well. Public administrators are governors. They exercise governmental authority over members of the political community. In so doing, they are subject to the same sort of checks and balances that affect officials in the nation's legislature or office of the chief executive. Appleby in particular sought to convince all who would listen that public administration is guided by the same forces that circumscribe other political activities.

Writers who promoted this political view were confronted early on with two challenges. First, they had to convince a field of study emerging from the bonds of orthodoxy that there was a governmental way to view public administration. Pendleton Herring's early work on the influence of interest groups on public administration and the trilogy by Paul Appleby were among the first to do this; a second wave was led by authors like Roscoe Martin, Alan Altshuler, and Francis Rourke. These books defined the issues of administrative governance in a political system: issues such as the source of bureaucratic power in the modern state, the political checks upon it, the ethics of public administration, and the reconciliation of bureaucratic forces with public participation and other democratic standards.

Second, the writers in the political school had to lay down a series of generalizations describing how politics affected administration. This was accomplished by Philip Selznick's study of administrative cooptation in the Tennessee Valley Authority, Herbert Kaufman's study of administrative disintegration in the U.S. Forest Service, Meyerson and Banfield's story of site selection for public housing in Chicago, Aaron Wildavsky's book on the politics of the budgetary process, Joseph Harris' book on legislative oversight, Marver Bernstein's analysis of the independent regulatory commissions, Graham Allison's analysis of bureaucratic politics in the Cuban Missile Crises, and A. Lee Fritschler's description of the iron triangle of bureaucrats, legislative committees and interest groups guiding government policy on tobacco smoking. These authors frequently made use of case studies or quasi-clinical studies of single agencies to explore the politics of administration.

Through their descriptions of reality, scholars from the political school revealed an administrative machine in the United States that was involved in policy making, pluralistic, decentralized, and geared toward participation of interest groups and clientele. Orthodox theorists, by contrast, had advocated an approach to governmental management that was centralized, bureaucratic, and isolated from the political process.

Despite their commitment to description, writers from the political school seemed rather fond of the mildly disorganized system of administrative pluralism found in the United States. A few theorists, including Paul Appleby and Emmette Redford, praised the pluralism of American public administration and the involvement of bureaucrats in the political process. It provided a political solution, they said, to the problem of limiting bureaucratic power in a state devoted to democratic principles.

In the United States people from the political school showed a great deal of interest in administrative pluralism, in the politics of administration, and in the power of the bureaucracy to influence government policy. These are only a few of the governing issues that arise in public administration. In developing nations, there is the issue of whether or not civil servants should act as entrepreneurs in the development process. In federal systems, there is the question of whether to administer national programs through state or provincial governments. In all countries, there is the problem of how to recruit and organize a civil service. There are problems of centralization, secrecy, citizen participation, of public employees in unions and more. A whole series of governing issues arise when one views public administration through the lens of the political approach.

Throughout the period of description, writers from the political approach struggled with the problem of how to relate their findings to the needs of practicing public administrators. Practitioners needed applications. To bridge the gap between description and application, writers produced case studies. Hundreds of case studies were written, most of them published as single monographs by institutions like the Inter-University Case Program. Occasionally case studies were bound together as a book on a single subject, such as Frederick Mosher's work on governmental reorganization. The case method encouraged the belief that if students read enough cases, they would gain a "feel" for the politics of the administrative process and in this way become better practitioners than if they simply committed to memory the orthodox principles of administration.

The Behavioral Revolution

While writers in the political school attacked writers in the orthodox school for being naive about politics and administration, a covey of social scientists attacked orthodox theorists for their failure to adequately explain human behavior in organizations. The behavioral revolution, as it came to be known, attracted scholars from sociology, psychology, and business administration, with the result that specialists in public administration were obliged to borrow extensively from disciplines not primarily interested in governmental organization. That did not serve to discredit the principles uncovered by behavioral scientists, however. In their eyes, organizations were organizations, pretty much the same wherever one found them. One could not, from their perspective, have one set of principles for organizations in government and another for organizations in general.

Quite a number of approaches to the study of organization theory and behavior arose during the descriptive period. Building upon the human relations movement, scholars continued to study behavior in organizations from the perspective of people within them, especially as those people formed groups. The best compilation of empirical research on small group behavior appeared in a volume edited by Dorwin Cartwright and Alvin Zander. Victor Vroom published a widely used review of research on personal motivation in the work place. Scholars like Philip Selznick helped to translate findings such as these into principles of institutional leadership.

Some social scientists studied organizational behavior from the perspective of psychology and anthropology. Robert Kahn, in one of the few works in this area that has been frequently cited, wrote a book on Organizational Stress. Other scholars explored the impact of individual perceptions on organizational reality, a perspective that allowed a few people to suggest that novels -- which often tell a story from one individual's point of view -- could be used to fathom administrative behavior.

A smaller group, building upon the Marxist belief that class determines behavior, examined worker attitudes and power struggles within organizations. Some of the best efforts in this area dealt with the social functions of conflict.

No single approach had as much influence during the descriptive period, however, as the study of organizations as formal systems. Principles were advanced to describe the operation of the organization as a whole, in the abstract, or with reference to some non-personal element within it such as the organizational decision.

Herbert Simon's explanation of decision making is representative of the non-personal nature of the subfield that came to be called organization theory. Simon was confronted with an explanation of decision making, drawn largely from economics, suggesting that organizations select courses of action calculated to maximize the achievement of their objectives. At first glance, that explanation seems plain enough. If an executive wants to maximize profit, then he or she -- one would expect -- would chose the best course of action designed to make money.

In reviewing empirical studies, Simon found little evidence to support the conclusion that organizations used this "rational comprehensive" approach to decision making in practice. Instead, he drew a picture of organizations engaged in "satisficing", searching through familiar behavior patterns for one that fit the situation and satisfied minimum standards. This, he said, was a much better explanation of organizational decision making as it actually occurred.

Decision making was only one of the multitude of organizational phenomena studied under the heading of formal organization theory. Building on Simon's earlier work, Cyert and March produced a behavioral theory of the firm. Herbert Kaufman, one of the few frequently-cited behaviorists to write primarily about government, produced a practical study of administrative feedback. Luce and Raiffa used game theory to describe administrative decision making. There were more studies of decision making (Mailick), more books by Herbert Simon, including a textbook on public administration, books on organizational research (Vroom) and, underneath it all, the massively difficult translation of Max Weber's theory of social and economic organization from German into English.

The books most frequently cited from this period are the great compendiums produced between 1958 and 1966, when the behavioral movement reached the zenith of its influence. March and Simon's Organizations, Bertram Gross' two volume Managing of Organizations, March's Handbook of Organizations, and Katz and Kahn's Social Psychology of Organizations dipped into all aspects of behavioral theory, from the behavioral assumptions underlying the orthodox principles of administration to the contributions of modern psychologists. Research and theory-building on motivation, communication, participation, group behavior, decision making, leadership, conflict, organizational equilibrium, power, authority, perception, stress, and change had grown impressively by the early 1960s. The compendiums attempted to weave these explanations together, with a passion for description and a search for overarching theories.

The result, fully condensed by the publication of Katz and Kahn's compendium in 1966, was the acceptance of the open systems approach as the principle means for unifying the elements of the behavioral revolution. Open systems theory admitted the importance of the old orthodox procedures, tacked on the influential findings on small group behavior, then embraced the findings of formal organization theory. The authors aligned these elements in an organization constantly struggling to stay afloat in a shifting environment. Only by repeatedly fine tuning their organization, especially in ways that motivated employees to respond to changes in the environment of the organization, could executives hope to create an "open system" that would continue to prosper from year to year.

This view of the organization bobbing up and down in its own particular environment helped to keep organization theory afloat. If organizations were sensitive to their environments -- especially the successful ones -- then one could explain why organizations differed so much by categorizing their environments. Amitai Etzioni attempted to do this in terms of authority (a prison is different than a church), James Thompson in terms of task and technology (running a university is different than operating a sewage treatment plant) and Lawrence and Lorsch in terms of the differentiation of the environment (a high technology firm is in a more fast-moving, differentiated environment than a corporation that manufactures containers). This contingency approach, an outgrowth of organization theory, helped to keep the behavioral mood alive as public administration moved into new areas of study.

Bureaucracy

One approach to behavioral theory is so distinct that it deserves to be discussed as a separate category. About 1940, sociologists like Robert Merton began to stress the vulgar side of organizational life: the rules, red tape, impersonality, and resistance to change. This approach was advanced considerably when in 1946 Max Weber's work on bureaucracy began to appear in English translations.

The writings of Weber, a German scholar, played a critically important role in helping European public administration expand beyond its traditional preoccupation with administrative law and into the realm of organization theory. Writing at the turn of the century, Weber set down his ideas on sociology, history, law, politics, economics and religion.

In public administration, Weber is most famous for his essay on bureaucracy, written about 1911. In this and other works, Weber explained in detail the phenomenon that many people would perceive only in outline form until Weber's works became more widely known. Of all the different types of organizations that have been developed to serve humanity, the bureaucratic type is only one. Weber defined its formal characteristics and explained why it was marching to dominance in the twentieth century.

Armed with Weber's theory, scholars were in a better position to understand why bureaucracies went awry. Outstanding studies of bureaucratic lunacy were produced by Alvin Gouldner, Peter Blau, Robert Merton, Robert Presthus, Victor Thompson, and the French sociologist Michel Crozier. Many focused on the manner in which executives used bureaucratic authority to force employees to pledge allegiance to organizational rules, curiously encouraging those employees in the process to disregard the goals for which the organization was created. Merton insisted that such "bureaucratic dysfunctions" were a direct outgrowth of the installation of bureaucratic principles and the misplaced assumption that such principles would always promote efficiency. Informal groups and personal indifference were advanced by scholars as healthy responses to the ill taste of bureaucratic life. Popular writers such as C. Northcote Parkinson and not a few novelists spread the vulgar view of bureaucracy, a view that the few dissenters such as Anthony Downs and Charles Perrow were hard pressed to refute. Perrow retorted that bureaucracy as a form of organization was "superior to all others we know or can hope to afford in the near and middle future" (Perrow, 1979, p. 6). By then, however, the debate had turned ideological, with writers like Dvorin and Simmons and Warren Bennis arguing that bureaucracy was not only ineffective but also inhumane.

The Heritage

The middle period, like the 1950s around which it was centered, was a period of calm when scholars could reassess their
beliefs about administration and sort out important findings.
Knowledge about administrative behavior was advanced considerably by the behavioral movement and studies of bureaucratic
sociology. The political approach disseminated a clearer picture of the conditions shaping governmental administration,
especially in the United States.

The knowledge gathered in the middle period, despite all of
the assaults on the orthodox beliefs, did not drive orthodox
public administration into oblivion. The great contribution of
the middle period was the establishment of two alternative
schools of thought to the orthodox approach: the behavioral
school and the political approach.

That contribution was both the strength and the weakness of
the middle period. It extended public administration, but it
also fragmented it. It expanded understanding, but provided
fewer prescriptions than the orthodox period had. Behavioral
theorists in particular, in their quest to build a science of
administration, demonstrated more interest in description than
prescription. Their theories might help practitioners better
understand why organizations worked the way they did, but left
practitioners with little advice on what to do about it. For
all of their shortcomings, the orthodox principles contained
prescriptions. So when government heated up again in the
1960s, modern scholars began to scramble through the descriptions in search of applications.

THE ERA OF APPLICATIONS

Through open systems theory, scholars described organizations
that adapted in order to survive. Well, public administration is
a system, albeit a loosely knit one, and it behaved according
to theory. When its environment changed, it began to adapt.

How did its environment change? Quite simply, government
expanded its administrative activities. In the United States

administrative expansion began in defense, where systems analysts led by an auto company executive (Robert McNamara)
sought to reform defense management. This was followed by
an impressive expansion of domestic programs, first for civil
rights and shortly thereafter by something called the "War on
Poverty." Spurred by federal grants-in-aid, state and local
governments began to gear up their administrative machinery.
Overseas, developing countries emerging from the era of formal colonialism sought to set up social and economic (and
often military) programs with Western assistance.

The demand for administrative expertise revived the reforming
impulse in public administration: the dissatisfaction with knowledge for knowledge's sake when the opportunity arises to apply
it to real problems. Public administration undertook an extensive search for relevant administrative strategies to counter
what one scholar called "the staggering ineptitude of governments struggling to launch new programs."

New specializations arose to meet the challenge. Five major
areas -- four new and one old -- dominated. The new areas
were policy analysis, management science, organization development, and comparative public administration; the old, a
metamorphosis of the now well established political school of
thought.

Ultimately, these areas were judged on the basis of the advice
they provided to practicing administrators, for this was the era
of applications. Laying as they did on the building blocks of
the past, since the older movements continued to influence
teaching and practice, these new areas extended the number of
schools of thought and areas of application within public
administration to the splintering point.

The new areas firmly established public administration as a
multi-disciplinary field of study. The reemphasis of applications strengthened the professional orientation of the field.
The eventual drive toward reunification -- a response to the
splintering -- strengthened its status among the social science
disciplines. Here are the movements that did it, beginning in
the 1960s.

The Rational School

Scholars who observed public administration during the era of description described a sloth-like, happily political governmental service. Pluralists called it incrementalism and marveled at the degree of participation it allowed. Behaviorists called it satisficing behavior, a concept practicing administrators recognized as the notion that a barely satisfactory program was "good enough for government work." A famous scholar in the area of intergovernmental relations praised "decentralization by mild chaos." Aaron Wildavsky revealed a politically charged budgetary process that seemed immune to reform.

Deep in the psyche of public administration lay an alternative mood, a commitment to science, rationality and reform. This commitment had crept in during the orthodox era in the form of Frederick Taylor's scientific management. It had been strengthened by the practice of operations research in the military services during World War II, by the practice of cost-effectiveness analysis in business firms, by ultra-rational think tanks like the RAND Corporation, and by branches of the discipline of economics not fully utilized by public administration in the past.

When public administration began to emphasize applications, practicing administrators turned to scholars for solutions and the rational school bloomed. Its advocates possessed solutions, something that scholars during the period of description had never fully worked out. Never mind that the solutions often failed, defeated by the political system in the case of budgetary reform and deadened by their own clumsiness in the case of Vietnam. Solutions were in demand. Two decades of demand allowed rationalists to sort out strengths and weaknesses, and in the end even a faultfinder like Aaron Wildavsky could be found praising certain aspects of policy analysis.

The Policy Approach

Two areas of application emerged from the rational school: policy analysis and management science. Of the two, policy analysis has had the greater impact on public administration. Policy analysis is the great success story of the era of applications. Initially, it drew its strength from the disciplines of economics and political science. Political scientists in particular saw it as a way of renewing their off-and-on-again interest in governmental administration.

Political science and economics were much more advanced than public administration in their use of scientific methods when this era began. Knowing a good thing when they saw it, public administration grabbed hold of the most useful applications to be found in the policy sciences. Program evaluation was a favorite theme. Evaluation experts such as Joseph Wholey, Carol Weiss, and Edward Suchman helped practitioners understand how to use empirical methods to verify the impact of their programs on the problems they sought to solve.

Policy analysts showed practitioners how to apply economic ways of thinking to the choice, scale, and design of public services. In the beginning, in books by Roland McKean and Hinrichs and Taylor, the emphasis lay on comparing costs and benefits. By the publication of the second edition of Haveman and Margolis' Public Expenditures and Policy Analysis, economic thinking was being applied to all sorts of expenditure problems in all sorts of ways, from the design of programs with multiple objectives to the creation of incentives that encouraged the public to comply with public policy.

Policy analysts used research strategies to analyze the causes of problems and test the efficacy of proposed solutions, tasks that encouraged the development of the highly elaborate technique known as systematic experimentation. Alice Rivlin's Systematic Thinking for Social Action remains one of the most widely-read books advocating such rational methods. In addition to systematic experimentation, Rivlin discusses survey research, benefit-cost analysis, program evaluation, performance measurement and that brand of budgetary reform from which policy analysis was barely rescued, PPBS. To answer the question, "what can policy analysts do?," E. S. Quade wrote the widely read Analysis for Public Decisions and Arnold Meltsner even wrote a book on what it was like to be a policy analyst advising public officials.

Policy analysts from political science and other disciplines spent a great deal of time trying to interpret the way in which government policy got made. The older, one-theory interpretations of American politics were revived, such as

Robert Dahl's study of American pluralism and David Truman's study of pressure groups. They were fit together with more elaborate studies of choice, strategy, and leverage by social scientists like Bauer and Gergen. To clarify this research for students of policy analysis, authors like James Anderson promoted the idea that policy could be studied in stages (identification, formation, implementation and evaluation). Others such as Thomas Dye used different models to explain different policy areas, pointing up the essential difference between the formulation of tax policy, for example, and the development of welfare programs. It was here that policy analysis broadened into the policy approach: the tendency to view government in terms of tax policy versus welfare policy rather than legislation versus administration. This, of course, was the situation that existed in the days before the formal study of public administration began, when a tax accountant studied more tax accounting in order to become a better public executive.

The most distinct intellectual challenge to the old-style public administration was offered by the so-called "public choice" school. In 1957 Anthony Downs wrote a book, using economic models, which concluded that a simple representative democracy would ever fail to maximize the general welfare as defined by public preferences. Five years later James Buchanan and Gordon Tullock endeavored to prove, again using economic models of thinking, that citizens would always get more government than they bargained for when the costs of participation were set as low as they were in the United States. Their bias against big government was recast in Tullock's 1965 study of bureaucratic aggrandizement in the public service. That same year Mancur Olson shocked pluralists by refuting the notion that interest groups possessed the capacity to directly represent the interests of their members. One of the strongest blows was delivered by William Niskanen in his 1971 Bureaucracy and Representative Government. Using economic theory and mathematical proofs, Niskanen attempted to demonstrate scientifically that government bureaucracies would always grow faster and perform less efficiently than competitive private industries.

The public choice school challenged public administration on two levels. Based as it was on the science of economics, the public choice school put forth a much more theoretically rich and empirically verifiable theory than people in public administration were accustomed to employing. This gave public administration an intellectual kick in the pants, creating an incentive for the field to become more consciously scientific or lose out to an approach that was. Second, the public choice school reminded people in public administration of the power of practical theory. This practical theory provided the intellectual justification for the efforts of conservative politicians to cut back the size of government and restructure the incentives that affect bureaucratic performance.

Public choice theory is based largely on the economic theory of competition. It is useful to review the competition model in some detail if for no other reason than to see what a practical, empirically verifiable theory of organizational performance looks like.

The competition model describes in general terms a series of events commonly experienced by business firms operating in a competitive market. The sequence of events begins when the public, for whatever reasons, decides that it must have more of a particular product. This sends out signals that producing firms generally receive in the form of higher profits and prices for the product in demand. The promise of economic profit attracts new producers, which in turn causes the market supply curve which economists love to draw to shift to the right. With more supply being produced, prices slide down the demand curve. A new equilibrium is reached eventually at a point of increased supply and lower price. As more and more of the product is produced and consumed, average costs of production approach the minimum and economic profit approaches zero. Throughout this cycle producers experience strong pressures to keep ahead of the profit squeeze by reducing costs, a pressure that frequently results in product and technological innovation.

Public choice advocates suggest that governmental bureaus can be treated as the providers of goods and services and that -- insofar as technically possible -- the incentives such as those encountered in the competition model can be used to force bureaucrats to cut costs and invent new methods of doing business. This would bring to bear on public administration the full resources of the discipline of economics, which for all of its problems is much further advanced as a scientific field of study than public administration.

As government moved out of the era of expansion and into the era of cut-back management, politicians paid more attention to the public choice idea of using methods from the free market system to improve the delivery of public goods and services. Many of these methods were sold under the collective heading of "privatization." Privatization means many things, from efforts to get business firms to take over selected public programs to efforts at making public agencies compete with one another. Privatization theory proved popular not only in the United States, but also in nations with centrally managed economies whose leaders sought incentives that might make state-run enterprises perform more effectively.

Public choice theory casts serious doubts on the ability of public administrators to improve agency performance through simple administrative reform. Using theories of economic choice, experts like Gordon Tullock and Anthony Downs have argued that governmental ineffectiveness is the natural result of bureaucrats rationally pursuing their self interest in a system that encourages modest levels of performance. Since people inevitably pursue their self interest, according to Tullock and Buchanan, nothing short of a major redesign of the whole governmental system will ever result in the high levels of administrative performance sought by administrative reformers.

This commitment to rational thinking, economic analysis, and scientific investigation dominates the policy analysis movement. Yet it was not always that way. In the beginning, when policy analysis was getting underway, the incrementalist interpretation of policy formulation held center stage. Supported on two sides by Simon's explanation of satisficing behavior and Appleby's description of administrative pluralism, Charles Lindblom and David Braybrooke defended incrementalism as the best available explanation of American public administration and, in addition, the best way to reconcile conflicting interests.

Being sensitive to the political element in governmental management, public administrators tended to side with the incrementalists. This placed them in the awkward position of having to defend the existing system of pluralism and administrative compromise as "the way things were." This gave the high ground, which public administrators historically had enjoyed as advocates of reform, to policy analysts who wanted to change the system. The incrementalists exposed themselves to arguments such as those advanced by policy specialist Yehezkel Dror, who insisted that incremental changes in the "base" would not solve social problems when the base was rotten. That criticism, plus the fact that the rationalists offered administrative reform, sunk the incrementalists, who frankly were more interested in describing reality than changing it.

Management Science

While policy analysts hoped for a breakthrough in administrative performance through their use of economic models, management scientists sought a breakthrough by applying mathematical models to organizational decision making. The large scale application of mathematics to governmental decision making began during World War II under the rubric of operations research. After the war ended, it lay dormant in "think tanks" like the RAND Corporation and in inconspicuous pockets of governmental activity. Most scholars were convinced that public executives "satisficed" on account of poor information and vague goals and thus remained skeptical about the saving grace of management science. In 1958 Roland McKean challenged the satisficing ideology with his Efficiency in Government Through Systems Analysis, a study of how benefit-cost analysis could be used to improve decision making in water resource programs. This was followed two years later by Hitch and McKean's Economics of Defense in the Nuclear Age. In 1961, Defense Secretary Robert McNamara, a former business executive, put Hitch and McKean in positions of power in the Pentagon and management science had its foot back in the governmental door.

To many, management science in these restoration years appeared to be preoccupied with management techniques. Hitch and McKean became famous for promoting the use of benefit-cost analysis and planning-programming-budgeting systems (PPBS). Defense and space programs proved a fertile environment for the development of operations research, PERT, large scale command and control systems, simulation, management information systems, linear programming, technology forecasting and project management.

It soon became apparent, however, that management scientists were talking about much more than simple management techniques. They began experimenting with decision making models that potentially could alter the nature of governmental administration.

In 1945, Herbert Simon had called upon public administrators to make the decision their basic unit of analysis. At the time, orthodox theorists tended to focus on organization structure -- exempified in the organization chart -- as the common element in all administrative activity. Simon argued that the decision was a much better choice. One might imagine it as the organizational equivalent of the atom in physics, the secrets of which once unlocked would open the door to the possible modification of all sorts of administrative phenomena. Simon suggested, moreover, that the "rational comprehensive" model of decision making, drawn from the discipline of economics and applied in areas such as policy analysis, went off in the wrong direction. Managers, he said, simply did not behave that way, an observation which once verified won for him the Nobel Prize.

Few people apparently understood at that time just where Simon was going. In public administration, people interpreted Simon's early work as just another justification for their disbelief in all types of rational decision making. As late as 1957 March and Simon continued to encourage this interpretation by writing about "satisficing" behavior in formal organizations, a model describing administrators as persons who would cast about through familiar patterns of behavior in search of any old alternative that met minimum standards.

Like Charles Lindblom, Simon had stated early on that information shortages were a primary cause of this "satisficing" behavior. So in 1960, when Simon published his New Science of Management Decision, he shocked many people in the field by announcing that a solution to the information shortage was at hand. The computer, he said, had broken the information barrier.

Simon's observation that computers could be programmed to make routine managerial decisions came as no great surprise to informed experts in public administration. Computers, after all, have been programmed to perform first level audits on income tax returns, a task once assigned to an army of clerks. Nor does anyone really doubt the technical capability of computers to supervise employees performing repetitive functions.

No, what surprised people in the field was Simon's interest in computers that could perform mid- and upper-level executive functions. The implications of Simon's interest in decision making now began to sink in. His work with James March and Richard Cyert on cognitive processes, where he had put forward his ideas on "satisficing," was only a first step. An understanding of the workings of the human mind in making decisions provided a bridge to the science of computer programming. Simon and his colleagues hoped to program a computer to make complex decisions: in effect, a computer that could think. Such a computer would have astonishing potential. It would allow the automation of mid- and upper-level executive functions, giving top executives previously unimaginable control over administrative decisions throughout the organization. A new generation of decision making theorists continue to work on just that -- the mathematical expression of cognitive processes in ways that will allow computer programming.

Management science simultaneously attracts and frightens people studying public administration. It attracts intellectually inspired people with its hope for a science of administration. It attracts reformers with its tough, technocratic belief that managers can solve society's problems if politicians will simply get out of the way. Altogether, it appeals to those who believe that good government can be achieved through good management. This faith in management runs deep in the psyche of public administration. It exerted its power during the period of description in a movement which drew people from schools of business and public administration together "to make government more business-like." Persons allied with this approach tend to view public administration more as a problem of management than a problem of politics or policy making. They tend to concentrate on problems of organization structure, administrative methods, institutional leadership, financial control, and effective decision making. Although public administration draws many books from the management approach (they are listed in the fourth part of this volume under the section on general public administration), only a few are frequently cited and some of those are more behavioral than managerial in tone.

Public administrators sometimes look to the literature on business management for guidance, to approaches such as Peter Drucker's "management by objectives" or Robert Anthony's Planning and Control Systems. Anthony is in part responsible for the fascination in business circles with the strategic planning process. In addition to its emphasis upon strategic planning, Anthony's book also reminds public and private managers of the steps that must be taken through managerial and operational control to assure that plans are actually carried out. Within public administration, Robert Golembiewski has promoted the management perspective, although he is best known for his books on organization development. Pfiffner and Sherwood once wrote a textbook on Administrative Organization and Harlan Cleveland has given advice to "future" executives. Although none of these books could be characterized as scientific, their general outlook has helped to keep alive the management emphasis in public administration.

Management science goes much further than this. It represents a new way of thinking about public administration: more rational, more scientific and less tolerant of human defects or political interference. More than any other movement affecting the field, it leans toward the attitude that management problems can be structured and broken down and that programs can be written that solve them. It echoes the orthodox belief that politics can be separated from public administration and revives Frederick Taylor's faith in the "one best way" of performing each job.

This frightens people familiar with the dependence of public administration upon political philosophy. Such people see management science as much more than a tool for improving governmental management. To them it represents a rejection of political philosophy, a charge that can be illustrated by considering the problem of governmental ambiguity. To make management science work, one has to remove a substantial amount of the ambiguity associated with the political process. Vague objectives conflict with the careful planned definitions that are necessary to start the programming process. Vague objectives, however, are the stuff of successful politics. They allow groups with conflicting objectives to agree upon a common cause so long as each group can convince itself that its objectives will be realized. Ambiguity allows compromise. Management science does not.

This sort of ultra-rationality scares many public administrators, a sense of fear well expressed in Ida Hoos' Systems Analysis in Public Policy and Robert Boguslaw's The New Utopians. Both authors charge that systems analysts remain ignorant of social and political processes for decision making and, in Boguslaw's view, tend to avoid political reality by creating machines to take the place of imperfect people.

In spite of such criticisms, management science continues to enjoy a favorable reception in the government. It is widely used in the defense department. (The American military still uses PPBS.) Planning and control systems have worked their way into domestic agencies. (The U. S. Department of Housing and Urban Development developed one of the best.) Operations research can be found in the cities (modeling the best distribution of fire stations in New York City, for example). Computers run the subways in San Francisco and Washington, D.C. Still, one does not find many books about management science cited frequently in the field of public administration, nowhere near the numbers found for the new rationality of policy analysis.

Management science has the potential to make the study of public administration suddenly more scientific if the computer revolution so long promised by Herbert Simon and his colleagues comes true. Some of the most exciting research frontiers that could be applied to public administration are being explored by persons who are highly skilled in the use of mathematics or computer programming. At the same time, people familiar with public administration seem to understand that should this technology become available, it could have a devastating impact on many of the political tenants underlying the field.

Organization Development

Organization development (often referred to simply as OD) shows in a marvelous way how a school of thought can make the transition from description to application. Ever since the Hawthorne Experiments, behavioral scientists have been building up knowledge about small group behavior and human motivation. While formal organization theory dominated the early behavioral revolution, studies of human behavior placed second.

When the formal theories proved incapable of doing much more than describing behavior, the experts on human behavior stepped forward with their recommendations for organizational change.

The most popular applications began to appear in 1960, just as professional managers began to clamor for advice. That was the year that Douglas McGregor published his influential Human Side of Enterprise, promoting the eternal "Theory X and Theory Y." McGregor's book was quickly followed by Rensis Likert's New Patterns of Management, prescribing a group-based, participatory scheme of administration. Chris Argyris continued his series of books with Integrating the Individual and the Organization. Warren Bennis began to make predictions about the death of bureaucracy the type of organization that would succeed it.

None of these people were professors of public administration. Most of them were social psychologists who served the business world. Argyris ventured into the U.S. Department of State with his theories for organizational change, only to have his efforts brushed aside. Robert Golembiewski, the leading public administration writer in this area, has had to spend a good bit of time explaining why public agencies are less receptive to organizational development strategies than business firms.

As an area of application, organization development presents the firm or the agency with a strategy for planned change. The strategy is generally designed to improve the performance of the organization: at solving problems, for example, or adjusting its mode of operation to a new technology. The strategy is also designed to improve the quality of work life for people in the firm. Organization development consultants are admittedly biased toward democratic, participatory organizations where authority is deemphasized and group problem solving enhanced. Authoritarian organizations, they believe, are simply bad for the mental health of their employees, irregardless of well or how poorly they perform. This belief owes much to the early work of psychologist Abraham Maslow, who laid down the doctrine that healthy people have a natural predisposition to want to move up a "hierarchy of needs" toward career growth and responsibility.

In studying the nature of this organizational crusade, it is wise to remember the distaste with which thinking people viewed bureaucratic life in the 1950s. It was portrayed, in a series of popular books and articles, as conformist, obedient, dull, and suburban. Organization development sought to erase that situation, to tap human potential, tear down facades, and encourage creativity. Early on, it did this with techniques like the T-group, the purpose of which Leland Bradford well explains. Later on, as Warren Bennis describes, OD adopted a wide range of intervention strategies. Clearly, it abandoned empiricism for action.

Despite its enthusiasm for applications, along with a tendency to display cures rather than discuss evidence, organization development does rest on a foundation of research findings. The most impressive collection of research findings is contained in Cartwright and Zander's Group Dynamics Research and Theory. A shorter and more popular treatment can be found in Edgar Schein's Organizational Psychology. Even the infamous T-group -- the device for beginning the democratization of organizations and the self-actualization of individuals -- grew out of research techniques utilized for small group studies in university laboratories.

Still, it is hard to prove empirically that OD "works" in the sense that it leads to higher levels of organization performance. Tom Burns, Alfred Marrow and Chris Argyris, in their much cited books on the use of OD techniques to produce organizational change, rely on case studies of particular firms to build support for their approach. As any research scientist knows, successful cases in the absence of appropriate scientific controls do not prove much of anything. Rensis Likert presents what is probably the best empirical argument for participatory management in his New Patterns of Management and Frederick Herzberg uses survey research to back up his claim that nothing motivates people more than an exciting job. Other social scientists, however, dispute such claims. Victor Vroom, for example, in his survey of motivational research, suggests that the data does not support the claim that increased job satisfaction leads employees to higher levels of productivity.

In an era of applications, however, success is defined not just in terms of scientific proof but also with regard to how well the approach is received by practicing executives. Judged in that sense, organization development is one of the leading success stories from the era of applications, especially in the business world and occasionally in public administration. The continued emphasis on small group research, moreover, may eventually provide OD with the empirical base that will establish its validity among the social sciences.

Comparative Public Administration

Here is a specialization within public administration that failed to make the transition from description to prescription. Comparative public administration made a mighty contribution, then collapsed, although hopes for its revival are high as the sense of world interdependence grows and people overseas recognize the importance of good administration for program success.

The comparative public administration movement began as an effort to export western know-how to developing countries. The Western nations, and the United States in particular, sought to export technology, agriculture, engineering, economics, airports and eventually public administration. In 1962, the Ford Foundation presented the Comparative Administration Group -- a special division of the American Society for Public Administration -- with one-half million dollars to study methods for improving the practice of public administration in third world countries. Even stalwarts like Luther Gulick could be found overseas (in Egypt), advising governments as to the proper mobilization of administrative and economic resources.

As Dwight Waldo had pointed out in The Administrative State, American administrative methods are deeply rooted in the American experience. In a country possessed by a different set of values, those principles might produce different results. The experts, even Gulick, suspected this. Experiencing it firsthand, however, was as bracing as the difference between dreaming about the joy of the first summer swim and actually jumping into the cold sea. Americans went abroad confident of their ability to adjust (the British issued warnings, generally ignored) and came home from their tours of duty with incredible tales of administrative failure.

The experts were anxious to share their misfortunes with others who had suffered similar adventures. Frustrated in their efforts at giving practical advice, they wrote papers which were largely theoretical and descriptive. The best collections can be found in anthologies by Nimrod Raphaeli, William Siffin, Ferrel Heady and Sybil Stokes: papers on administrative systems, on administrative problems, on modernization, and on the development of this emerging field of study. Heady produced a textbook on comparative public administration, among other things suggesting an intriguing relationship between the types of political regimes that ran different countries and the styles of administrative organization they tended to adopt. A few years later, Naomi Caiden and Aaron Wildavsky explained the process of planning and budgeting in developing countries, where poverty and political instability made western methods especially difficult to adopt.

It fell to Fred Riggs, one of the leaders of the Comparative Administrative Group, to weave this together into one of the most creative theories ever to emerge from the pen of a public administrator. Riggs constructed an "ecological" theory of public administration, complete with its own vocabulary, to describe what happens when administrative institutions from a Western nation are squeezed into a non-Western culture. A theory of administrative development, it reveals how administrative institutions become intertwined with the social, economic, and political necessities of a transitional society. It provided the first full-blown ecological theory of public administration.

Alas, the Ford Foundation had not paid for abstract theory. They, along with the Agency for International Development, the World Bank, the United Nations and other international organizations wanted practical theory, not abstractions explaining why reforms were so hard to implement. If the public administration experts did not know how to remedy failing development programs, then the international organizations would let the economists or someone else do it. No one, of course, possessed a complete set of remedies, a fact that was amply demonstrated from Iran to Vietnam. In 1971, the Ford Foundation terminated its support, and the Comparative Administrative Group disbanded, although public administrators are creeping back onto the multi-disciplinary teams that travel abroad to rescue wrecked economies and implement development programs.

ADMINISTERING PUBLIC PROGRAMS

The field of public administration came into the 1980s with at least nine major schools of thought and areas of application. The orthodox school, the political school, the behavioral school, the rational school, the study of bureaucracy, policy analysis, management science, O.D., and comparative public administration all possessed their own distinct interpretations of public administration. As if that were not enough, there were schools within schools, such as the "public choice" advocates within policy analysis, who wanted to mold public administration along even different lines. Reviewing this situation in 1974, Dwight Waldo lamented:

> Public Administration is suffering from an identity crises, having enormously expanded its periphery without retaining or creating a unifying center. (Waldo, 1974, p. 185)

All of the lists folded into the new edition of this bibliography were prepared after Waldo issued his warning. People in the field must been listening, for the pattern that emerges shows a distinct reorientation toward a unifying center for public administration.

That unifying center is the political school of thought, already well developed during the era of description by people like Paul Appleby and Aaron Wildavksy. After flirting with the idea that business and public administration could be taught in the same breath -- a legacy of the management approach and the behavioral revolution -- scholars concluded that the unique aspects of governmental administration required separate treatment.

This placed the political school in the position of being the vehicle through which findings from the outlying schools of thought could be applied to governmental administration. In A New World, for example, Jay Shafritz takes findings on motivation and participation from the modern behavioral sciences and applies them to traditional public personnel administration. The findings, like many of those utilized in the field, are borrowed from people not primarily concerned with public administration. Still, they are filtered through persons like Shafritz who have a well developed sensitivity to the nuances of governmental affairs. The job of filtering was made possible in large part by the tremendous growth of university programs for public affairs and administration during the 1970s and, with them, the growing body of scholars for whom public administration remains their primary field of study.

The political school, like the movements on which it drew during the 1960s and 1970s, experienced a shift in emphasis toward applications. In this case, the shift moved the political school toward a concern for the problems of administering public programs. The shift was subtle at best. Some of the books produced in the "new" period, such as Harold Seidman's work on the politics of government organization, are indistinguishable in tone from "older" descriptions of reality such as Aaron Wildavksy's Politics of the Budgetary Process. Conversely, public administration has always been in the business of giving advice. The shift toward applications, therefore, was not as dramatic in the political school as it was, say, in the behavioral sciences.

Nonetheless, newer books in the political school tend to have more of an advisory tone. Guy Benveniste shows this with his book on the politics of planning. Martha Derthick explains how the federal government uses conditions attached to grants-in-aid to force reforms on public administrators in state government. Harold Wilensky isolates the dangers, causes and remedies of the "groupthink" phenomenon that invades intelligence gathering. James Sundquist, Steven Bailey, and Daniel Patrick Moynihan summarize the lessons gained from administering the new domestic programs coughed up by the American Congress during the expansion of government in the 1960s. Lewis Mainzer describes the principle methods by which governmental bureaucracies can be held accountable to the public and political will.

Nowhere was the advisory tone more deliberate than in the area known as implementation studies. Pressman and Wildavsky's study of the failure of the Economic Development Administration to promote employment opportunities among the poor in Oakland helped to launch this emphasis. Their book deals with the shortcomings in program design and the terribly complex job of mobilizing otherwise independent federal, state, and local administrative agencies in a cooperative venture. People working in this area seek to isolate those factors that contribute to (and distract from) successful program implementation. Technically a branch of policy analysis, implementation studies have been snapped up by public administrators anxious to give advice on the problems of administering public programs.

The triumph of the political school of thought as the central pillar of the field has had an important impact on the way in which people approach the principle areas of application. First, it has continued the preoccupation with administrative processes, an orientation that the field of study took up in its early years. The processes of personnel administration, budgeting and finance, and professional city management continue to be primary areas through which experts in public administration influence public laws and administrative policy, especially in the United States. Second, the political school of thought revitalized the importance of political theory in public administration. Political theory provides a justification for treating these areas of application not only as problems in management or economic efficiency, but also as problems of governing and social stability. This development is very apparent in the area of public personnel administration.

Public Personnel Administration

The principles of public personnel administration are as old as the systematic study of public administration -- perhaps older, since the passage of the original civil service reform act in the United States predates Woodrow Wilson's call for administrative studies by four years. Personnel administration in those early years was full of a sense of purpose, application, and reform. It was out to change government by changing the rules for hiring and promoting the people who ran it.

Once the merit system was firmly in place, personnel administration went through a phase when, in the words of Wallace Sayre, technique threatened to dominate purpose (Sayre, 1948). With the purpose largely accomplished (enactment of the merit system), personnel administration got down to the nuts and bolts of making the system work.

A number of books written during the era of applications helped to reverse the concern with technique. Perhaps the most impressive was Samuel Krislov's Representative Bureaucracy, issued in 1974. Technically a book on equal employment opportunity, the most important new reform in public personnel administration, Krislov's study quickly turned into a book on the purpose of government employment. That purpose, not as some efficiency expert might imagine, exists to minimize social conflict and preserve a willingness among the general public to be governed by the government. Unlike the judiciary or the legislative branch, which tend to be dominated by lawyers, the bureaucracy offers the principle opportunity for a wide range of ethnic, social and interest groups to take positions of influence within the regime and thus gain a larger share in the governing process. Representation is more of a problem of political representation than administrative efficiency, and Krislov's analysis places public personnel administration squarely in the political context.

Krislov cites findings from more than a half dozen Western and non-Western countries, including the United States, to make his point. Brian Chapman adds a similar dimension to the public service--public government nexus with his description of civil service systems in Europe. Paul Van Riper gives historic depth to this perspective with his political history of the U.S. civil service movement. Frederick Mosher offers his classic Democracy and the Public Service, observations on the potential conflicts between non-elected public servants and democratic ideas.

The political emphasis spawned a number of books on the politics of personnel administration. Among the most frequently cited were Frank Thompson's study of civil service politics in Oakland and Hugh Heclo's masterful study of the sparring that goes on between political appointees to the federal executive branch and top career civil servants. The political emphasis also revitalized the reforming impulse that had helped to launch this specialization, as research studies on top career executives by David Stanley, John Corson and Paul Shale helped lay the groundwork for another round of civil service reform in the United States. Once again, personnel administration became a mechanism for achieving social goals, in this case, equal employment opportunities for women and minorities. Research findings on motivation, supervision, and training were filtered through personnel administration textbooks by Jay Shafritz and even the traditional O. Glenn Stahl, while offices of personnel administration became one of the primary vehicles for feeding ideas from the behavioral sciences into public organizations. Finally, specialists in personnel administration grabbed onto one of the hottest political issues in all of government: the unionization of government employees, described in detail by Jack Steiber and a score of other authors. With all of these developments, public personnel administration no longer had to face a dismal future with little to do but classify positions and standardize salaries.

Budgeting and Finance

Like personnel administration, the area of budgeting and finance received from the political school a renewed sense of purpose. In this case, purpose came packaged as budgetary reform: the creation of new methods that would allow budgeting to be used as a tool for planning public policy.

In the orthodox era, budgeting was seen as a more or less neutral tool for controlling and measuring agency performance. Aaron Wildavsky, in the most frequently cited book in public administration, convinced nearly everyone in the field that budgeting was also a political tool, designed to set the rules affecting who got money and who got cut. In this context, budgetary reforms created a debate over not only appropriate methods, but a game of guessing whose policies would triumph and how much more they would get to spend if the rules of budgeting were changed in any significant way.

The major effort to change the rules came in the proposal for the institution of Planning-Programming-Budgeting Systems (PPB). Among authors of the most frequently cited books, Charles Schultze, David Novick, Fremont Lyden and Ernest Miller, and Leonard Merewitz and Stephen Sosnick lined up behind PPB with varying degrees of enthusiasm. Peter Pyhrr promoted zero-base budgeting, a shorter-lived reform. The most frequently cited critic was Aaron Wildavsky.

The best accounts of the pain of budgetary reform came from the states, perhaps because their administrative systems were more primitive to begin with. Primitive they did not remain, but neither were they able to swallow PPB whole, for reasons well explained by Allen Schick, John Crecine, and Thomas

Anton. Rational budgeting comes slowly, but it is coming, according to Kenneth Howard, who documents in a political context the growing acceptance of rational methods in his Changing State Budgeting.

The issue of the 1980s turned out to be money, where to get it and how to make the best use of it once it arrived. Here public administration drew on the expertise of economists who had distinguished themselves in the field of public finance. For years, through standard textbooks by James Maxwell, Otto Eckstein, and the Musgraves, students had been introduced to the economic principles underlying taxation. Now confronted by scarcity, the finance texts and their companions went considerably beyond this. The Musgraves, for example, spend two-thirds of Public Finance in Theory and Practice discussing economic principles and their application to the programs on which the government spends its tax dollars. The two Ott's, in their book on Federal Budget Policy, treat the budgetary process as an economic problem, investigating such questions as the appropriate aggregate level of government spending. L. L. Ecker-Racz, in his study of state-local finance, takes up political and administrative questions. Robert Haveman and Julius Margolis, in Public Expenditures and Policy Analysis, show how spending levels in individual programs can be subjected to economic investigation. Joseph Pechman deals with the use of tax incentives to achieve social and economic goals. User charges, government regulation, public debt, pensions and their funding: these and other aspects of public affairs are being treated as economic problems subject to economic analysis.

State and Local Administration

Concern over municipal mismanagement provided much of the motive force behind the professionalization of public administration. In 1871 the reform movement scored its first big victory over Boss Tweed in New York City, in 1904 Lincoln Steffens aroused national sentiment for municipal reform with his Shame of the Cities, and in 1906 the Bureau of Municipal Research (a philanthropic good government group) began to lay the groundwork for the "scientific" study and teaching of public administration. The International City Management Association (ICMA) was organized in 1913, promoting the idea that mayors and city councils should appoint trained managers to administer city government professionally. Today, ICMA continues to publish practical guides to effective city management and is joined in this endeavor by authors like Willis Hawley and David Rogers. Books on state and local administration, including its various political and social underpinnings, constitute one of the more significant bodies of literature on public administration.

As public administration entered its period of expansion in the 1960s (and local government expanded its work force threefold), books on state and local government continued to give advice. Appropriate to the era, however, such advice dealt less with the nuts and bolts of effective administration (although that was still present) than with the broader political question of the relationship of the federal government to the states and cities.

In his Cities and the Federal System, Roscoe Martin argued that the federal government should bypass the states and deal directly with the institutions that dealt directly with the people. Although the federal government continued to funnel most grant-in-aid programs through the states, Martin characterized state government as a relic left over from an age of agrarian simplicity. Arguments by people like Martin, increasing in popularity, eventually drew rebuttals from defenders of state government such as Terry Sanford and Daniel Elazar. Even political scientists who had traditionally viewed state government as relatively unworthy of serious scientific study began investigations that emerged in collections by people like Herbert Jacob and Kenneth Vines.

The renewed interest in intergovernmental relations led social scientists to seek to conceptualize the web of activity created by America's maze of governments, a task made difficult by the ideologically pure but factually inaccurate doctrine of "dual federalism" (the principle of separation). James Fesler struggled with the inherent conflict created by the need to relate governments both by area (e.g., Tennessee) and by function (e.g., education) and W. Brook Graves exhausted readers with his 1,000 page description of American Intergovernmental Relations. It remained for Morton Grodzins, however, to fully explain the nature of bureaus and administrators dealing across governmental lines. With his characterization of the American system as a "marble cake" of shared functions, he dismissed the traditional belief in a "layer cake" of separate functions. Grodzins' insights arrived just as the federal government began to expand its assistance programs through the federal system and thus helped to lay the groundwork for the reconsideration of American intergovernmental relations.   That reconsideration spawned block grants, revenue sharing and various proposals for "new federalisms."   These developments are summarized in a mercifully short book by Michael Reagan and John Sanzone, while the grand experiment with revenue sharing is evaluated in a much longer two-volume study led by Richard Nathan.

THE HERITAGE: A "SCIENCE" OF PUBLIC ADMINISTRATION?

The emphasis upon applications brought public administration back to the practical orientation that launched the field of study one hundred years earlier.   Today's civil service reform has its roots in the war against patronage in the 1880s. Modern efforts to improve city management echo the early years of municipal reform.   New attempts to restructure the budgetary process memorialize the budgetary struggles of the 1920s. Public administration emerged from the era of applications being what it was in the beginning: an applied science committed to solving the practical problems that affect governmental performance.

Much has changed since those early days of orthodoxy. Public administration has taken on new approaches, incorporated new disciplines, and explored new areas of specialization.   The behavioral sciences have evolved from the primitive human relations techniques of the 1920s into the carefully orchestrated methods of organization development.   Management science, once consisting of little more than Frederick Taylor's early experiments on time, motion, and the layout of work, has moved into the computer age.   Policy analysis has brought quantitative analysis and scientific experimentation to public administration.   Comparative public administration has worked to promote an ecological perspective, helping to reveal why an approach that produces miracles in one setting produces disasters in another.

In their search for understanding, people who study public administration have reached into more than a few fields and disciplines for lessons that can be applied to government. The era of applications firmly established the principle that public administration is bigger than political science, that it extends through social psychology, economics, mathematics, computer science, business administration, policy studies and beyond.

Through their influence on public administration, outlying fields and disciplines such as these have helped to lay the foundation for a more scientific field of study. The American Society for Public Administration states that its goal is "to advance the science, process, and art of public administration" (italics added). For a variety of reasons, public administration has lagged behind other social sciences in its use of scientific methods as a basis for testing propositions and building theory. When it turns to other fields and disciplines for knowledge, it often encounters those methods. Some of them rub off. The tendency within the field to borrow books and ideas from out-lying fields gives people within public administration a chance to see what scientific standards look like in practice.

Policy analysis, through practical applications such as program evaluation, reminds people in public administration of the importance of empirical verification. To say that a certain program produces certain results is to invoke scientific stand-ards of causality. Policy analysts helps to clarify those stand-ards in governmental administration, making it harder for practitioners or scholars to claim that public programs or management reforms "work" when the evidence supporting those claims is faulty.

Management science and organization development remind peo-ple in the field that sciences are often built around common units of analysis. Management science uses the decision; organization development concentrates on the small group. Since every organization is made up of people making decisions and people working in small groups, any improvement in those processes is likely to improve overall performance in the organization. Understanding how those processes work is the first step toward learning how to improving them.

Policy analysis, through the insights supplied by the public choice approach, reminds people of the importance of theory building. To many practitioners, the word theory is synony-mous with the word irrelevant. Few things, however, are as powerful in shaping governmental operations as a good theory with practical implications. Public choice theory digs into the conditions, such as the lack of competition, that affect government operations. It suggests that those conditions are often more important in shaping the performance of single agencies than government-wide administrative reform. Conditions like competition, which the American space program faced in the late 1950s, can force agencies to adopt new ways of doing business that the agency might otherwise resist. Whatever one might think of their particular theory, public choice advocates make an important contribution when they build theories that explain how external conditions such as competition shape administrative performance.

It seems amazing that public administration as a field of study could absorb all of these approaches and specializations and still remain intact. This is the major heritage of the era of applications. In spite of the splintering of the field, people backing the political approach were able to promote it as the principal means of orientation through which outlying ideas could be applied to the administrative needs of government.

People in outlying schools of thought do not always have government in mind when they formulate their principles. Even the public choice approach, which at first glance seems to be designed for government, actually turns out to be based on the theory of competition formulated for the business world. A theory formulated for business firms may not be applicable to agencies in government. Business firms come into being because individual consumers think that they must have a product and will part with their money to pay for it. Public agencies come into being because political communities conclude that governmental intervention is necessary largely without regard to the costs involved. One is a commercial transaction, the other a political act. They are, as Wallace Sayre liked to say, only similar in their unimportant respects.

The maintenance of this sensitivity to the political implications of public administration was strengthened considerably during the era of applications. It was strengthened in large part because it was challenged. Such challenges forced people in the field of study -- at the same time they were reaching out to other fields and disciplines -- to reconsider many of the political theories upon which governmental administration is based.

VALUES: A PERIOD OF RECONSIDERATION

Public administration is more than a technical management problem. When one asks the question, "what sort of public administration should we have?", one in fact is asking the question "what sort of government should we have?" Does one, for example, want a government dominated by large, non-discretionary bureaucracies (such as the Social Security Administration), organized along business lines, using computers to distribute benefits to which citizens are entitled by law? Or does one want public administrators to govern (as they do in the area of environmental policy), working with state and local officials and private firms to develop plans that meet federal standards.

The answers to these questions emerge in a number of ways. They emerge from the political theories, from 18th century liberal thought to 20th century socialism, that dominate modern societies. They emerge from the different types of governments that those theories help to produce. Answers are pushed out by events, especially as those events accumulate to form the broad economic, social and technological trends that push societies toward one form of administration or another. In more than a modest way, answers emerge from the approaches taken by scholars in the fields and disciplines. Books that scholars write often provide the intellectual justification for political and administrative movements that shape broad points of view.

Anyone who has come this far in this essay will probably guess that a body of knowledge has grown up around these things too. Some of it is borrowed from people writing about history, society or politics in general. Some of it is taken from people writing about public administration. Much of it is cited by people working in the field. It has been around for as long as the field itself, and always part of any genuinely intellectual approach to the subject.

Early in the twentieth century, writers began to worry about the consequences of the transition then underway from societies based on relatively simple agrarian principles to societies organized around large bureaucratic institutions. Commentators observed that institutional control in bureaucratic societies, both in the public and private sectors, seemed to be passing from the "owners" of organizations to the people who were in charge of managing them. In the public sector, the owners who were losing control included the public. The managers, of course, were the bureaucrats who ran the organizational society. In 1941 James Burnham examined the implications of this "managerial revolution," predicting that a new elite composed of well trained professionals would use the state bureaucracy to solidify their position as the dominant class in society. John Kenneth Galbraith expressed a similar concern through The New Industrial State, in which he warned of the damage being done to the entrepreneural spirit and the idea of limited government by professional managers concurrently in charge of corporations and government bureaus. Dwight Waldo began his career by worrying about the values that public administrators were embracing, particularly the gospel of efficiency, and whether they were compatible with the other political values that societies had been pursuing for longer periods of time.

Public administrators seemed content to simplify Waldo's concern to a single dominant question: how could a large bureaucractic state be held politically accountable using political institutions created in the eighteenth century under a philosophy of government that never anticipated the power of bureaus? Influenced as they were by the American experience, the leading writers on this subject tended to buy the pluralistic solution to the apparent conflict between bureaucracy and democracy. Check bureaucratic power by letting bureaucrats compete in the political arena, accountable not only to Congress and the President, but also to special interest groups, public interest groups, citizens, unions of public employees and anyone else who could get organized. The acceptance of this philosophy of administrative pluralism was helped enormously when Paul Appleby pointed out that this was the way that modern government actually worked. At least, this was the way that it worked in America, in the middle of the twentieth century, where wide-scale participation was the norm, helped along by a period of affluence that provided a steadily rising pot of revenues available for distribution to the groups lined up to participate.

Not everyone bought this tidy little solution to the political problems posed by bureaucratic government. In fact, three different lines of attack appeared. In 1966 Grant McConnell helped to expose how private interests "participate" under the cloak of the public interest only to promote their own well being. Three years later Theodore Lowi, in a book predicting The End of Liberalism, chastised the pluralistic ideology for paralyzing American government and weakening its ability to respond to emerging problems. That same year Kenneth Culp Davis published a treatise that attacked the foundation of pluralistic public administration: the presumption that public servants ought to have the discretion to, in Appleby's words, "make policy." Both Lowi and Davis argued for a government of nondiscretionary bureaucrats, forced to enforce the law equitably instead of entering into compromises bargained out with the groups having special interests in the policy being administered.

A group of young public administrators, soured by the products of government in the 1960s and egged on by Dwight Waldo, forced the second attack. The bureaucracy, they claimed, had grown too repressive and conservative. It was unresponsive to the issues that mattered: to the destruction of the environment, for example, and poverty. It was too preoccupied with efficiency, when values like social equity mattered at least as much. Known generally as the "new public administration," the tenants of this movement appeared in collections edited by Frank Marini and Dwight Waldo. Its advocates argued for a proactive bureaucracy in place of the theoretically neutral one for which they had been trained to serve. They pressed the case for a humane and adaptive civil service instead of an inflexible one. They insisted on the elevation of the value of social equity -- the use of governmental power to give citizens equal opportunities in society -- at least to a par with efficiency. Whereas Lowi and Davis wanted a nondiscretionary bureaucracy of jurists, the New PA wanted a proactive civil service of social reformers. This was met by the arguments of elders like Victor Thompson who pointed out that a proactive bureaucracy could just as easily be proactive against social welfare programs as for them (Thompson, 1975).

Against was what they got. The third attack on pluralistic government came from people who wanted to make the bureaucracy significantly smaller. This movement was given intellectual coherence by a group of writers who used economic theory to attack the sluggishness and undemocratic nature of bureaucratic government. These authors, among them Anthony Downs, Gordon Tullock, James Buchanan and William Niskanen, provided the intellectual justification for conservatives who wanted to dismantle social programs, "privatize" them, and let the forces of the market govern that which government had previously claimed at its domain. These authors endeavored to prove that government bureaucracies were far too sluggish to effectively serve an entrepreneural society and, what was worse, that the mechanics of pluralism tended to produce more government than the public generally wanted.

The "public choice" advocates, as they came to be known, embraced a utilitarian interpretation of direct democracy in which individuals secured their preferences through direct access to goods and services, just as they would do in a perfectly functioning private market. From the public administration community, Vincent Ostrom criticized the old guard for dodging the opportunity to embrace this market-place democracy. Instead, he said, people in public administration continued to travel the road toward the Wilsonian-Weberian model of bureaucratic professionalism. Ostrom characterized the "public choice" perspective as the modern counterpart of the Jeffersonian spirit of democratic government upon which the American republic was founded.

A significantly different public service, guided by significantly different principles, would emerge if any of these three countermovements took over the mainstream of public administration. Lowi and Davis would turn public servants into jurists, equitably enforcing the law. In this perspective, they acquired a fair measure of support from orthodox theorists who believed that interest group interference in administration significantly weakened the performance of government agencies.

Advocates of the "new" public administration would turn career civil servants into social reformers, trained to recognize justice as well as good management. Their brand of public administration received considerable support from the behavioral sciences, especially those in the organization development movement, whose advocates maintained the importance of employee initiative and participation in promoting organizational excellence.

Public choice advocates would turn public servants into organization men, public counterparts of corporate managers providing public goods and services. They received significant support from business interests upset with what they perceived to be an overly ambitious government and conservative politicians who won control of the executive branch of government in the U.S. presidential election of 1980.

When the era of applications got underway around 1965, few people gave much attention to higher level questions such as these. Spurred by the faith in pluralism and what seemed to be an endless prospect of revenue growth, most people in the field of public administration began the era of applications apparently content to perform the job of advising public managers on the various methods necessary to oil the governmental machine. The issues that characterized the early era of applications, to the extent that issues were even discussed, converged on internal administrative techniques. PPB, PERT, program evaluation, zero-base budgeting, merit pay, and transactional analysis were promoted through books that seemed tailored more for government training sessions than university seminars. Among the newly cited books initially climbing into positions of prominence in the field, over sixty percent were "how-to-do-it" books. They taught readers how to do benefit-cost analysis, how to calculate user fees, how to motivate employees, how to conduct social experiments, along with an occasional critique of faulty methods.

Attention to governance issues took hold as a countermovement to this early emphasis upon applications. The books were already there. They always had been, for the intellectual tradition goes back all the way to the beginning when reformers wrestled with questions like the proper relationship between political parties and public administration.

A number of factors combined to make value loaded political questions the central issues for public administration in the 1980s and initiate a period of reconsideration. The era of revenue growth was replaced by an era of financial crises, both in the United States and abroad. Public confidence in government, which opinion pollsters follow closely, dropped sharply, a phenomenon attributed in part to public dissatisfaction with governmental performance. Educational programs in business management acquired a reputation for toughness not

matched by educational programs in public affairs, a measure
of prestige that was reflected in an increased willingness
among public executives to turn to corporate executives for
advice on how to make government more businesslike. Finally,
the election of Ronald Reagan as President of the United
States created at least a symbolic turning point in the general
philosophy of government that had dominated the U.S. since
the pluralistic era began.

These trends affected the knowledge base of public administration -- the books being used and cited. As the era of applications drew to a close, the number of "how to do it" books
being frequently cited dropped from sixty percent to forty
percent of the whole, more in keeping with their traditional
position in the field. Books that questioned basic tenants or
suggested new approaches were cited with increasing frequency.
It did not seem to matter which position they took. Dvorin
and Simmons could call for a more humane, proactive bureaucracy; Charles Perrow could call for a more bureaucratic one.
Krislov could call for a more representative bureaucracy;
Ostrom could call for one more limited in scope. Ida Hoos
could attack systems analysis; Alice Rivlin could praise it. It
did not seem to matter what the new books advocated so
much as the fact that they advocated something.

Most important, the prescriptions to come out of books such as
these drew on political and social philosophy. The newly cited
titles by Marini, Waldo, Krislov, Ostrom, Hoos, Dvorin and
Simmons all drew on political and social theory. Even Charles
Perrow, writing what appeared to be a textbook on organization theory, paused long enough to point out the movements in
social philosophy -- such as the desire for equality under the
law -- that bureaucratic organizations tended to fulfill.

The reconstruction of these political and social issues strengthened the political school of thought as the central pillar in the
field of study. Because it treats public administration as a
problem in governing -- and less as a problem in administrative
efficiency -- the political school relies upon political and social
philosophy in its consideration of administrative issues. Dwight
Waldo, in his classic work on The Administrative State, took
orthodox administrative principles and stood them up against
classic questions of political philosophy. What, he asked, was
the position of early administrative scientists on the purpose of

government, the role of government in promoting "the good life," and the choice of who should rule? Waldo shocked those who thought that the orthodox administrative science movement was "value free" by pointing out that the engineers of government promoting the orthodox view had published definitive answers to questions such as these.

Other authors unsettled the field of study by raising questions about the philosophic foundations of governmental administration. Public choice theorists, in the process of sniping at modern governmental administration, reintroduced the important philosophic question of whether a direct democracy might not be superior to a representative one. In their ideal democratic state, citizens would select the goods and services they wanted directly from the administrative arm of government rather than allowing elected representatives do that for them. When public administration is guided by political philosophy, all sorts of interesting issues arise. Alan Altschuler, in a book of readings that comes as close as one can to this political point of view, raises issues like secrecy, news management, and the role of the public interest in public administration.

Having the political school of thought serve as the mainstream of public administration draws attention to issues such as these. The political perspective helped to create the period of reconsideration, where administrative questions that superficially might seem to be matters of efficiency and effectiveness could be turned into debates about government and society and how one wished to see these things organized. Insistence on this point of view in recent years has strengthened Appleby's dictum that "government is different" when it comes to discussing administration, different in particular than the administration of business enterprises. Appleby was a practitioner, and it often takes a practitioner to remind the uninitiated of that. When a recent President, one of two in the last century to be trained as an engineer, sought to institute a business-like merit pay system in the public sector, a practitioner from the National Park Service rose at a Presidential town meeting to remind him.

> Unlike much of private industry, the work of government can only rarely be evaluated on profit and loss statements or in the products of an assembly line.

> Most of the career people . . . draw their principle
> rewards from highly intangible, albeit deeply felt
> satisfactions of helping to try to make a difference in
> the quality of national life. (Carter, 1978, p. 1362)

In practice, there is no law of nature that says that the
administrative machinery of government must be considered
from a different point of view. The latitude for choice is
great. Government can be run like a business if it is set up
that way. It can be as bureaucratic as the governors make it.
Programs to combat poverty can be run with the participation
of the poor or they can be packaged and delivered up like
insurance policies. Park rangers can take an active role in
environmental protection or parks can be privatized and run by
concessionaires. Bureaucrats can be responsive to clientele
groups or they can be ciphers.

So long as public administration deals with applications, a
motive remains for turning it into a science of efficiency for
a government managed by nonentities. Make no mistake about
it -- public administration is strongly oriented toward applications. Fully forty percent of the most frequently cited books
to be found in the next section are little more than elaborate
"how to do it" manuals. Another forty percent are descriptions of administrative practice or organizational behavior.
Only twenty percent of the 181 books that follow prescribe
values or deal with political theory. Nonetheless, public
administration maintains a sufficient amount of political and
social theory at its core to prevent the triumph of a purely
mechanistic approach to governmental administration. It seems
to be getting more. The period of reconsideration is forcing
people concerned with public affairs to address questions such
as the value of pluralism in an era of cut-back management or
the utility of allowing government to perform functions that
could be left to the private sector. Still, the full volume of
public administration consists of knowledge and applications
drawn from a wide variety of sources. Any one of those
sources, from business management to the behavioral sciences
or the economic theory of "public choice," have the opportunity to supplant the primary orientation. They constantly try,
as the mainstream political school is tested by competing ideas
and approaches.

SUMMARY

Public administration is an area of practice based upon a body
of knowledge. In the arena of applications, it has increasingly
taken on the characteristics of a professional field of practice.
Professional practice above all means that practitioners turn to
a body of knowledge and experience for their expertise.
Increasingly the process of building that body of knowledge,
viewed especially from the perspective of those who specialize
in producing it, has taken on the twentieth century characteristics of an academic discipline.

As people who study the subject well know, public administration is based upon many bodies of knowledge. The orthodox
period contributed the principles of administration. The era of
description produced the behavioral school and the mainstream
political school through which many of the outlying sources of
knowledge are filtered. Policy analysis, management science,
comparative public administration, and organization development reached maturity during the era of applications. The
period of reconsideration has helped to reestablish the principle
that good administration remain as much a question of political
philosophy as managerial efficiency.

Public administration draws upon the disciplines and fields of
economics, sociology, psychology, political science, business
administration, labor relations, philosophy, history, mathematics
and law. It applies what it knows from a wide range of fields
and disciplines to a wide variety of administrative areas, from
personnel administration, budgeting, finance, state and local
administration to modern problems like implementation, evaluation, representation, and bureaucratic responsiveness.

Different approaches bid for dominance, but the political
school of thought has served as the mainstream of scholarly
study for the last forty years. Even so, public administration
has not been guided entirely by the political approach. It has
shown the ability to collect knowledge and theories from a
variety of sources. Public administration accumulates. In
scholarship and practice, public administration retains a
remarkable ability to remember the past and retain the peri-
pheral, picking up knowledge from wherever it needs it. As
the field turns new corners, the past will not die, no more
than the orthodox principles of administration have disappeared

even though their shortcomings have been known for at least fifty years. As new events bring prominence to new specializations and even new schools of thought, they will come to rest upon the building blocks of the past that form the knowledge base of the field that is public administration.

REFERENCES

Carter, Jimmy, 1978. "Federal Service Reform and Reorganization," Weekly Compilation of Presidential Documents, Vol. 14, No. 31, August 3, 1978. Washington: Government Printing Office.

Fayol, Henri, 1916. General and Industrial Management. New York: Pitman Publishing Company.

Gulick, Luther, 1937. "Science, Values and Public Administration," in Luther Gulick and L. Urwick, eds., Papers on the Science of Administration. New York: Augustus M. Kelley Publishers, pp. 191-195.

Nisbet, Robert A., 1976. "Social Sciences, History of," The New Encyclopedia Britannica. Macropedia, Vol. 16. Chicago: Encyclopedia Britannica, Inc.

Perrow, Charles, 1979. Complex Organizations, 2nd ed. Glenview, IL: Scott, Foresman & Company.

Sayre, Wallace, 1948. "The Triumph of Techniques Over Purpose," Public Administration Review. 8 (Spring, 1948) 134-137.

Thompson, Victor, 1975. Without Sympathy or Compassion. University, AL: University of Alabama Press.

Waldo, Dwight, 1975. "Education for Public Administration in the Seventies," in Frederick C. Mosher, ed. American Public Administration. University, AL: University of Alabama Press.

Webster's Third New International Dictionary of the English Language (Unabridged). Springfield, MA: G. & C. Merriam Co., 1976.

Wilson, Woodrow, 1887. "The Study of Administration," Political Science Quarterly, June 1887; reprinted in 56 (December 1941) 481-506.

III The Most Frequently Cited Books in Public Administration, with Reviews

The number of books written about public administration or borrowed from other fields and applied to public affairs easily approaches two thousand. Since its inception in 1940, for example, the editors of the Public Administration Review have selected some 1,700 books to appear in their book review sections. In constructing the new ranking for this bibliography, over two thousand books were identified. Obviously, this is a frightening large number for a student or practitioner who only has time to review the most important works in the field. Where should such a person begin?

Out of that larger group of books, a few hundred have achieved the status of classics or are so frequently used that their contributions deserve to be known to all persons working in the field. This section identifies one such list of books, based on the frequency with which they are cited by experts also working in the field. The books, along with brief reviews of them, are presented in alphabetical order.

In order for a book to place in this top ranking division, it generally must be cited by persons working within a number of the areas that contribute to our understanding of public affairs and administration. The bibliography is constructed in such a way as to produce this effect. If a book is used only within a single area, it generally will not receive sufficient citations to climb into the most frequently cited category. It may have made a valuable contribution to that area of specialization, but unless it is cited by persons working in other areas as well it will not appear below. The books that follow, as a result, tend to belong to the field as a whole. The top-ranked Politics of the Budgetary Process, by Aaron Wildavsky, provides a good illustration. Ostensibly written for students of public budgeting, this book is used widely by persons working in other areas such as policy analysis, organization theory, and administrative politics.

The use of citations to create this bibliography produces another important effect. Books do not arrive in the "most frequently cited" category until they have been around long enough to prove their importance. The ranking system is set up in such a way as to highlight established works, especially those that are recognized as classics in the field. It favors books that have been around long enough to acquire recognition; conversely, it is slow to recognize new titles on their way up the list.

A series of code numbers and letters reveal the relative importance of each book in the cross-referencing scheme. The citation for the top-ranked book in the bibliography, Aaron Wildavsky's classic study of the budgetary process, appears as follows:

> Wildavksy, Aaron, The Politics of the Budgetary Process. Boston: Little, Brown and Company, 1964. Subsequent eds. O-B-P-M-U-T-G-F (15 + 21 = 36)

The numbers reveal the frequency of citation. Out of the eighty-one lists merged to create this bibliography, Wildavsky's book can be found on thirty-six, or nearly half. In addition, the book is being cited with more frequency today than two decades ago when it was first published. This is indicated by the two numbers that add up to the citation frequency. Wildavsky's book received fifteen citations on the forty lists used to create the first ranking, lists representing the field as people viewed it in the mid to late 1960s. The citation frequency

increased when the new ranking was created. On forty-one
new lists, which reflect views of the field in the late 1970s
and early 1980s, Wildavsky's book was cited on twenty-one.

To gain entrance to this section containing the most frequently
cited books in public administration, a book had to receive a
combined ranking of at least seven citations. At least three
of those citations had to come from the new ranking. A new
book -- defined as one with no standing in the first ranking --
needed six citations to break into this top division. The rankings from the two periods were combined deliberately. This
was done in such a way as to insure that books totally
removed from favor would move out while classics still being
cited, although with less frequency, would remain. Had only
the new ranking been used, whole sections of the field -- such
as the study of comparative public administration -- would
have disappeared.

Accompanying the numbers are a series of letters which indi-
cate the areas within public administration where each book
tends to be used and cited. The citation for Herbert Simon's
pioneering work on administrative behavior, one of top four
books in the combined ranking, is followed by seven letters.
Nine are possible. All of them are shown in Table 4.

Simon, Herbert S., Administrative Behavior. New York:
The Free Press, 1945. Subsequent eds. O-B-P-M-
U-T-G (14 + 16 = 30)

Table 4. Codes Used to Categorize the Eighty-One Lists
Cross-Referenced to Create the Bibliography

Code   Area From Which the List Came

O   Organization Theory and Behavior
B   The Study of Bureaucracy
P   Policy Analysis
M   The Study of Public Management and
            Personnel Administration
U   State and Local Public Administration
T   Management Science
G   General Overviews of Public Administration,
            as in a general textbook
C   Comparative Public Administration
F   Budgeting and Public Finance

As each of the eighty-one lists was fed into the bibliography, the list was categorized and labeled on the basis of the area from which it came. A list of books covering organization theory, for example, would be tagged with the letter "O." The citation for Simon's book indicates that it can be found on thirty lists from seven different areas of public administration. Not only is Simon's classic cited by people working in the area of organization theory, but by people working in six other areas as well. This reaffirms the tendency of the most important books to belong to the field as a whole rather than to any single specialization within it.

Finally, the bibliography reveals when the book first appeared by listing the original date of publication rather than the date of the most recent edition. Where later editions have emerged, the original date of publication is followed by the notation "subsequent ed(s)."

By noting the original year of publication, the bibliography calls attention to the period when the book began to have an impact upon the field of study. The influence of most important books, as well as their principle contributions to the field, commonly rests with the first edition. Simon's book provides a good example. It had a major impact on the field of public administration when it first appeared in 1945. In the revised editions, Simon has added some new features, but the most important material from the first edition of the book remains intact. In those cases where an author has significantly changed a book through a revision, that is described in the review of it.

Because these books belong to the field as a whole, it behooves the student or practitioner of public administration to become familiar with the entire section. These 181 books are the principal knowledge base upon which the practice of public administration is based. To introduce these books, short reviews follow, outlining the most important contribution of each book to the field, the specialization from which it comes, its major findings or points of emphasis and the range of topics with which it deals.

Allison, Graham T., Essence of Decision: Explaining the Cuban
Missile Crises. Boston: Little, Brown & Company, 1971.
G-P-M-T (0+8=8) The book that helped to launch the
"bureaucratic politics" interpretation of executive policy
making. Actually, Allison interprets the events of the
Cuban missile crisis through three schools of thought,
without favoring any one in particular. The first two,
however, had previously been laid out in some detail, so
that the introduction of the third -- the bureaucratic politics interpretation -- created the most interest. Allison
spends two chapters interpreting the crisis through the
"rational actor" approach, set in calculated, strategic
choices. He then repeats the analysis through the lens of
Simon's organization theory, revealing a sluggish, disorganized scenario propelled by familiar organizational behavior
patterns and routines. Following this, he reinterprets the
events as if they were bargaining games played by top
policy-makers and organizations jockeying to promote their
own perception of the crises and maneuver themselves into
positions of greater influence: the bureaucratics politics
school. Allison ends by suggesting that the latter two
interpretations deserve as much attention as the rational
approach.

Altshuler, Alan A., The Politics of the Federal Bureaucracy.
New York: Dodd, Mead & Company, 1968. Subsequent
eds. B-U-P-G-O (3+4=7) A book of readings on the politics of administration from the point of view of an academic political scientist. Altshuler would like to convince
people in the discipline of political science "that American
public administration can very fruitfully be studied as a
branch of American politics," as if public administration
had not long since abandoned political science in search of
wider perspectives and friendlier allies. Still, one is curi-
ous to see what public administration might look like under
those terms, and the book supplies a view that is much
more public interest conscious than the standard fare.
Altshuler's selections begin with the "fundamental issues:"
bureaucracy and hierarchy versus democracy and decentralization. Through the readings, he explores the likelihood
of executive supremacy and the methods (news management
receiving equal time with budgeting, for example) by which
executives reduce conflict and reenforce control. A final
section throws the reader onto a philosophic plane, with

theoretical pieces on the nature of the public interest in
public administration and the "responsible" exercise of executive discretion.

Anderson, James E., Public Policy-Making. New York: Holt,
   Rinehart & Winston, 1975. Subsequent eds. P-M-G-U
   (0+6=6) An introductory textbook for students studying the
   policy making process and persons wondering what policy
   analysts do. The book is organized into chapters that cor-
   respond to the "stages" of policy development: the policy
   environment, where problems are identified and political-
   socio-economic factors set the stage for the policy debate;
   the formation process, where the policy is adopted; implementation, where the policy is carried out; and evaluation,
   where the impact of the policy is gauged. Two additional
   chapters discuss special issues in the policy sciences: the
   different models that policy analysts use to describe the
   process, the different ways of categorizing public policies
   so as to study the differences between them, the methods
   by which government agencies attempt to enforce compliance with their policies, and the elusive concept of the
   public interest. The chapters are supported by careful
   summaries of leading policy studies and by practical examples from government programs.

Anthony, Robert N., Planning and Control Systems. Boston:
   Graduate School of Business Administration, Harvard University, 1965. G-T-M-P-F (5+5=10) A basic classification
   scheme for students of management science which identifies the major elements of any planning and control system. In essay fashion, Anthony defines and explains
   strategic planning, management control, and operational
   control. He then goes on to examine the special problems
   of processing information and "reporting financial information about the organization to the outside world." Speaking through the confusion of the literature, he urges
   administrators and scholars to think in terms of these
   three elements of administration, rather than in terms of
   time, techniques, functions, or types of organization.

Anton, Thomas J., The Politics of State Expenditures in Illinois. Urbana: University of Illinois Press, 1966. F-P-U-G
   (2+6=8) A case study on the chaos of state budgeting in
   Illinois in the early 1960's by a participant observer. In

separate chapters, Anton examines the role of the state legislature, a joint executive-legislative Budgetary Commission, the Department of Finance and its Superintendent of Budgets, the Governor, and the various administrative agencies, with the latter having the most influence over expenditure decisions and the legislature acting in near-complete ignorance. With colorful political lore, Anton characterizes the system as incremental, haphazard, and occasionally corrupt. The book is usefully read as a companion to Kenneth Howard's and Allen Schick's books on state budgeting reform, allowing the reader to contrast traditional budgeting with the emerging system based in policy analysis.

Appleby, Paul H., Policy and Administration. University, AL: University of Alabama Press, 1949. O-G-M-P-B-C (6+4=10) In one of the leading rebuttals of the politics-administration dichotomy, this journalist turned administrator turned academic sets out the general themes that were to guide the political school of thought in public administration. Appleby contends that "public administration is policy making," and as policy making is subject to the same constraints as other major political processes such as elections and enacting legislation. He uses the first two chapters to lay out this argument, disarming the fallacy that administration may be treated separately from policy and describing administration as "the eighth political process." It is here that Appleby lays out his definition of public administration, emphasizing his view that public administration is much more a matter of governing than of management. Public administration, he says, is "the government in direct action on behalf of and in restraint of citizens; policy making in administration is the exercise of discretion with respect to such action." In the remainder of the book (four chapters) Appleby takes up special problems that confront public administrators given this definition: the reconciliation of partisan politics and administrative expertise, the need for an administrative structure that allows the public organization to respond to public demands, the checks upon arbitrary administrative action, and the influence of ideology and demands for citizen participation upon public administration.

Appleby, Paul H., <u>Morality</u> <u>and</u> <u>Administration</u> <u>in</u> <u>Democratic</u>
    <u>Government</u>.   Baton Rouge: Louisiana State University
    <u>Press, 1952</u>.   O-M-B-G (3+5=8) Joined with <u>Big</u> <u>Democracy</u>
    (1945) and <u>Policy</u> <u>and</u> <u>Administration</u> (1949), this volume
    completes Appleby's trilogy on the nature of public admin-
    istration.   As such, it is much more a book on Appleby's
    theory of political administration than strictly a work on
    ethics.   Appleby continues his "goldfish bowl" analogy,
    arguing that government executives in the public eye are
    expected to observe much higher ethical standards in mak-
    ing policy than business executives.   A business executive
    may hire friends and accept gifts from contractors, but a
    public official who uses his or her office for private gain
    triggers public outrage.   Many problems in government
    ethics, Appleby suggests, occur because political appointees
    bring with them into the public service the ethics of the
    business world.   The public sector, moreover, imposes spe-
    cial moral expectations on an already difficult situation.
    Through his discussion of these expectations, Appleby pre-
    sents the most refined version of his political theory of
    public administration.   He discusses democracy and the
    public interest, the special role of law and formal adminis-
    trative procedures, the problem of balancing administrative
    responsibility with the many institutions to which the
    administrator must be accountable, the way in which poli-
    tical accountability works to prevent bureaucratic rigidity,
    the efforts of pressure groups to influence administrators,
    and the problems of building effective public organizations
    in a political system where the public tends to distrust the
    government.   In the final chapter, Appleby returns to mor-
    ality, outlining the pattern of administrative responsibility
    that he finds most compatible with the special require-
    ments of a political democracy.   Like the two books
    before it, this is a series of lectures based largely on
    Appleby's twelve years of service with the federal govern-
    ment.

Argyris, Chris, <u>Interpersonal</u> <u>Competence</u> <u>and</u> <u>Organizational</u>
    <u>Effectiveness</u>.   Homewood, IL: Richard D. Irwin, Inc.,
    1962.   O-M-T-G (7+5=12) Argyris applies a program of
    behavioral change to a large corporation in the American
    Mid-West.   His basic hypothesis is that "the present organ-
    izational strategies developed and used by administrators
    lead to human and organizational decay."   This hypothesis

is based on earlier theoretical and empirical work in which
Argyris argued that increased managerial controls and use
of technology tended to create greater tension, anxiety,
and unproductive conflict among the work force. His
"research" for testing this hypothesis consists of interviews
with the 18 company executives who went through his program of behavioral change. The book consists of four
parts: a theoretical section on interpersonal relations in
formal organizations; data and propositions gathered from
the diagnosis of executives behavior during the program; a
description of the structure and underlying philosophy of
T-group education; and a section which attempts to
confirm the positive impact of the program on the executives who participated in it.

Argyris, Chris, Integrating the Individual and the Organization.
New York: John Wiley & Sons, 1964. G-O-T-M-B (8+5=13)
A more mature and elaborate version of his earlier Personality and Organization, in which Argyris had concluded,
after reviewing existing research, that there was a "lack of
congruence between the needs of healthy individuals and
the demands of the formal organization." In this book
Argyris presents his "mix model" -- a continuum of six
essential properties determining the presence of a healthy
work environment -- and searches through existing empirical studies for examples of the ideal firm. He then moves
about propositions on how organizations might be rede-
signed to enlarge worker responsibilities and eliminate
first-line supervision, focusing on managerial rewards and
penalties, manpower development, and the structure of
work. The first section is a restatement of earlier writings with a defense against charges of middle-class bias.

Bailey, Stephen K., and Edith K. Mosher, ESEA: The Office of
Education Administers a Law. Syracuse: Syracuse University Press, 1968. O-P-M (5+3=8) An excellent case study
of program development relating the role of the U.S. Office of Education to the legislative and administrative
genesis of the Elementary and Secondary Education Act of
1965. The authors focus on the process by which an old-
line agency with ties to traditional education groups learns
to innovate while tripling the size of its budget. It
demonstrates how bureaucratic organizations can create
responsive change through incremental and pluralistic

methods. The first two chapters describe the enactment of the ESEA; the following chapters explain the reorganization of the Office of Education and the development of specific programs under the various titles of the Act. They authors conclude with a inventory of administrative policy problems that affected the implementation of the ESEA, including the question of how much federal control the agency should exercise over program participants and the effectiveness of program evaluation.

Barnard, Chester I., The Functions of the Executive. Cambridge: Harvard University Press, 1938. O-B-P-M-U-T-G (13+17=30) A book which is credited with helping to inspire the behavioral revolution. It was written by a practitioner, the President of New Jersey Bell. Barnard felt that the orthodox theories of Frederick Taylor and Henri Fayol did not adequately explain his own experiences as a manager. Encouraged by Elton Mayo and his colleagues at Harvard University, where Barnard had studied many years before as an undergraduate, Barnard began to set his own experience down on paper. The result was a book that helped to propel the relatively simplistic human relations principles collected by Mayo and F. J. Roethlisberger into the richly baroque social systems theory of scholars like Herbert Simon. Barnard turned orthodox management theory on its head. The organization, said Barnard, is not created from above, as Luther Gulick and Fayol had proposed. It is made up of a collection of work groups that are inspired to work together because their cooperation satisfies individual needs. Barnard begins his definition of organization at the group level: "a system of consciously coordinated activities or forces of two or more persons." The function of the executive class -- simply another work group in the organizational collage -- is threefold. It must maintain the willingness to cooperate, maintain the system of communication, and maintain the purpose of the organization. To explain the willingness to cooperate, Barnard presented his famous theory on the "economy of incentives," likening the motivation of workers to buyers with widely varying wants expressing their desires through a market. His thoughts on communication tore away the assumptions behind bureaucratic authority. Authority, Barnard insisted, did not exist "in the office" or on an organization chart. Authority is nothing more than the ability to issue a communique and have it carried out, a process that depends largely on the consent of the recipient and the existance of redundant channels of communication created by the informal organization. Barnard wrote the book for practicing administrators as much as for scholars; as a result the book is not organized like a scholarly tome. In the first part Barnard works to convince the reader that organizations are social systems made up of cooperating groups and individuals; in part two he describes the social factors that are necessary to bring the organization into equilibrium, including the informal organization. In part three he presents his views on specific elements of organization life, including specialization, incentives, authority, and decision making. The fourth and final section is devoted largely to a discussion of the tasks and moral responsibilities of executives.

Bauer, Raymond A., and Kenneth J. Gergen, eds., The Study of Policy Formulation. New York: The Free Press, 1968. O-P-T-F-G (5+5=10) Policy analysts are intensely interested in how policy gets made. This early collection of nine papers searches for scientific models and a research strategy that can be used to explain the policy formulation process. The backgrounds of the authors betray the models upon which they will rely. The Harvard Business School and its friends, the Harvard Economics Department and the Swarthmore Psychology Department, outnumber the lone political scientist. The result is a book that reads much more like a treatise on organization theory than American politics. The most memorable papers are the four that take the reader through a series of formal models that explain in an abstract way how politicians handle problems of choice, priorities, uncertainty, strategy, and leverage. Three papers apply the models to particular policy issues. One paper assesses different research methods and Bauer contributes his impressions on various aspects of this developing area of study.

Bennis, Warren G., Kenneth D. Benne, and Robert Chine, eds., The Planning of Change: Readings in the Applied Behavioral Sciences. New York: Holt, Rinehart & Winston, 1961. O-T-M-C-P-B-G (9+7=16) Warren Bennis is one of the leading contributors to the organization development field, an area of study that is fundamentally concerned with the process of social and organizational change. In this ambitious collection of over 80 papers, he and his coauthors explore various aspects of social change. Through their arrangement of the papers and extensive introductory remarks before each chapter, the authors seek to apply social science research to the "urgent needs" of persons attempting to manage change. The twelve chapters are arranged into four sections on the origin of efforts to plan and control change, basic conceptual approaches to social systems and models of change, the phenomenon of social influence, and particular techniques for managing change, especially small group techniques. Most of the papers are theoretical or research-oriented.

Bennis, Warren G., Changing Organizations. New York: McGraw-Hill, 1966. G-O-T-P-M (10+7=17) Within the behavioral sciences, Bennis is most widely known for his prediction that bureaucracy as we know it will die out within the next fifty years. As a form of organization, he says, bureaucracy cannot respond to the modern pressures placed upon it: the rapid pace of technological change, the "inevitability" of democracy as "the only system which can successfully cope with the changing demands of contemporary civilization," and the increasingly large number of organizational employees who count themselves as members of professions. In the first half of the book, Bennis presents his death of bureaucracy thesis along with some thoughts on emerging trends in the behavioral sciences and how they are changing conventional views of organizational leadership. The second half offers optimistic guidance from the behavioral sciences that can be used to assist organizations in making the transition from bureaucracy to the post-industrial adhocracy, mainly through laboratory training. Excellent reviews of existing organizational theory are included. This book was the basis for Alvin Toffler's only chapter on administration in his best selling Future Shock.

Bennis, Warren G., and Philip E. Slater, The Temporary Society. New York: Harper & Row, 1968. O-M-B-G (2+5=7) Another expression of Bennis' belief that bureaucracy is dying, although in a slightly different context. Bennis, who has studied large public and industrial organizations, teams up with Slater, an expert on the family.

The result is six short essays that examine the impact of complexity and chronic change on social institutions large and small. Bennis argues that organizations must become more adaptive and that new forms of organizational leadership must emerge, while Slater examines the emergence of the "democratic family" and the development of intense but temporary human relationships. Together the two argue that democracy is inevitable for society as a whole as those societies encounter the demands of contemporary civilization.

Bennis, Warren G., Organization Development. Reading, MA: Addison-Wesley Publishing Co., 1969. O-G-M-T (4+5=9) The first in a six volume set by different authors on the emerging field of organization development. In this small book, Bennis offers up a broad survey on the origins and practice of OD and one of the best definitions of what its advocates are up to. Bennis puts forth his belief that "every age develops an organizational form most appropriate to the genius of that age," and offers his prediction that the old form is dying. He defines OD as an "educational strategy" designed to help manage the transition from older forms to the new form which, he believes, can best occur by changing the "culture" of the organization. Bennis is at his best describing the humanistic, democratic, self-awareness ideology of the "change agents" who promote the development of the new organizational culture. The book also contains some practical advice on the mechanics of organizational intervention for those who would be change agents and those managers who would invite them in, followed by a short chapter on one of the earliest intervention strategies in this fast moving field -- sensitivity training. In a final chapter titled "reconsiderations," some of the nervousness about whether all of this will work shows through.

Benveniste, Guy, The Politics of Expertise. Berkeley: Glendessary Press, 1972. Subsequent ed. G-B-M (0+7=7) A perceptive book on planning in government that labors to convince the reader that planning must be treated as part of the political process. The primary purpose of planning, Benveniste argues, is to reduce uncertainty to tolerable levels by pointing out what is possible given "the multiplicity of alternatives" created by technology and the problems of implementing programs in highly differentiated, interdependent societies. This, he says, is a distinctly political function. When their statements are perceived as true, planners have a "multiplier effect." Their statements about the future, such as what to spend on national defense, become the basis for decisions by governmental and business institutions about courses of action they might take. Within this definition of public sector planning, Benveniste discusses the official and unofficial functions that planners perform, the way they think, and how planning works in a variety of countries from Russia to western Europe, the U.S. and the third world. The second half of the book is devoted to an examination of "how experts acquire power," the tactics they use, the coalitions they form "to bring about the multiplier effect," and the strategic decisions they make about what to plan. The book is based largely on Benveniste's insights gained from years of government service and a selective review of the planning literature.

Bernstein, Marver, Regulating Business by Independent Commission. Princeton, NJ: Princeton University Press, 1955. P-G (3+5=8) A classic study of the purpose and operation of independent regulatory commissions. Bernstein traces the development of the regulatory movement from the 18th century and the progressive movement to the present time. He presents his famous "life cycle" of commissions: gestation, youth, maturity, and decline. He reviews, without much sympathy, the arguments for strict, judicial-like independence of commissions. He considers a variety of problems in regulatory practice, including the difficulties of promoting expertness in commissions, the movement to establish uniform regulatory procedures, and the effectiveness of commissions in enforcing compliance with their decisions. Through the book, Bernstein stresses the theme that regulation is "inescapably political." Regulatory commissions operate amidst an intense struggle between groups "for political and economic advantage." Bernstein faults the legal theory of regulation, with its impossible quest for judicial style independence and court-like procedures, for ignoring the political realities required for successful administration. To be effective, Bernstein concludes, regulatory commissions must develop regulatory practices (he lists thirteen) that are far more political and managerial in character than legal. The book is based generally on the literature on regulation, backed up with plenty of examples from the seven most important regulatory commissions in the United States.

Blau, Peter M., The Dynamics of Bureaucracy. Chicago: University of Chicago Press, 1955. O-B-M-P-G (9+3=12) One of the most important books on the sociology of bureaucracy. Blau examines the activities of low-level officials in two bureaucracy settings: the adjustment in behavior following the introduction of a statistical performance appraisal system in a subunit of a state employment agency; and the informal work arrangements among members of a subunit of a district office of a federal law enforcement agency. (Both contained about 20 employees.) The congenial, work-facilitating behavior of the federal bureaucrats produced efficiency, but violated departmental rules. Blau concludes that bureaucrats do not inherently resist change, but only under certain conditions, the chief one being status insecurity.

Blau, Peter M., and Marshall W. Meyer, Bureaucracy in Modern Society. New York: Random House, 1956. Subsequent eds. M-G-T-B-D-C (5+5=10) A tightly written summary of the bureaucratic perspective on public administration. It contains an excellent summary of the writings of Max Weber joined together with modern studies of "bureaucracy's other face:" informal groups, bureaucratic power, and bureaucratic pathology. There are chapters on the rationalization of modern life, the theory and development of the bureaucratic form of organization, informal behavior and bureaucratic ideology, bureaucratic authority, research findings based on the comparative study of organizations, and the problems of change and democracy in a bureaucratic society.

Blau, Peter M., and W. Richard Scott, Formal Organizations: A Comparative Approach. San Francisco: Chandler Publishing Co., 1962. T-B-M-G (6+8=14) A textbook on the sociology of bureaucratic forms of organization. It focuses on the formal and informal aspects of large organizations, bringing together extensive findings from existing social theory and empirical research. The authors' aim is to "explain some of the principles that govern organizational

life." Those principles encompass the writings of Max
Weber, a typology of organizations, the relationships between organizations, their publics, and the total social system, peer group relations, the informal structure of work
groups, communication and task performance, supervision
and hierarchical authority, managerial control and manipulation and organizational change.

Boguslaw, Robert, The New Utopians. Englewood Cliffs, NJ:
Prentice-Hall, 1965. O-T-P-B-G (4+4=8) A fascinating
book about computers, the people who use them, and the
impact that computer system technology is having upon the
modern world. Boguslaw intended to write "a relatively
straightforward description of problems in the analysis and
design of contemporary large-scale computer-based command and control systems," and the book does provide a
nontechnical description of linear programming, game
theory, operating unit design, and other models utilized by
the new computer priesthood. The more he wrote, however, the more Boguslaw became impressed with the
"intellectual underpinnings" of computer science and the
"formulations of social theorists in the Utopian tradition."
In some detail he discusses the intellectual posture of systems designers, the type of world they are trying to
create, and the lack of influence that the majority of the
people have over modern technology. Traditionally, utopians have been impatient with human imperfections.
Boguslaw warns that the new utopians plan to deal with
human imperfections by using machines as substitutes for
people, by substituting calculations of efficiency for
humanistic ideals, and by relying upon technological control.

Bradford, Leland P., Jack R. Gibb and Kenneth D. Benne, eds.,
T-Group Theory and Laboratory Method. New York: John
Wiley & Sons, 1964. O-P (6+3=9) One of the best collections of papers on laboratory training or T-groups as
developed by the National Training Laboratory in Group
Development. T-groups were one of the earliest techniques
used by organization development specialists in their
efforts to promote organizational change. The authors
examine how T-groups help participants learn about themselves, about individual motivation, and about interpersonal
relations in groups. The first five articles introduce the

reader to the history and operating techniques of T-groups. The next nine articles treat various aspects of T-group learning goals and processes. A third section of four articles compares T-groups to other educational techniques and presents a survey of research on the subject.

Braybrooke, David, and Charles E. Lindblom, A Strategy of Decision: Policy Evaluation as a Social Process. New York: The Free Press, 1963. O-G-P-F-B (7+5=12) A highly theoretical book which develops Lindblom's ideas on bargaining and incrementalism. In fact, this is two books: five chapters on social science and policy making by Lindblom and four chapters by Braybrooke on philosophy and ethics. Both are upset with their academic colleagues for adopting analytic models that do not account for the complexity and uncertainty "that beset social analysts in the real world." Lindblom is upset with analysts who adopt the rational-deductive approach or try to promote the highly mathematical calculation of a general welfare function. Braybrooke is upset with the inability of anyone to calculate a solution to a real problem using the doctrines of utilitarianism. Lindblom suggests that the most effective method of using information and reconciling values is through "disjointed incrementalism," i.e., making choices that are in the close neighborhood of the status quo. Braybrooke believes that disjointed incrementalism supports what he calls a "felicific census" (felicific means to make happy) that allows utility to be considered in cases where different policies are in dispute. Braybrooke's proof will seem foggy to anyone lacking a background in philosophy; Lindblom's arguments on why the doctrine gets used in practice sound more familiar. The book was significant inasmuch as it offered a full-blown analysis of incrementalism, a concept which at that time Lindblom had been developing for about ten years.

Buchanan, James M., and Gordon Tullock, The Calculus of Consent. Ann Arbor: The University of Michigan Press, 1962. B-P-F-G (3+6=9) A distinctly original interpretation of democratic politics and an influential piece in the intellectual development of the "public choice" school of policy analysis. Buchanan and Tullock begin with the general theory of rational behavior contained in the study of economics. They assume, based on this theory, that individuals in society seek to minimize the costs imposed on them by collective decisions (such as taxes or government regulation) as well as minimize the costs that they personally incur when they seek to organize collective action to solve a problem. Under what conditions, then, will individuals turn to government for collective action (as opposed to solving problems through private firms or associations) and with what consequences? Drawing on the theory of games, Buchanan and Tullock analyze governmental arrangements that provide collective action to individuals at low participation costs (rule by simple majority.) These, they endeavor to prove, will result in overinvestment in the public sector (relative to the advantages of private collective action) and do ultimate damage to the assumed desire of individuals to minimize the costs imposed on them by collective decisions. It is more efficient, and ultimately more rational, say the authors, to insist upon unanimous consent rules (such as checks and balances) to initiate governmental action. Regardless of what one thinks of the authors' ideological conclusions (their preference for less government), the analysis of constitutional decision making through the theory of rational behavior sets out an important intellectual challenge.

Burkhead, Jesse, Government Budgeting. New York: John Wiley & Sons, 1956. F-G-M-T (5+8=13) One of the standard textbooks on the budgetary process, emphasizing public expenditures in the federal government. An economist, Burkhead views the budgetary process as a rational mechanism for allocating public resources and planning public policy, including the use of the budget for fiscal control and economic development. The eighteen chapters are divided into four sections: the historical, institutional, and procedural foundations of budgeting; the classification of budgetary concepts, including performance and capital budgeting; the budgetary process from agency to audit; and special budgetary problems such as revenue estimation and government corporations.

Burnham, James, The Managerial Revolution. Westport, CT: Greenwood Press, 1941. O-M-G (4+3=7) An influential book, in a number of spheres. For the study of business management, Burnham described the the death of entrepreneural capitalism, foreshadowing discussions of the "new industrial state" by John Kenneth Galbraith and others. In the area of social thought, Burnham repudiated communist governments for failing to achieve their goal of a "classless society" where workers would control the means of production, accusing them instead of lodging control of the economy in unresponsive totalitarian states. (Burnham himself was a former Marxist.) In public administration, the book was instrumental in defining the rise of a professional managerial elite. This elite, Burnham predicted, would use their control of the bureaucracy in such a way as to weaken the power of democratic institutions such as the legislative branch. In the book, Burnham argues that the second world war, the communist revolution, and the American "New Deal" were manifestations of a much broader revolution, more persistent than the rhetoric surrounding those events. That persistent revolution is the passage of economic control from the owners of business firms to professional managers who owe their power to technical ability, to the career system (promotion from within), and to their control of the state. The book is principally remembered for this "passage of control" thesis, which in fact as Burnham admits was a point made some ten years earlier by Adolph Berle and Gardiner Means in a book titled The Modern Corporation and Private Property. Burnham goes much further than this, describing how the managerial revolution will create new economic, political, social and ideological orders. He predicts that government will take over control of industry, that entrepreneurs and labor will disappear as classes, and that the managers will use their newly found power to redirect income and privileges to the managerial elite. The book, first published in 1941, inspired George Orwell to write 1984, a fictional account of life under the fully established managerial order.

Burns, Tom and G. M. Stalker, The Management of Innovation. London: Tavistock Publications, 1961. O-T-P-G (6+4=10) A seminal work in organization development, best remembered for articulating the need for different types of management systems under different conditions. It is also one of the leading European contributions to behavioral theory, based as it is on studies of twenty industrial firms in Scotland and England. Fifteen of the firms under study were attempting to move up in the rapidly changing field of electronics; another was a rayon mill. The authors describe the management processes within the firms as tending toward either the "mechanistic" (i.e. bureaucratic) or "organic" model. In spite of academic opinion to the contrary, people working under the mechanistic system in the rayon mill did not feel aggrieved or belittled. The firm, moreover, was growing and prosperous. This led the authors to suggest that the mechanistic approach -- with its emphasis upon specialization, hierarchy, rules and vertical coordination -- might be appropriate for firms facing stable conditions. This sets up the authors discussion of the electronics firms, which were clearly facing changing conditions and forceful technological change, factors that would seem to favor the organic form. In fact, managers in the Scottish electronics firms (seven out of the fifteen) fought the organic model, lacked enthusiasm for moving into the electronics field, and only moved when forced to do so by a shrinking market for traditional products. The electronics firms in England (eight in all) were more progressive. The authors suggest that three variables work to push firms toward the mechanistic or organic form; these variables form the principal subject matter of the book's three sections. The first part takes up the shaping forces of technical and market change. The second section demonstrates how personal struggles over power and status encourage firms to resist the organic form. The last third of the book examines how leaders at the top of the organization can make the difference by defining the need for change and securing individual commitment to it, reversing the tendency of the firm to revert to the mechanistic form.

Caiden, Naomi & Aaron Wildavsky, Planning and Budgeting in Poor Countries. New York: John Wiley & Sons, 1974. B-F-G-C (0+6=6) One of the most realistic books to come out of the comparative administration movement. The book attacks comprehensive planning and annual budgeting as totally inappropriate to the needs of poor nations and describes the process by which financial decisions there are actually made. Three chapters on budgeting reveal the strategies that policy makers and department executives use to grab funds given the widespread practice in developing nations of constantly remaking the budget during the year as conditions change. The three chapters on planning contain fewer strategies that work, in part because the authors believe that central planning itself does not work. The planners they describe lack the power to control events in society or even the power to veto spending decisions that are incompatible with the country's master plan. A chapter describing the impact of poverty on public administration sets the stage for an early chapter on the failure of "expert" advice and a conclusion where the authors recommend methods better adapted to conditions in poor countries. The book is based on in-depth studies of twelve countries and surveys of the situation in seventy more.

Cartwright, Dorwin, and Alvin Zander, eds., Group Dynamics Research and Theory. New York: Harper & Row, 1953. Subsequent eds. B-O-T-G-M-P (16+5=21) Small work groups are at the heart of any administrative activity. This collection of papers shows how far research scientists can go in mounting a systematic, empirical attack on administrative phenomena, one that tests assumptions and establishes facts "through careful use of objective methods." The book begins by describing the breakthroughs in research techniques that allowed social scientists, beginning in the late 1930s, to recreate group behavior in the laboratory and, later, to conduct genuine experiments within natural groups. These experiments laid the groundwork for a scientific approach to professional practices in the fields of social work, psychotherapy, education, and administration. In administration, the science of "group dynamics" was applied most successfully through the various group-building techniques of organization development. This collection of some two-score papers chronicles the development of the science of group dynamics, the theoretical issues, and the major findings. The findings are arranged into sections that conform to the major areas of application: how people come to form and join groups, how they promote conformity to group norms, how they influence their members, how they are led, how they set goals and motivate members, and how structure affects their operation. Cartwright and Zander are both psychologists; most of the papers in the book are in the form of research reports.

Chapman, Brian, <u>The</u> <u>Profession</u> <u>of</u> <u>Government</u>: <u>The</u> <u>Public</u>
<u>Service</u> <u>in</u> <u>Europe</u>. Westport, CT: Greenwood Press, 1959.
G-O-M-C (4+3=7) A comparative study describing civil
service practices in Western Europe, prepared during the
1950's by a British scholar. The countries compared are
Belgium, Denmark, France, Germany, Great Britain, Hol-
land, Italy, Spain, Sweden and Switzerland. Chapman
begins with an historical overview, from Rome through the
Napoleonic reforms to the modern period, so as to explain
the emergence of the European civil services as a distinct,
classical profession. In sixteen chapters, Chapman then
examines the training and recruitment of civil servants,
their conditions of service, the methods of controlling
administrative acts, and the system of political accountability. The latter sections are most informative, with
their discussions of administrative courts, financial control,
the ombudsman, politics and administration, and public service trade unions.

Cleveland, Harlan, <u>The</u> <u>Future</u> <u>Executive</u>. New York: Harper &
Row, 1972. G-M (0+6=6) Cleveland's description of exe-
cutive management in organizations with "nobody in
charge" is one of the most widely read descriptions of
administration in the future. The book contains ten short
essays written at different times and based on Cleveland's
personal reflections as a public executive and university
president. Cleveland begins by describing trends underlying
business and public organizations: their free-wheeling complexity, the disappearance of organizations where executives can bark out orders and expect them to be uncondi-
tionally obeyed, and the increasing "publicness" of private
enterprise. A second section focuses on the qualities that
future executives need to possess, especially the skills
needed to choreograph a fast moving situation where
administration requires consultation and consensus building.
In the third section on "purposes," Cleveland calls on
future executives to think of planning and decision making
"as a continuous improvisation on a general sense of direction." The best test of a good decision is whether it will
withstand public scrutiny, says Cleveland. Institutional
leadership will be very unstructured, he concludes, and
exhilarating for the executives who can master it.

Corson, John J., and Paul R. Shale, <u>Men</u> <u>Near</u> <u>the</u> <u>Top</u>. Baltimore: Johns Hopkins University Press, 1966. G-O-M (4+4=8) A study of the people who occupied the supergrade levels in the federal civil service in the early sixties, based on questionnaires returned by 424 of them and in-depth interviews with eighty. The authors focus on the system of plural accountability in the senior civil service, allowing the respondents to describe that system in terms of the work they perform. Those patterns of work are gathered into three categories: career executives who manage programs, officials who serve as support staff to political or career executives, and high ranking officials who serve in a professional capacity as lawyers, economists, scientists, or other technical roles. The latter part of the book deals with the career patterns of senior civil servants and discusses issues that here in their primitive form would later blossom into civil service reform: recruitment, mobility, compensation, and planned career development.

Crecine, John P., <u>Governmental</u> <u>Problem-Solving</u>: <u>A</u> <u>Computer</u> <u>Simulation</u> <u>of</u> <u>Municipal</u> <u>Budgeting</u>. Chicago: Rand McNally & Co., 1969. P-T-F (2+5=7) Management science meets the politics of the budgetary process in this computer simulation of municipal budgeting. Crecine, while a graduate student under Herbert Simon, developed a model of municipal budgeting based on the Simon-Lindblom-Wildavsky theories of decision making. In essence, the model presumes that the allocation of resources for existing programs can be predicted using historic levels and trend data, given the total resources available as the major constraint. Crecine depreciates the "pressure group" model of policy making, suggesting through his model that while external forces do influence the total amount of resources available (tax decisions, for example), the distribution of those resources between programs is an internal bureaucratic process. The central part of the book describes, in fairly technical language, how Crecine fit his model to a computer program, then checked its validity by comparing its predictions to actual budget allocations in Pittsburgh, Detroit, and Cleveland. The opening and concluding chapters relate the model to the general literature on budgeting and decision making.

Crozier, Michel, The Bureaucratic Phenomenon. Chicago:
University of Chicago Press, 1964. O-C-G-T-B-P
(8+13=21) One of the best empirical studies of bureaucratic behavior to be found in the social sciences. Crozier, a French sociologist, conducted what he called "clini-
cal" studies of two French bureaucracies. The first, a
clerical agency, had a reputation for being rigid, standard-
ized, and impersonal. The second, a state owned monopoly
producing a simple commodity, was totally disconnected
from its market and from the need to fight for revenues.
Crozier found that the highly bureaucratic character of the
clerical agency served important functions for its employees: it created a shield that protected them from having
to engage in face-to-face relations or become personally
dependent upon someone who could act arbitrarily, situations that the employees could not bear. Turning to the
industrial monopoly, Crozier explains that a struggle for
power supports its bureaucratic character, with different
groups competing to gain the status that would come from
knowing how to deal with the few remaining areas of uncertainty that the monopoly could not subject to routine
procedures. In order for the power struggles to reach an
equilibrium that can sustain the bureaucratic character of
the organization, Crozier observes, four elements must
come together. The organization must adopt impersonal
rules, centralize decision making, isolate workers at different strata, and set up parallel power relationships
around the remaining areas of uncertainty. This results in
what Crozier calls a "bureaucratic vicious circle, since it
builds up pressures for even greater impersonality and centralization in decision making. Only when the pressures
become so great that a crises ensues will the fundamental
relationships change, says Crozier, after which the new
organization will quickly slip back into the old pattern of
routine. The book contains not only Crozier's theory, his
famous definition of bureaucracy ("an organization which
cannot correct its behavior by learning from its errors")
and the lessons to be found in the two case studies. It
also contains a long section -- often skipped by American
readers -- explaining how bureaucratic patterns of behavior
are reenforced by French culture.

Cyert, Richard M., and James G. March, A Behavioral Theory
of the Firm. Englewood Cliffs, NJ: Prentice-Hall, 1963.

O-T-B-M-P-F (8+4=12) One of the boldest attempts to design a comprehensive theory of organization behavior based on the observation of Herbert Simon and others that firms "satisfice" rather than engage in economically rational behavior. The book represents the challenge directed at classical economic beliefs by professors associated with the Carnegie Institute of Technology, a challenge that eventually won for Professor Simon at Carnegie Tech the Nobel Prize. The first six chapters of this book lay out the general theory, the heart of which is expressed in four concepts. The authors see the firm as a coalition of members in which conflicts over goals are never fully resolved. That uncertain coalition forces the company to adopt strategies that satisfy the need for some profit while meeting the other demands of the members and reducing uncertainty at practically any cost. When problems arise, the members of the firm search through familiar patterns of behavior for the first solution that meets minimum standards of acceptability. Finally, organizations "learn" like humans do, by applying familiar approaches to new problems and modifying them gradually over time as experience accumulates. As a demonstration of the utility of their model, the authors create two computer simulations based on their theory and use them to predict pricing decisions in a department store and investment decisions in a bank. Their largely accurate predictions bear little relation to what most people would recognize as profit-maximizing behavior. The book concludes with three chapters specially written by other authors on problems of managerial rationality, predictability, and the use of computer models.

Dahl, Robert A., Who Governs? Democracy and Power in an American City. New Haven: Yale University Press, 1961. U-P-M (5+3=8) One of the most famous descriptions of how American pluralism works at the local level. Dahl attacks the elitist theory of urban politics with an exhaustive empirical analysis of community power in New Haven, Connecticut, using historical analysis, case studies, and survey techniques. He discovers no "power elite" but citizens broadly organized into three loose patterns of influence: separate spheres of interest, executive centered coalitions, and rival sovereignties. Dahl presents material on the political and social history of New Haven; leadership patterns in political nominations, urban redevelopment, and public education; the three patterns of influence; the distribution of political resources contrasted to their actual use; and a final section on the role of elites in a democratic system.

Davis, James W., ed., Politics, Programs and Budgets. Englewood Cliffs, NJ: Prentice-Hall, 1969. F-U-G (3+4=7) A collection of some twenty-eight articles dealing with current issues in American budgeting, almost exclusively at the national level. The book is distinguished by the willingness of Davis to reach beyond academic journals into publications such as Business Week for more popular and readable treatments of budgeting and national politics. The anthology covers three general areas: the size of the federal budget and its impact on society and the economy, the politics of budget formulation, and the impact of PPBS, including the full text of President Johnson's now-historic statement requiring all federal agencies to adopt PPBS, and the subsequent memoranda from Johnson and OMB as the agencies continued to resist the reform.

Davis, Kenneth Culp, Discretionary Justice. Urbana: University of Illinois Press, 1971. M-P-G-B (3+5=8) The purpose of public administration, Davis writes, should be to observe, describe, and criticize governmental processes. Davis sets right out to do that. This is an angry book about the injustice and unequal treatment that results when administrators exercise large discretionary powers. Davis, well known for his books on administrative law, argues that 80 to 90 percent of all administrative action "escapes both formal proceedings and judicial review" and has become increasingly discretionary. He is satisfied that highly bureaucratic, procedurally bound agencies such as the Internal Revenue Service -- whose decisions can be appealed -- are reasonably well run, at least from the standpoint of granting justice. He turns instead to the discretionary activities of police officers, social workers, public housing managers, contracting officers, parole boards, immigration officers, public prosecutors, and some special areas such as the regulation of corporate mergers. The first two chapters explain what discretionary power is and why so much of it has come to be vested in public administrators. Paradoxically, Davis dismisses the traditional method of limiting discretion as unpromising -- the legislating of more exact standards -- in part because so much discretion is based on "administrative assumption of ungranted power." Instead, he wants to confine, structure, and check discretionary power, and spends three chapters outlining reforms in each of these areas. He would, for example, impose formal rule-making procedures on police departments. In two final chapters Davis attacks the tendency of the government to selectively enforce the laws, the absence of procedural safeguards where "privileges or gratuities" such as welfare payments are involved, and the powers of public attorneys to make decisions about who shall and shall not be prosecuted. The book was originally delivered as a series of lectures, which accounts for its conversational tone and the use of analogies rather than research findings.

Derthick, Martha, The Influence of Federal Grants. Cambridge: Harvard University Press, 1970. G-U-F-P-M (2+5=7) A study of how the federal government, through the conditions imposed for the receipt of grants-in-aid, influenced the administration of public assistance programs in the state of Massachusetts. The federal government, says Derthick, had five goals. It wanted the state to provide more adequate assistance; that is, more money. It wanted the state to provide it equitably. At the least, that meant uniformity of treatment. It wanted to improve the efficiency of program delivery in the state, especially by eliminating politics from the selection of state and local public assistance personnel. It wanted the state to provide social services, mainly social work, along with financial assistance. Finally, it wanted to professionalize state and local personnel by requiring, among other provisions, a college degree for hiring and promotion. Derthick examines the methods used by Congress and the federal bureaucracy, through their ally, the central state agency, to force these changes on state legislators and public assistance workers. The result, Derthick concludes, was a shift in power to a more centralized state agency whose personnel were tapped into the national public assistance subgovernment. Derthick concludes with a chapter on the new federalism, suggesting that its authors want to reverse the tendencies affecting public service programs revealed by this case, namely the capture of programs by state bureaucracies and professional associations of public employees.

Downs, Anthony, An Economic Theory of Democracy. New York: Harper & Row, 1957. O-P-B-F-G (5+3=8) A pioneering work in political science and public policy analysis, this book laid the groundwork for much of the "public choice" literature that was to follow. Economic theories of government were by no means rare when the book was published. Downs' theory is distinguished by the way he treats the motives of people in government. "Our main thesis," he says, "is that parties in democratic polities are analogous to entrepreneurs in a profit-seeking economy. . . They formulate whatever policies they believe will gain the most votes, just as entrepreneurs produce whatever products they believe will gain the most profits." Downs has a similar view of voters, suggesting that they also behave in an economically rational way. Almost immediately this rather utilitarian model of government "begins to disintegrate," for a reason that Downs is prepared to handle. Some six years earlier economist Kenneth Arrow, in a work which won him lasting fame, proved that a government facing a particular combination of public preferences (conveniently known as an Arrow problem) could never produce rational public policy because a majority of voters would always prefer some other alternative. A ruling political party which tries to formulate a rational public policy dooms itself to defeat at the next general election. The same thing will happen to the party which replaces it. Downs insists that this does not doom the economic theory of democracy for the very simple reason that voters and public officials do not quite know what they are doing. (Social scientists call this the problem of uncertainty.) By combining a discussion of uncertainty with other elements of the model, Downs proceeds to generate some two dozen propositions about political parties and voting behavior in a simple democracy. He discusses, for example, why economically rational behavior forces political parties to adopt similar positions in a two party state. Of more importance to public choice theorists, he explains why governments are "highly unlikely" to give the public what it wants. The technical term used to describe a perfectly balanced public policy is known as a Paretian optimum, a situation in which no redistribution of benefits can make someone better off without significantly harming someone else. Much to the glee of public choice theorists, Downs argues that governments are much less capable of of aggregating the preferences of individual citizens in this way than -- by comparison -- institutions in the private sector.

Downs, Anthony, Inside Bureaucracy. Boston: Little, Brown & Co., 1967. G-O-U-P-T-F-B   (9+12=21) Another fairly influential piece in the development of the "public choice" school of governmental behavior, although Downs wrote the book more as a study of bureaucracy than as a trumpet for any particular perspective. The book remains impor- tant because Downs, an economist, was one of the first to calculate the consequences of applying maxims of economic rationality to official behavior in bureaus. Downs begins by proposing that bureaucrats act rationally and that high among their goals is the desire to maximize their self-in- terests. From these two propositions -- along with the more traditional observation from sociology that bureau- cratic structure affects bureaucratic behavior (and visa versa) -- Downs proceeds to formulate 16 laws and a lar- ger number of propositions. The laws are not that surpris- ing: organizations tend to become more conservative as they grow older, requests for free services always rise to meet the capacity of the producing bureau, bureaus that cannot charge money for their services are obliged to devise techniques for rationing them, and any attempt to control one large bureaucracy generally tends to generate another. What is unique is Downs's effort to defend such laws as a consequence of the economically rational, self- maximizing behavior of bureaucrats. In all, Downs pro- duces 21 chapters, plus 19 pages of propositions, on sub- jects including how specific types of officials behave, control problems in bureaus, the rigidity cycle, bureaucratic decision making, bureaucratic change, ideology and indoc- trination in bureaus, and territoriality. Downs also offers his opinion on the value of bureaus to society in a hard nosed economic way. Although he mildly agrees with the public choice conclusion that citizens tend to get more bureaucracy than they bargain for, especially in the short run, he is more interested in demolishing the fuzzy headed conclusion that bureaucracies destroy individual freedom. Bureaucracies, he argues, have helped to produce "greater

freedom of choice" than ever existed before the rise of
bureaucratic society.

Dror, Yehezkel, Public Policymaking Reexamined. San Francisco: Chandler Publishing Co., 1968. O-G-P-F-C-B-M
(7+9=16) A plea for rational public policy formulation by
one of the leading policy analysts in public administration.
Dror argues that "there is a significant gap between the
ways individuals and institutions make policy and the available knowledge on how policies can best be made." Dror
would rely upon net output to ascertain the real quality of
policy making, the implications of which he examines in
modern and developing states. He constructs an ideal
model of policy making, contrasts it to the "muddling
through" approach, and advocates needed reforms. The
book is most famous for Dror's effort to refute the claim
that lack of knowledge necessitates the use of incrementalism. Dror draws on political science, behavioral sciences, and systems analysis for this largely theoretical
book, which may account for the difficulties in style and
language.

Dvorin, Eugene P., and Robert H. Simmons, From Amoral to
Human Bureaucracy. San Francisco: Canfield Press, 1972.
U-G-O-M (0+10=10) A short book containing seven short
essays on the nature of bureaucratic power in the modern
democratic state. The book sets out to disprove a number
of myths founded in high school civics, including the existance of majority rule and legislative supremacy.
"Bureaucrats," the authors insist, "originate policy." But
bureaucrats are afflicted by myths as well, especially the
myth of value neutrality. Dvorin and Simmons attack
value neutrality and propose a new ideology: a humane,
proactive bureaucracy that has the training and capacity to
promote the public interest. The argument is largely rhe-
torical.

Dye, Thomas R., Understanding Public Policy. Englewood
Cliffs, NJ: Prentice-Hall, 1972. Subsequent eds.
G-F-C-P-M (0+6=6) An introduction to policy analysis
with a heavy emphasis upon the process of policy formulation. Dye gathers up the major analytic models in political science and begins to apply them to major policy
areas. Different policy areas, Dye discovers, are best

explained by different models. Thus tax and budget policy is explained by incremental theory, welfare and health are examples of sloppy rationalism, civil rights is a case of elite-mass interaction, and urban policy is a product of institutional and administrative arrangements. There are seven models in all (incremental, rational, elite, institutional, group, game, and systems approach) applied to nearly a dozen policy areas, with a bonus chapter on program evaluation and three chapters providing an overview of policy making and policy analysis.

Ecker-Racz, L. L., The Politics and Economics of State-Local Finance. Englewood Cliffs, NJ: Prentice-Hall, 1970. U-F (2+5=7) An examination of a large number of economic, political, and administrative issues in state-local finance, with the author presenting his opinions. Ecker-Racz argues that America has the means "to support adequate government services," but is prevented from doing so by archaic fiscal systems supported by an uninformed public. He discusses various proposals for reforming taxes large and small, from the income, sales and property tax to inheritance, local sales and income taxes and taxes on farmland on the urban fringe. The middle section is concerned with borrowing, survival in the bond market, tax exempt bonds, industrial development bonds, and constitutional limits on state-local debt. In the final sections, Eckert-Racz discusses solutions requiring intergovernmental cooperation, from grants-in-aid and revenue sharing to federal tax credit for state income taxes and federal collection of state taxes. The arguments are like essays, uncluttered by technical data or empirical evidence.

Eckstein, Otto, Public Finance. Englewood Cliffs, NJ: Prentice-Hall, 1964. Subsequent eds. F-T-G (3+4=7) A short but sophisticated introduction to the economic principles underlying public finance. The book looks at public finance in the broad sense, presenting not only the principles of efficiency and equity in tax decisions, but also examining the economics of public debt, the theory of fiscal policy, efficiency criteria in budgetary decisions, the growth of government expenditures at different levels of government and the fiscal problems this creates, including a special chapter on the fiscal fragmentation of large metropolitan areas. The book is designed to give readers the economic framework to answer such questions as: how much government is too much, at which level of government should a service be provided, how do tax policies affect the economy, and how much public debt should we have?

Elazar, Daniel J., American Federalism: A View From the States. New York: Thomas J. Crowell Company, 1966. Subsequent eds. U-P-M-G (3+10=13) A book written in praise of the states as "the keystones of the American governmental arch" at a time when the federal government was beginning to emphasize programs directed at urban centers and community organizations. This book, along with the volume published the same year under Morton Grodzins' name, propelled Elazar and his university-based Center for the Study of Federalism to the forefront of American intergovernmental relations. The book analyzes in detail three major subjects: the constitutional, political, and administrative status of the states in the intergovernmental system; the political cultures of the states (including an interesting tripartite classification scheme); and the response of the states to the new era of intergovernmental partnership. The book is based both on research findings and Elazar's own insights.

Etzioni, Amitai, Modern Organizations. Englewood Cliffs, NJ: Prentice-Hall, 1964. O-T-B-M-G-P (4+9=13) A short introduction to the theory of organizations by a leading sociologist. The book has two purposes. First, it serves as a basic textbook on approaches to organization theory, reviewing scientific management, human relations, Weber's theory of bureaucracy, and what Etzioni terms the structuralist approach. Second, the book serves as a review of Etzioni's own work in the field, which he characterizes as being in the structuralist school. Etzioni probably is best remembered for his comparative typology of organizations, based on their means of control (coercive, utilitarian, and normative-social). The final chapters examine special issues of interest to sociologists studying organizations: the organization of knowledge through professions, client relations in large-scale bureaucracies, and the conditions in society at large that permit and maintain massive organizations.

Fenno, Richard F., The Power of the Purse: Appropriation Politics in Congress. Boston: Little, Brown and Co., 1966. F-P-G-S (4+9=13) One of the most widely respected books in political science. Fenno spent nearly six years prowling the halls of Congress collecting quotations and anecdotes from leading participants in the Congressional appropriations process. The result is a remarkable blend of academic generalization and political entertainment. On the academic side, Fenno locates the behavioral expectations, adaptations, images, sanctions, roles and resultant structures that serve to distribute, integrate and protect decision-making powers. On the political side, Fenno allows the words of the politicians to explain how these things really work. At the heart of his analysis is the House Appropriations Committee which, sitting at the center of a system that involves executive agencies, Senators, and challenges from the House floor, seeks almost tribal-like unity among its committee members in order that its decisions might be upheld. Equally fascinating is Fenno's contrast of the hard-working, budget-cutting, specialists from the House committee and the less-informed but politically adept members of the Senate, an explosive combination when they meet in conference committee.

Fesler, James W., Area and Administration. University, AL: University of Alabama Press, 1949. O-M-U-B-G (6+4=10) The leading treatment of the distribution of governmental authority into governmental areas: the field service areas set up by administrative departments, the special purpose districts set up to provide particular services, and the general governmental areas that outline the jurisdictions of cities, counties, states and other general purpose units of government. Fesler focuses on the difficulty of reconciling geographic areas with functional specializations, which in practical terms appears as the question of whether to emphasize area-based popular control or the effective delivery of specific functions when officials draw up governmental areas. Fesler shows how these two tendencies can be reconciled through structural reforms and cooperative techniques, illustrating these concepts with practical examples and identifying the factors that retard their execution. As part of the book he provides a careful summary of the factors that an administrative department must take into account when realigning its regions and districts in the field. He then proceeds to outline the procedures that generalist administrators use in their attempts to simultaneously decentralize authority and coordinate specialists that have been sent out to the districts. (Here he offers his famous observation that administrators cannot coordinate those functions in the field that are left uncoordinated at the center.) He concludes with a review of what at that time were emerging patterns of areal cooperation, beginning with the Tennessee Valley Authority and ending with multi-county planning councils. The book consists of six lectures delivered at the invitation of the publishing university.

Follett, Mary Parker, Dynamic Administration: The Collected Papers of Mary Parker Follett. Edited by Elliot M. Fox and L. Urwick; New York: Hippocrene Books, 1940. G-M-P-B-O (9+4=13) Mary Parker Follett was a leading exponent of human relations principles which she derived from her participation in various social work movements in the Boston area in the early 1900s. This book contains 14 papers which she wrote during the 1920s. Mary Follett believed that the productivity of the modern organization depended upon an understanding of individual and group motivation. She searched for true principles of organization that would coordinate "the vital forces of human progress." Among her most famous principles was the "law of the situation," found in her paper on "The Giving of Orders." Orders, she said, do not emanate from superiors, but are dictated by the situation. Insofar as two persons in the same organization confront the same situation, she concludes, more effort should be spent improving the methods by which they "discover the order integral to (that) particular situation" than trying to get one to give and the other to receive a formal command. The papers collected here discuss power, the psychology of control, participation, conciliation, leadership, giving orders, management becoming a profession, responsibility, individualism in a planned society, and constructive conflict. They raise many issues still of great interest in modern studies of organization behavior and development.

Fritschler, A. Lee, Smoking and Politics: Policymaking and the Federal Bureaucracy. Englewood Cliffs, NJ: Prentice-Hall, 1969. Subsequent eds. T-U-P-G (4+6=10) One of the most widely used studies of bureaucratic power in national policy making. The book is a case study interpreting the efforts of a proactive Federal Trade Commission to require a warning on tobacco products, and the efforts of Congress to curb the power of the FTC. Fritschler interprets the case using the subsystem model of American politics, examining the "iron triangle" alliances built between bureaucrats, Congressional committees, and interest groups. Though technically a case study of a regulatory decision, the book is a rich source of information on subsystem politics, advisory committees, the delegation of policy making powers to administrative agencies, regulatory procedures, rulemaking and Congressional oversight of public administration.

Galbraith, John Kenneth, The Affluent Society. Boston: Houghton Mifflin Co., 1958. Subsequent eds. M-P-F-G (4+3=7) A book on economics that helped to provide much of the philosophic foundation for the growth of social and environmental programs in the sixties and seventies. Galbraith faults traditional economists for their preoccupation with production, efficiency, and the redistribution of wealth. In a carefully drawn argument, he shows how these concerns (which evolved in times when most people lived on the margin of human survival) lose their relevance in an affluent society. In particular, he criticizes businessmen for maintaining the myth of scarcity, which encourages a public preoccupation with the consumption of private goods, and government for joining in the promotion of production as a means of creating a rising standard of living, which the leaders of society believe will minimize the potential for social conflict. The consequences, Galbraith argues, will be inflation and an general unwillingness to forgo personal consumption in exchange for general progress. He calls on society to marshall its affluence to support public education, health, a clean environment, and the removal of pockets of persistent poverty.

Galbraith, John Kenneth, The New Industrial State. Boston: Houghton Mifflin Company, 1967. T-P-M-B (6+3=9) An ambitious book on the death of the entrepreneural corporation and the end of limited government. Galbraith offers four major observations: that the control of modern corporations has passed to managers in the technostructure; that the technostructure is more concerned with stability than profit; that the consumer and the market system are less important than planned demand, including advertising; and that the public sector is converging with the corporate sector because of the necessity for the government to maintain demand for goods and stabilize wages and prices. Much of the book is written as a jousting match with neo-classical economists who profess allegiance to free enterprise theories.

Golembiewski, Robert T., Frank Gibson and Geoffrey Y. Cornog, eds., Public Administration: Readings in Institutions, Processes, Behavior, Policy. Chicago: Rand McNally & Co., 1966. Subsequent eds. G-U (3+5=8) A book of readings on public administration, consisting of some forty selections, with a distinctive managerial-behavioral tone. The readings were chosen to fill in Golembiewski's view of the administrative process, with the result that a number of little known or specially prepared selections appear in the volume. Broadly speaking, Golembiewski and his co-editors want to call attention to three aspects of administration: the behavioral world of the administrator, the institutional settings that shape administrative action, and the administrative methods that are the tools of management. The selections are arranged in alphabetical order, by author, emphasizing the interdependence of these three aspects of public administration and the fact that the best lessons do not fit any single construct.

Goodnow, Frank J., Politics and Administration. New York: Russell and Russell, 1900. G-O-M (4+3=7) This is the book most often credited with popularizing the politics-administration dichotomy. Published at the turn of the century, it is an insightful and realistic analysis of public administration and political parties under the patronage or "boss" system, especially in state and municipal government. Goodnow was a reformer, and not the last political scientist to be fascinated by European political systems. In the book, he calls for two major reforms: strong national political parties, rather than the decentralized boss system; and the centralization of public administration in the states, based on the model of the national administrative system. Goodnow argues that centralization of administration under the control of the chief executive prevents removal of administrative officials for political reasons, blocks party bosses who would otherwise obstruct administration, and promotes administrative efficiency. He further insists that centralized administration by itself without strong parties will lead to "political manipulation" just as fast as the boss system does, bolstering his argument for reforms that would subordinate local party chiefs to the national party machinery and make the party more responsive to the public will. The argument is sprinkled with informative references to political and administrative practices in many types of government, both in Europe and the United States and to state, municipal, and national functions within them. The book opens with his famous call for the separation of politics and administration.

Gouldner, Alvin, Patterns of Industrial Bureaucracy. New York: The Free Press, 1954. T-B-O-G (9+4=13) Gouldner's case study of bureaucracy in a gypsum plant and mine in the Great Lakes region helped to construct a theory of informal organization as an amendment to the works of Max Weber. The case develops as a change in top management displaces routine bureaucratic behavior. Gouldner describes three responses: a "mock" bureaucracy, where neither management nor workers pay attention to formal rules; a "punishment-centered" bureaucracy, where managers enforce rules and workers resist; and a more stable "representative" pattern wherein rules are both enforced and obeyed.

Graves, W. Brooke, American Intergovernmental Relations. New York: Charles Scribner's Sons, 1964. U-G (3+4=7) An exhaustive study of American intergovernmental relations, over one thousand pages long. Written prior to the explosion of intergovernmental programs in the mid-sixties, the text retains a classical approach to intergovernmental relations. This is reenforced by Graves' own prescriptions for reform, which are largely administrative and draw on classical principles (coordination, consolidation, and better communication, for example). There are twenty-six chapters spread over six sections: historical origins, a mini-textbook on American government ala intergovernmental relations, federal-state relations in four policy areas, fiscal relations (interstate, state-local, interlocal, and more), and a full section on emerging trends and efforts at reform.

Grodzins, Morton, The American System. Chicago: Rand
    McNally and Co., 1966. U-P-G (7+5=12) Morton Grodzins
    pioneered the idea of what he called "cooperative federal-
    ism" before politicians found it popular to promote shared
    responsibilities and intergovernmental reform. He saw in
    America not the neatly layered doctrine of separation
    advanced by proponents of dual federalism, but a
    federalism of shared functions which he characterized as
    the "marble cake" of American government. That federal-
    ism, he said, rested on a foundation of citizen access
    through "multiple cracks" in the body politic created by
    undisciplined political parties and "a little chaos."   He
    found the system democratic, responsive, and decentralized
    to real centers of power. This book of essays, prepared by
    Daniel Elazar from Grodzins' unfinished work, contains 16
    chapters defending his "marble cake" view of federalism.
    Grodzins explains the early triumph of cooperative federal-
    ism in American history, shows how the system works,
    describes what the sharing looks like from the local per-
    spective, elucidates how it is held in place by the uniquely
    decentralized character of American political parties, and
    rails against those who would promote an "orderly" decen-
    tralization of governmental functions.   The system is
    already happily decentralized, he argues, to genuine centers
    of power. The reformers, he accuses, would centralize
    power first in the name of an orderly decentralization --
    and who could trust them to give the power back once
    they had taken it up?

Gross, Bertram M., The Managing of Organizations: The
    Administrative Struggle, 2 volumes. New York: The Free
    Press, 1964. O-G-B-M-P (8+4=12) One of the most com-
    prehensive reviews of organization theory ever written.
    Gross seeks to display empirically based theories as if they
    were answers to "the major questions asked by both
    administrators and scholars concerning the governance of
    organizations." For nearly 900 pages he leads the reader
    through the history of administration and administrative
    theory, fundamental aspects of administration, including
    some proverbs, the motivation of people in organizations,
    the purposes or ways of calculating administrative effec-
    tiveness, and some notes on administrative science and
    organizational democracy in the future. One of the more
    frequently read chapters reviews major administrative

thinkers from Plato to Herbert Simon. In the section on administrative purposes he discusses interest satisfaction, output and operations, efficiency and profitability, survival, mobilization of resources, observance of codes, and rationality. Within such practical themes he manages to present the findings of over 400 authors in the field. The book was reissued in 1968 in a condensed form (a mere 700 pages) as Organizations and their Managing.

Gulick, Luther, and L. Urwick, eds., Papers on the Science of Administration. New York: Augustus M. Kelley Publishers, 1937. G-O-M-P-B-F (11+15=26) This classic work appeared at the zenith of the administrative science movement, a widely supported effort to discover the the underlying principles of good administration. Gulick called for a science of administration in which "the fundamental objective . . . is the accomplishment of the work at hand with the least expenditure of manpower and materials," i.e., efficiency. Gulick's paper "Notes on the Theory of Organization" reveals principles of administration such as unity of command, span of control, and POSDCORB. Although said to represent the "high noon of orthodoxy," the anthology contains important contributions from Elton Mayo and Mary Parker Follett on the psychological and social basis of administration as well as more orthodox papers from Urwick, James Mooney, Henri Fayol and others.

Harris, Joseph P., Congressional Control of Administration. Washington, D.C.: The Brookings Institution, 1964. G-M-F-P-O-U (6+6=12) Some political scientists have observed a reversal of roles in the traditional separation of powers, with the Chief Executive writing legislation and the Congress overseeing its administration. Harris' book is a legal-historical review of the efforts of Congress to control administrative operations in detail, an important contribution to the "political" understanding of public administration. He reviews the powers of Congress over the creation of departments and their procedures, the budget and appropriation process, the audit, the civil service, the legislative veto, control by investigation, and discusses various proposed reforms, mainly in the area of budgeting.

Haveman, Robert H., and Julius Margolis, eds., Public Expenditures and Policy Analysis. Chicago: Rand McNally Publishing Co., 1970. Subsequent eds. P-G-F-M (0+11=11) A primer on public expenditure economics, or the "application of economic analysis to the choice, scale, and design of services." The book helps readers understand the growing importance of economics in public administration and the implications of a preoccupation with economic efficiency. The work begins with a lengthy introduction to what the authors call the field of public economics and the basic concepts that underlie it: public goods, individual utility, weighing, markets, pareto efficiency, externalities, collective action and income redistribution. The bulk of the book consists of an application of economic principles to policy analysis, program evaluation and cost-benefit analysis, along with a number of applications to current policy issues. The authors conclude with some of the leading criticisms of economic methods in public decision making and comments on the resistance that techniques like cost-benefit analysis have encountered. The first edition gave much attention to PPPS, an emphasis which passed out at the second edition.

Hawley, Willis D., and David Rogers, eds., Improving the Quality of Urban Management. Beverly Hills, CA: Sage Publications, 1974. Subsequent abridged edition. M-U (0+6=6) A collection of nineteen papers on various aspects of urban management. The papers take up various approaches to the improvement of urban management: evaluation, better analysis, decentralization, alternatives to bureaucracy, and ways to use the private sector, such as contracting out selected services. Although many noteable academics are represented among the contributors, the tone of the papers is practical and the improvements they propose are realistic. A final section examines obstacles to change and suggests a limited number of methods for dealing with them. An abridged version, consisting of nine articles dealing "most directly...with ways of measuring, organizing and delivering public services" was issued in 1976 by the editors under the title Improving Urban Management.

Heady, Ferrel, and Sybil L. Stokes, eds., Papers in Comparative Public Administration. Ann Arbor: University of Michigan Press, 1962. C-M-O-B (5+3=8) A collection of ten papers written during the formative years of the comparative public administration movement. The papers examine the history and status of this field, present some conceptual models comparing administrative systems, and analyze what Dwight Waldo in the introduction calls "substantive" issues of administration in developing countries. Heady reviews the concerns and priorities of comparative public administration and Fred Riggs presents a condensed version of his ecological model. Other authors try their skill at model-building using cybernetics and Weber's analysis of bureaucratic development. Edward Weidner criticizes all of the models. The book then turns to the substantive concerns, where the authors deal with more practical issues but nonetheless manage to retain the abstract quality of the model builders. Here the contributors examine the problem of securing loyalty to development goals among units in the field, the forces that retard the exercise of control or the generation of a sense of responsibility among bureaucrats in developing countries, the process by which three different countries go about developing an indigenous public service, and the way in which national governments tend to purge the society of particularistic loyalties and promote "universalism," a paper that is based on the experience of Israel.

Heady, Ferrel, Public Administration: A Comparative Perspective. New York: Marcel Dekker, 1966. Subsequent ed. O-G-M-B-C (4+6=10) Considered by many to be the leading textbook dealing with comparative public administration. The book grew out of the era of preoccupation with public administration in developing countries and the problems of implanting Western administrative methods within them. Heady uses this as a point of departure, focusing on the various ways that different countries adjust to the growth of public bureaucracies. The analysis utilizes the ecological approach to explain the role of public bureaucracies in developed and developing countries, and Heady is most impressed by the relationship between bureaucracies and the political regimes within which they operate. Heady deals with a dozen different political and administrative systems, including all of the modern varieties from the civic culture of the USA to strongman military systems and communist totalitarian states, along with the major historic antecedents in the west. Much of the existing literature on comparative public administration is summarized, and there are plenty of examples to illustrate the various systems.

Heclo, Hugh, <u>A Government of Strangers</u>. Washington, DC: The Brookings Institution, 1977. M-P-G (0+7=7) The leading book on the relationships between the 700 or so political appointees in the executive branch of the federal government and the top level career employees. Heclo describes political appointees performing management work and career executives performing political chores. One of the few differences between the two groups is that while the first holds office for about two years, the other holds tenure for from 17 to 25 years. The heart of the book consists of two chapters on the strategies utilized by the short-term appointees "to handle their bureaucratic relations in a more productive, or at least less self-destructive, manner than others." The other five chapters contain more conventional personnel administration material: the operation of the executive branch, the development of the executive corps, the selection and assignment of political executives, the mechanics of the upper career service system, and a chapter on reform that foreshadowed the creation of the Senior Executive Service and the Office of Personnel Management. The book is based in large measure on interviews with about 200 government executives from various administrations.

Heller, Walter W., <u>New Dimensions of Political Economy</u>. New York: W. W. Norton & Co., 1967. F-P-U-B-G (6+6=12) A personal account of the coming of age of the "new economics" by the Chairman of the Council of Economic Advisors who sold Presidents John Kennedy and Lyndon Johnson on the use of fiscal policy to spur economic growth. A number of themes in the book converge around the role of the economist in government as a scientist, state counselor, and consensus seeker. The three essays were originally presented as the Godkin Lectures at Harvard University. The first essay is a review of the politics of advice, drawing on the relationship between the Council of Economic Advisers and the President of the United States. Chapter two is an essay on the elements of modern economic theory relevant to growth policies in government. In the final essay Heller examines fiscal issues in the federal system and presents a strong case for revenue-sharing.

Herzberg, Frederick, Bernard Mausner and Barbara Snyderman, The Motivation to Work. New York: John Wiley & Sons, 1959.   O-T-M-G   (5+5=10)   A straightforward, empirical study of employee attitudes in nine Pittsburgh area business firms.   The authors ask: what do people want from their jobs?   The authors distinguish between the motivating desire for career growth and self actualization and "hygienic" working conditions such as fair compensation, supervision, and administrative practices.   They conclude that improvement of working conditions alone does not lead to higher productivity.   It merely creates a situation in which the real motivators -- achievement, recognition, responsibility, and work itself -- can be made to work.   In the final two chapters the authors consider the implications of their findings; most of the material which precedes this is in the form of a research report.

Herzberg, Frederick, Work and the Nature of Man. New York: Thomas Y. Crowell Co., 1966.   O-T-M-G   (2+5=7) Herzberg is best remembered for his theory that "work itself" is the principle source of motivation on the job.   In this rather broadly written but entertaining book, Herzberg restates the arguments that he uses to present his motivation-hygiene theory in front of practicing managers.   He suggests a religious analogy as a way of introducing the twin needs of people at work.   Adam represents the employee's need to avoid pain (the hygiene factors) while Abraham represents the need to grow psychologically (the motivators). Herzberg relates this theory to the development of management thought, concentrating on what he calls "the myth of economic man," to evolutionary theory and its description of the biological and psychological needs of the human species, and to the concept of psychological growth.   Forty percent of the book is spent summarizing additional empirical studies which lend support to Herzberg's original research.   In the final chapter Herzberg summarizes what must be done to convert his theory into practice, presenting between his caustic comments on the ignorance of business managers proposals for Divisions of Motivation and methods such as what came to be called job enrichment (the restructuring of highly specialized tasks into more satisfying units of work, thereby allowing employes to develop a sense of responsibility for their jobs).

Hinrichs, Harley H., and Graeme M. Taylor, <u>Program Budgeting</u> <u>and Benefit-Cost Analysis</u>. Pacific Palisades, CA: Goodyear Publishing Co., 1969. P-F-T-M (0+6=6) A primer on benefit-cost analysis, carefully set in the context of program budgeting and actual government decision making. The volume balances theory and practice by mixing fifteen case studies with seventeen commentaries by practitioner-analysts. The case studies provide the relevant data for readers to work out, for example, the choice of program budget categories for the Postal Service or a proposed timber sale in a national forest. The commentaries that they illustrate come from the top, in the sense that they are written by persons such as Robert McNamara, James Schlesinger, Charles Schultze, and Allen Schick, who are more concerned with discussing the purposes of analysis than selling particular techniques. The commentaries take up the analytic principles, their limits, and special issues such as objective-setting, program structure, output measurement, and discount rates.

Hitch, Charles J., and Roland N. McKean, <u>The Economics of</u> <u>Defense in the Nuclear Age</u>. Cambridge: Harvard University Press, 1960. G-B-P-F (6+6=12) A complex RAND Corporation research study put together by the people who would become Secretary McNamara's "whiz kids." Hitch and McKean announce that all military problems may be treated as "economic problems in the efficient allocation and use of resources," an approach which they claim will be so obvious and widely accepted that it will reduce interservice rivalry and bureaucratic conflict. There are sections on the size of the defense budget; the application of economic analysis; and papers on special problems such as research and development programs in the military, military alliances, disarmament, nuclear deterrence, and others. A total of seven authors contributed to the book.

Hoos, Ida R., <u>Systems Analysis in Public Policy</u>. Berkeley: University of California Press, 1972. M-B-P-T-G (0+8=8) This is a book on management science, organized like a text on management science, written by a "close professional associate" of C. West Churchman, one of the "fathers" of systems analysis and management science. It is, nonetheless, a blistering attack on systems analysis in public administration. Plenty of practical examples, representing most major policy areas, provide the evidence. The causes of misapplication vary from one policy area to another. Some criticisms, however, tend to reappear: the ignorance of systems analysts, whose "outsider" status gives them no advantage in understanding the social and political nuances in a particular policy field; the tendency of systems analysts, while claiming objectivity, to make "discriminatory value judgements" throughout the course of their analysis; and the willingness of analysts to transfer unperfected techniques to unfertile fields in order to win a government contract. Hoos presents an overview of systems theory, examines its practical development from defense to the civilian sector and the process by which its techniques are transferred between sectors, analyzes various techniques (including simulation, PPBS, cost benefit analysis, and MIS); and concludes with a blast at the study of "futures."

Howard, S. Kenneth, Changing State Budgeting. Lexington, KY: Council of State Governments, 1973. G-F (0+6=6) A comprehensive study of emerging trends in budget preparation in the American states. Howard describes the shift from traditional budgeting, with its short time horizon and efficiency/control emphasis, to rationalistic budgeting, which draws on a number of ideas and approaches from policy analysis. He is skeptical of budgetary fads, such as PPBS, and spends half of the book discussing the political, economic, and intergovernmental constraints on state budgeting and the reaction of governors and state legislators to budgetary change. Within this context he presents five detailed chapters on rationalistic budgeting, change strategies, planning, and capital budgeting. The book was sponsored by the National Association of State Budget Officers and based on interviews of budget officials in a number of states.

Jacob, Herbert, and Kenneth N. Vines, eds., Politics in the American States. Boston: Little, Brown and Co., 1965. Subsequent eds. P-U-F (4+3=7) A well integrated collection of essays by a group of leading political scientists who use the techniques of comparative analysis to explain the dynamics of state politics. The essays are clearly steeped in the behavioral tradition, replete with comparative models and empirical data. There is a section on participation in state politics, with chapters on parties, interest groups, and voting/opinion. Legislative, executive, administrative, and judicial power in the fifty states are compared. Finally, there is a section on public policy in the states, with in-depth examinations of taxation, highways, education, welfare, and the added bonus of a chapter on experimentation and innovation in the states.

Kahn, Robert L., et al., Organizational Stress: Studies in Role Conflict and Ambiguity. New York: John Wiley & Sons, 1965. G-O-T (5+4=9) This book is part of a larger research program on "the influences of the contemporary environment on mental health." As a behavioral study it focuses on two sources of organizational stress: role conflict and role ambiguity. The authors summarize the largely unhealthy consequences of conflict and ambiguity on organizational productivity and individual behavior in Part II of the book. The following chapters are more detailed: an exploration of the sources and and functions of stress and a detailed investigation of the effect that personality characteristics exert on individual response to stress, including neurotic anxiety, introversion-extroversion, flexibility-rigidity, and achievement orientations. The book is based on a field study of six large industrial plants and a nationwide survey.

Katz, Daniel, and Robert L. Kahn, The Social Psychology of Organizations. New York: John Wiley & Sons, 1966. Subsequent ed. O-G-P-M-T-C-B (8+13=21) The last major attempt to construct a formal theory of organization before the more popular applications from the organization development (OD) field took over. Katz and Kahn recognized the need to treat people as a critical resource in the functioning of formal organizations -- hence the emphasis upon "social psychology" in the title. At the same time, Katz and Kahn wanted to build upon what they saw as a rich collection of complex theory laid down by Talcott Parsons, F. H. Allport, Marxists, and people who wanted to treat organizations as "general systems." Katz and Kahn thought that they could link the two perspectives through what they called "open system theory." The organization in open system theory constantly adjusts in response to its supporting environment, adjustments which must be made if the organization is to avoid "entropy" or nature's tendency to let systems run down. Open system theory is also famous for its emphasis on "throughputs," in particular the willingness of people within organizations to be activated in ways that permit their organizations to interact effectively with their ever changing environments. Katz and Kahn spend the first third of this rather long book laying out their theoretical approach. While eliminating the mechanistic character of "closed system" theory and avoiding the simplistic quality of OD theories, open system theory tends to sacrifice clarity in its search for deep understanding. The actual theory seems unnecessarily complicated, but the concept of organizations bobbing up and down in their own particular environments caught the attention of scholars in the field. The last two-thirds of the book ostensibly applies open system theory to a variety of organizational issues. In fact, it turns out to be an excellent summary of existing research which the authors learned about in their earlier association with the human relations movement. The research issues summarized include authority, incentives, motivation, communication, decision making, leadership, stress, conflict, change, and a far reaching summary of alternative forms of organization, from Weber's bureaucracy to Maoist doctrine.

Kaufman, Herbert, The Forest Ranger: A Study in Administrative Behavior. Baltimore: Johns Hopkins University Press, 1960. O-G-P-M-T-B (7+9=16) One of the best studies of administrative behavior to emerge from the period of description and one of the only ones to focus on public administration. Kaufman prepared the book after conducting a field study of the U.S. Forest Service. The book reviews the strong tendencies towards administrative fragmentation arising from the decentralized field management practices in the Forest Service. Formal procedures for achieving integration of policy -- such as rules, clearance procedures and the budget -- are largely punishment centered and, Kaufman concludes, not as powerful as the power of professionalism in promoting a will to conform in the personal habits and attitudes of Forest Rangers.

Kaufman, Herbert, Administrative Feedback. Washington, DC: The Brookings Institution, 1973. G-O-B-M (0+7=7) In The Forest Ranger, Kaufman analyzed the tendencies toward administrative fragmentation in one large government organization. In Administrative Feedback, Kaufman and collaborator Michael Couzens examine the ways in which top-level officials go about finding out whether their organization has fragmented to the point that subordinates are not complying with central goals and directives. Nine federal agencies, all operating in the domestic sphere, were examined. Kaufman identifies five major and three minor sources of information about subordinate behavior gathered by headquarters. Both formal sources, such as reports and inspections, and informal sources, such as "the grapevine," are discussed. The authors conclude that the system of feedback in the nine agencies puts top officials in a good position to monitor subordinate behavior, then examine the circumstances under which those officials either deliberately or incidentally ignore alarm signals sent back through the feedback system.

Krislov, Samuel, Representative Bureaucracy. Englewood Cliffs, NJ: Prentice Hall, 1974. C-M-O-G (0+7=7) Technically, this is a book on the problems of building a government service in which women, minorities and other special sectors of society can gain jobs and promotions. In fact, the book goes well beyond this relatively narrow question, granting the reader an erudite commentary on the political realities of operating a government and its bureaucracy under a wide range of conditions. Krislov begins by investigating the relatively recent emergence of the doctrine of "representative bureaucracy" and its wide range of meanings. He sees in it a fundamentally political issue, for the composition of any bureaucracy "is the blood, bone and sinews of political power." He goes on to explain why bureaucracies can never become fully representative, pointing out how even the ancient Athenians (who chose their civil servants through a lottery) were forced to modify this purely representative device. Krislov explains why the bureaucracy offers the most fertile ground for special interest representation -- much more so, for example, than the judiciary, with its stronger compositional bias. He offers up a number of examples of recruitment to the bureaucracy and how recruitment has been used, both successfully and unsuccessfully, to minimize social conflict and preserve control. Krislov presents seven major cases, from colonial India to Lebanon and finally the United States, the latter which in relative terms he treats as a representative model. All along "quotas" and "fair shares" are presented as political problems. Groups with any sort of power in society want access to the governmental service. Stability in the political system requires that they receive it, notwithstanding the restraints imposed by the principles of merit, which Krislov shows to be compromiseable in practice anyway.

Lawrence, Paul R., and Jay W. Lorsch, Organization and Environment. Homewood, IL: Richard D. Irwin, 1969. O-T-M-B-0-P (3+5=8) A comparative study of complex organizations by two professors of organizational behavior which greatly advanced the contingency approach to business and public administration. The book operates at two levels. First, it reviews traditional organizational theories, along with their limitations, and advances the case for a contingency theory which sorts out the applicability of different theories under different conditions. Second, it is a research report on the determinants of organizational success and failure and how this can be explained through a contingency approach. Through their research, Lawrence and Lorsch compare ten firms in three different types of industry. They show how the different environments of the three industries create the need for different levels of differentiation, then relate the success of each firm to its ability to achieve the required state of differentiation and subsequently its ability to adopt integrating strategies that counter the required level of differentiation. The authors focus on the integrating strategies for conflict resolution, showing how tremendously these strategies must vary given different levels of differentiation.

Lee, Robert D., and Ronald W. Johnson, Public Budgeting Systems. Baltimore: University Park Press, 1973. Subsequent eds. G-F-M (0+7=7) One of the most successful "new" textbooks on government budgeting. Structurally, the book follows a traditional format: an overview of governmental growth and the nature of public budgeting, a section tracing the history of budgetary reform, a detailed discussion of the steps in the budgetary process (preparation, analysis, approval and execution) and a section on special issues which takes up subjects such as capital budgeting, intergovernmental fiscal relations, and the role of government in the economy. In its content, however,

the book is a product of the PPBS, program planning,
program analysis era during which it was written. While
not entirely embracing the rational model of budgeting, and
generally pointing out its political and technical deficiencies, the authors nonetheless conclude that budgeting will
continue to emphasize results rather than resources consumed and the types of program analysis that support this.

LeLoup, Lance T., Budgetary Politics. Brunswick, OH: Kings
Court Communications, 1977. Subsequent ed. G-F-P
(0+6=6) A very practical explanation of the federal budgetary process, typically used to introduce students to the
mysteries of automatic stabilizers, budget uncontrollability,
concurrent resolutions, covert budgeting, tax expenditures
and other essential concepts. The book combines definitions and timetables which outline the formal facts of
budgeting along with the political realities that push the
process along. Thus not only does LeLoup describe the
"Fall Review" timetable at the Office of Management and
Budget (OMB), he also examines the efforts of recent Presidents to politicize OMB and place it under the control of
short-term political appointees. The core of the book consists of chapters on budget composition and controllability,
agency assertiveness, OMB review, Presidential objectives,
Congressional processes, authorization, appropriation, and
budget execution. A chapter reviewing major budgetary
reforms allows LeLoup to conclude that the process has
not lived up to hopes that it could be made into a process
"for major reallocation" of monies or "as a device for
national planning." LeLoup also includes chapters on the
relationship between fiscal policy and budgetary decision
making, the tax burden, and the beneficiaries of federal
largess. An introductory chapter reviews the different
ways of viewing the budget process, from the perspective
of the formal budget cycle to the competing theories of
budgeting. LeLoup relies upon lots of current events and a
few case studies to illustrate the federal budgetary process
and the research that has been done on it.

Likert, Rensis, New Patterns of Management. New York:
McGraw-Hill, 1961. O-T-M-P-G-U (10+7=17) The validity
of the organization development approach to business and
public administration is an issue of much controversy in
the social sciences. Critics ask: where is the empirical

evidence that participatory management works; that all other things being equal, the OD management style gives organizations that use it an edge over organizations that do not? In the most empirically based summary from the OD field, Rensis Likert attempts to supply that evidence. Backed up by the files of the University of Michigan's Institute for Social Research (he was its director), Likert argues that "managers achieving better performance (ie., greater productivity, higher earnings, lower costs, etc.) differ in leadership principles and practices from those achieving poorer performance." He characterizes the behavior of higher producing managers with what he calls "the principle of supportive relationships" in which all members of the organization view their experiences at work as supportive and helping to maintain their sense of personal worth and importance. The managers accomplish this, says Likert, by avoiding the traditional person-to-person organizational style and treating workers as members of teams. Only in this way, Likert explains, "can management make full use of. . . its human resources." The book can be read in three parts. Likert presents the evidence linking participatory management to organizational performance in chapters 2, 3, 4, 9 and 10. In chapters 5, 6 and 7 he struggles to explain why managers -- given what he feels is conclusive evidence -- are so slow to adopt this theory. He blames their reluctance on the lack of methods for measuring human assets and the situational nature of leadership. If managers were forced to defend the impact of their supervisory practices on the human assets of the firm in the same manner that they are obliged to defend the impact of their decisions on the financial net worth of the firm, Likert believes that managers would not be allowed to use supervisory practices that destroy human assets in order to produce short term financial gain. Likert's admission that leadership is situational curiously seems to compromise his commitment to participatory management as the "one best way," a point on which critics such as Charles Perrow have been quick to jump. (See Perrow's Complex Organizations, chapter 3.) In the remaining chapters of the book (seven in all), Likert summarizes his theory, comments on the nature of highly effective work groups, and moves toward the presentation of four styles of management of which his "participative group" (System 4) is the highest. Here he introduces two

of the concepts with which he would become famously
associated: the group based "linking pin" concept that he
wanted to see replace the hierarchical "man to man"
approach to coordination and the "interaction-influence"
principle in which he argued that managers would not lose
power if they allowed their subordinates to influence them.
They would, he said with regard to the latter principle,
gain influence in the firm as a result of their willingness
to interact with the people on their teams.

Likert, Rensis, The Human Organization. New York:
McGraw-Hill, 1967. G-O-T-B-M (8+9=17) In this book,
published six years after New Patterns of Management,
Likert presents his theory in a form that managers can
more easily understand along with additional research findings that support it. He begins where New Patterns left
off, with the four styles of management and the argument
that "System 4" results in the highest levels of productivity. Results from the Harwood Manufacturing Company
experience -- reported in Management by Participation by
Alfred Marrow -- are offered as support. Likert elaborates
on the four systems of management, showing how they
affect not only leadership styles, but also communication,
motivation, interaction-influence processes, decision making,
goal setting, and management control. He also argues that
they constitute consistent management styles in practice: a
manager who uses System 2 leadership methods, for example, is likely to use System 2 control processes as well.
Likert discusses once again the "interaction" principle and
the "linking pin" concept, then elaborates on a third idea:
the concept of "human asset accounting." The current
value of the human organization and the goodwill this produces among customers, he argues, should be measured
with the same degree of precision as the financial assets
of the firm -- although he does not explain in detail how
this might be done. As in New Patterns, Likert grapples
with the fact that managers are slow to adopt his theory.
Here he forthrightly admits that research studies as a
whole fail to establish a consistent relationship between
leadership, employee attitudes and productivity. This time
he raises the time factor: the need to measure productivity
changes over "an appreciable period of time."

Lindblom, Charles E., The Intelligence of Democracy: Decision Making through Mutual Adjustment. New York: The Free Press, 1965. B-G-O-P-F (6+4=10) Most students encounter Lindblom's theory of incrementalism through his article on "The Science of Muddling Through," which appeared in the Spring 1959 issue of the Public Administration Review. Here Lindblom presents his theory in a more elaborate form. Lindblom is an economist whose specialization is mutual adjustment through markets. He applies this outlook to political bargaining in government, suggesting "that people can coordinate each other without anyone's coordinating them, without a dominant common purpose, and without (written) rules." He presents a sophisticated theory of pluralism that incorporates methods of partisan mutual adjustment, two models of government (centralist and pluralist), the utility of mutual adjustment for rational decision making, the shortcomings of planned central coordination, and the manner by which mutual adjustment produces a reconciliation or balance of values in the political system. The theory is frequently illustrated with examples from American government. The book is a follow-up to his Strategy of Decision, listed under co-author David Braybrooke's name.

Lindblom, Charles E., The Policy-Making Process. Englewood Cliffs, NJ: Prentice-Hall, 1968. Subsequent ed. P-F-M-G (5+10=15) A short but intellectually challenging textbook on government policy, which Lindblom begins by investigating "the conflict between analysis and politics in policy making." Lindblom, an economist, thinks that political science has oversimplified its descriptions of the policy process by presuming that policy making proceeds sequentially from initiation to evaluation. He proposes to consider policy making in a quite different way. In the first part of the book, he discusses the role of information and analysis in policy making, focusing to no one's surprise on the shortcomings of the latter and what he believes to be the fruitless efforts -- from Plato through Marx to contemporary political analysts -- to treat policy "scientifically." Analysis, he says, "is not conclusive," therefore people must solve policy disputes by trying to influence or control each other. (Analysis, Lindblom asserts, is just another method for trying to gain control.) The second section of the book takes up "the play of power" and the complica-

tions imposed on government policy making by democratic
rules, bureaucratic politics, the privileged position of business in policy making, interest groups and political inequality. In the third and final section Lindblom belittles the
impact of voting on public policy and makes a most star-
tling allegation. Using the market system as an analogy,
he suggests that citizens simply get that for which their
leaders teach them to ask. He ends in pessimism,
recounting his earlier test of a good policy as one that
emerges from a good process, but concluding that "policy
making in the United States . . . does not repond well to
popular control."

Lowi, Theodore J., The End of Liberalism. New York: W. W.
Norton & Co., 1969. O-P-U-G-M (3+8=11) A powerful
indictment of administrative pluralism by a leading political
scientist. Lowi traces the origins of "interest group liberalism" from the constituency agencies -- agriculture, com-
merce, and labor -- to the extension of the philosophy in
federal regulatory, national security, welfare, urban, and
civil rights programs. At the heart of the liberal philosophy, says Lowi, is the tendency of Congress to delegate
difficult political issues to administrative agencies, which
are then expected to negotiate solutions with the major
interests involved. The result, Lowi says, is not democracy, but a plethora of special interest groups deadlocking
democracy by fighting to maintain the status quo and pre-
venting the body politic from planning and instituting
effective social change. In his concluding chapters, Lowi
calls for a return to a "juridical democracy," in which
Congress would return to the task of drafting specific sta-
tutes and administrative agencies -- to the extent that any
discretion remained with them at all -- would return to
rule-making through open, formal procedures.

Luce, R. Duncan, and Howard Raiffa, Games and Decisions.
New York: John Wiley & Sons, 1957. T-O-M-P-G-B
(6+3=9) A comprehensive but not difficult introduction to
the use of game theory in the behavioral sciences. The
authors emphasize the use of game theory to explain the
decision making process in an environment of conflict, risk,
and sometimes uncertainty. They present material on general game and utility theory, theories of two-person games,
games with more than two players, games under conditions

of uncertainty, and group decision making. Public administration scholars may focus on chapters 2, 4, 6, and 14, which present basic theories for arbitration, social welfare planning, and group behavior.

Lyden, Fremont J., and Ernest G. Miller, eds., Public Budgeting: Program Planning and Implementation. Englewood Cliffs, NJ: Prentice-Hall, 1968. Subsequent eds. G-U-P-M-F-T (7+13=20) Lyden and Miller assembled nineteen articles on the PPB phenomenon during the last year of the Johnson administration when program budgeting was still the hottest managerial innovation in the federal government. As if to show how fast budgetary fads change in public administration, only two of the original nineteen articles remained in the book issued fourteen years later. By 1982, the date of the fourth edition, the attention of budgeteers had shifted to the role of government in society and what is sometimes called expenditure analysis. In the meantime PPB, zero-base budgeting and Management by Objectives had come and gone. In fact, budgetary issues change so fast that the first four editions might as well be viewed as separate books. A good library would contain at least the second edition (the pinnacle of rationality) and the fourth. By the publication of the fourth edition a bit of the emphasis on rational budgeting had worn off, as consideration of overall government spending prompted the editors to deal a bit more extensively with what they called the "macro-issues" of budget making. Nonetheless, the book continues to deal principally with the sort of planning, analysis, forecasting and evaluation that one associates with rational budgeting. Political and historical factors are treated deftly, but this is still a book for people who want to be professional budget analysts and program planners in the civil service. The book offers instruction in the history of government spending and budget reform, budgeting and the political process, program planning, lots of analytic techniques, program implementation, program evaluation, and a critique of the arguments for and against rational approaches to public budgeting.

McConnell, Grant, Private Power and American Democracy. New York: Alfred A. Knopf, 1966. P-U-G (3+4=7) A steady attack on the underlying premise of American pluralism, which holds that out of the clash of partial interests emerges the public good. McConnell weaves a complex rebuttal to pluralistic doctrine. Wealthy and well-organized interests have emerged to "participate" in government in order to promote their own well-bring, says McConnell. They speak for only a narrow segment of the population and some, like industries, do not even have "members" (in the conventional sense, as in an association of citizens). Government, including the administrative system, is kept fragmented, a strategy that McConnell says enhances the power of special interests. The book is divided into two sections. The first is a more or less historic review of the growth of private power in American government. It reminds the reader that when, at the turn of the century, private interest lobbying was first acknowledged, it provoked a storm of public discontent. McConnell analyzes the failure of the progressive movement to create an effective counterbalance to the power of private interests and reviews what he sees as the rather incomplete way in which private interests have tried to justify their existance as their power has grown. He concludes the first section with attempts to demolish two myths that representatives of private power would like the public to believe: the idea that local government is closest to the people (local government accentuates inequality in policy making, says McConnell) and the idea that private associations are the natural home of democratic process since associations represent people with similar interests (private groups are chock full of conflict, McConnell observes, conflict largely unaffected by basic freedoms because the Bill of Rights does not apply to private groups). In the second part of the book McConnell attacks the pluralistic notion that pressure group government is democratic because the groups check and balance each other. Pressure groups and their allies in government, McConnell insists, operate rather autonomously in their different spheres of interest. He argues this point by reviewing the development of state government, the politics of land and water policy, business regulation, and the deterioration of the labor movement. The book ends with a chapter on the public interest in which McConnell sets out a program of political centralization which he wishes would provide a check to the particularistic centers of private power.

McGregor, Douglas, The Human Side of Enterprise. New York:
McGraw-Hill, 1960. B-G-O-T-M-P (12+12=24) McGregor's
book is probably the most popular treatment of motivation
and supervision in large organizations to be found in the
behavioral sciences. McGregor postulates two contrasting
assumptions about human nature which managers bring to
the task of organizational influence and control. Theory
X, the traditional view, assumes that the average human
dislikes work and wants to be directed. Theory Y, its
opposite, assumes that most humans will exercise self-di-
rection and seek responsibility in an organization encouraging individual creativity and personal growth. Although
McGregor hoped that his "theories" would spur self-evalua-
tion among managers, the book is generally interpreted as
an oration on behalf of applying a Theory Y managerial
style to administrative tasks and problems.

McGregor, Douglas, The Professional Manager, edited by Caro-
line McGregor and Warren G. Bennis. New York:
McGraw-Hill, 1967. O-T-M-G-B (6+3=9) An incomplete
book published posthumously. It expands upon McGregor's
plea for a set of managerial attitudes which enhance trust,
self-motivation, and the integration of personal with organizational goals. McGregor agains begins by stressing how
much a manager's view of the world -- what he terms
"cosmology" -- affects that manager's behavior. McGregor
labors to show managers how they can bring their world
views more into line "with what psychology has learned
about human behavior," discussing those findings and how
they can transform managerial behavior, the organization
of work, control systems, the exercise of power, team
work, and conflict resolution.

McKean, Roland N., Efficiency in Government Through Systems
Analysis. New York: John Wiley & Sons, 1958.
O-B-M-P-F (4+5=9) An early ground-breaking attempt to
set the stage for the extension of benefit cost analysis
into government decision making. This volume, dealing
largely with water resource programs, preceded Hitch and
McKean's book on systems analysis in defense programs,
which in turn was followed by the McNamara reforms in
the Department of Defense. Both books were prepared
through the Air Force "think tank," the RAND Corporation.
In this volume, McKean spends seventy-six pages discussing

the problems involved in applying the efficiency criterion to public administration. He discusses suboptimization, spillovers, uncertainty, time streams, discounting, and the pros and cons of various ways of comparing benefits and costs. These general points are then illustrated with examples from water resource programs, including case studies of two water projects in Kentucky and California. In a final section, McKean speculates about how this form of economic analysis might be used to compare the value of different government programs, as well as judge the relative merits of alternative methods for accomplishing a single program objective. This is accompanied by a discussion of the need for reforms in governmental budgeting.

Mailick, Sidney, and Edward H. Van Ness, eds., Concepts and Issues in Administrative Behavior. Englewood Cliffs, NJ: Prentice-Hall, 1962. G-O-T-U-M (5+3=8) A collection of 13 papers prepared for two university-based executive development programs and addressed in rather practical terms to the executives who participated in them. Scholars such as Martin Landau, Edward Banfield, Norton Long, Robert Presthus, and Daniel Katz attempt to use decision making as an integrating theme for explaining various aspects of public administration and administrative behavior. They discuss decision making research, innovation, planning, values, the environment of administration, organizational politics, authority and legitimacy, communication, human relations and motivation. Only six of the 13 papers deal directly with decision making, the rest revealing how difficult it turned out to be to bend concepts like authority and communications to the decision making theme. Those six give only a hint of the rush of decision theory toward mathematical calculations (such as game theory) and computer programming.

Mainzer, Lewis C., Political Bureaucracy. Glenview, IL: Scott, Foresman and Co., 1973. G-C-B-M (0+8=8) A general review of "the principal means to secure responsible governmental bureaucracy," interspersed with summaries of the major academic theories on bureaucratic government. The authors begin with an attempt to explain the difficulties of attaining within the bureaucracy the perfect combination of responsiveness, technical competence, and individual initiative. A chapter on "public administration under law" examines the rise of administrative regulation, the role of the courts and the requirements of due process in checking administrative discretion. Political methods of accountability through the executive, legislature, parties, and interest groups, along with the attempts to depoliticize administration, are summarized in "public administration under politics." The fourth and final chapter examines the movements toward more bureaucracy, unionization, representative bureaucracy, and decentralized or democratic administration.

March, James G., and Herbert A. Simon, Organizations. New York: John Wiley & Sons, 1958. F-G-O-M-T-B-P (14+17=31) One of the most widely used texts on organization theory, produced at the high point of the behavioral revolution. Intended to be a comprehensive inventory of the field, it represents the best and worst in formal organization theory. A good amount of it is common sense restated as behavioral jargon. The language is often convoluted. Some sections, however, such as the discussions of bounded rationality, motivation, organizational equilibrium, and innovative problem-solving did more than summarize; they advanced the state of knowledge. The book begins with an attempt to draw an analogy between "the human organism" and the organization, an effort that March and Simon hope will allow them to treat organizations as "decision-making, problem-solving organism(s)." They then review "classical" organization theory, essentially Taylor and Gulick, pointing out five shortcomings in the orthodox approach which become the subjects for the next five chapters of the book. Those chapters take up the motivation of employees to produce in ways that satisfy organization goals, the motivation of employees to participate in the organization in the first place, the role of conflict and bargaining in organization behavior, the attempts of decision makers in the organization to behave rationally given their "limitations as . . . complex information-processing system(s)," and the way in which people in organizations go about solving new or innovative problems. The latter two subjects expand on the earlier and separate work of both March and Simon on routine and heuristic decision making, where they "contrast the concept of rationality that has been employed in economics and statistics with a theory of rationality that takes account of the limits on the power, speed, and capacity of human cognitive faculties," a point of contrast that won for Simon the Nobel Prize. March went on to develop this model into a behavioral theory of business firms, described in a book listed under co-author Richard Cyert. Simon launched himself into the field of artificial intelligence.

March, James G., ed., Handbook of Organizations. Chicago: Rand McNally & Co., 1965.   G-O-T-U-P   (14+8=22) An enormous compendium of specially written papers which summarize the knowledge on organization theory gained from the behavioral movement. In the introduction, March identifies the books "most frequently cited in the recent literature on organizations." He locates contributions from sociology, business administration, psychology, economics, and political science, noting the lack of theory produced by practicing managers. The 28 papers follow the same pattern: scholars from different disciplines with a shared language and common set of concerns discuss foundations, methods, theory, specific types of institutions, and applications.

Marini, Frank, ed., Toward a New Public Administration. Scranton, PA: Chandler Publishing Co., 1971. G-M-O-C-B (2+12=14) This is the book that marked the arrival of the "new" public administration. In 1968, Dwight Waldo invited a small group of young intellectuals to the Minnowbrook conference center in the mountains of upstate New York. Most shared a common sense of frustration with the impersonal, mechanistic approach that seemed to dominate professional public administration at that time. Anger over the war in Vietnam, political assassinations, urban unrest, and the disintegrating "War on Poverty" added to the mood of turbulence. The book itself consists of the papers delivered at Minnowbrook, with comments, plus four chapters assessing the impact and content of the movement. The papers and comments deal with diverse theoretical issues. The urgent mood that emerges from them is more straightforward: the wish for a "proactive administrator" with positive values to supplant the so-called "impersonal" bureaucrat, the desire that "social equity" at least match efficiency as a goal of public administration, the emphasis upon adaptive and client-centered organizations rather than bureaucracies, and the revolt against "value-free" social science, to be replaced by social relevance.

Marrow, Alfred J., David G. Bowers, and Stanley E. Seashore, <u>Management by Participation</u>. New York: Harper & Row, 1967. G-O-T-B (3+6=9) A field study of planned behavioral change in a single manufacturing firm guided by the techniques of organization development. The changes took place in the Weldon Manufacturing Company, which in 1962 was acquired by the Harwood Manufacturing Company. Both manufactured pajamas. The Harwood Company made an interesting case, inasmuch as its president, Alfred Marrow (the senior author of this book), had been working since 1939 with Kurt Lewin and others to install participatory management in his firm. The directors of the Weldon company, on the other hand, employed authoritarian methods and a paramilitary system of management control. Their company was failing. The book is the story of how teams of managers, research scientists, engineers, and "change agents," using techniques such as survey research, sensitivity training, and job redesign, made Weldon healthy again through participatory management. Although a partisan book, it does present data on behavior and performance at Weldon in the period surrounding the change.

Martin, Roscoe C., <u>The Cities and the Federal System</u>. New York: Atherton Press, 1965. U-G-P-M (4+4=8) An analysis and advocacy of America's large metropolitan areas as equal partners in the federal system, written at a time when the level of skepticism about the ability of state governments to address the social and economic problems rooted in the cities was at its height. Martin describes the shift from an agrarian to urban society, links it to the constitutional status of the cities in the federal system (they are creatures of the states), and analyzes the causes of the diminishing relevance of state government. He then turns to the emergence of direct federal-urban assistance in the civil aviation field, its expansion in housing and urban renewal programs, and the different perspectives on the new partnership from the point of view of Washington, the states, and local communities. He concludes with the suggestion that the new partnership will strengthen American democracy, since urban government is closest to the people while the national government attracts the most popular interest.

Martin, Roscoe C., ed., <u>Public</u> <u>Administration</u> and <u>Democracy</u>.
Syracuse, NY: Syracuse University Press, 1965.
M-G-C-O-F-P (6+5=11) Fifteen leading scholars in public
administration honor Paul H. Appleby, the man who worked
so effectively to establish the mainstream political
approach. Each contributes an essay emphasizing the relevant value-conscious approach which Appleby brought to
the analysis of the public side of administration. The
essays, including two by Appleby, are divided into five
sections on the study of public administration, basic processes of administration, public administration and people,
comparative public administration, and ethical issues in
administration.

Maslow, Abraham H., <u>Motivation</u> and <u>Personality</u>. New York:
Harper & Row, 1954. G-O-T-M (6+6=12) Maslow is often
identified as the spiritual father of the organization development movement. This is the first major statement of
his "hierarchy of needs," written before he began to apply
his psychological theory to organizations. Maslow rejects
stimulus-response behaviorism in favor of a positive,
dynamic theory of human maturation. He identifies a
hierarchy of deficit and growth needs: physiological, safety,
belongingness and love, esteem, and self actualization. Not
until the lower needs are gratified will a superior need
begin to create its drives. The popular press picked up on
Maslow's work during the 1970s when the "self actualized"
person became the highest form of incarnation for the
"me" generation. Maslow describes the self actualized
person as someone who has an exceptional ability to perceive reality, solve problems, accept givens, be spontane-
ous, and retain a sense of privacy and self satisfaction.
Maslow also presents his thoughts on instinct, aggression,
love, cognition, and the origins of threat and neurosis.

Maxwell, James A., <u>Financing State</u> and <u>Local Governments</u>.
Washington, DC: The Brookings Institution, 1965. Subsequent eds. G-U-F (4+5=9) A relatively brief, non-technical
textbook on state and local finance by a leading authority
in the field. The book first appeared when state and local
governments were beginning to break the fiscal sound barrier, propelled by postwar expansion and service demand.
Maxwell reviews the various revenue choices open to state
and local governments and correctly predicts that they will

have to be retapped. There are chapters on grants-in-aid, various state taxes, the property tax and other local taxes, user changes, and debt, supplemented by chapters comparing financial sources in different states and discussing special problems in state budgeting created by earmarking and capital expenditures. This volume, along with the books by the Otts and Joseph Pechman, constitute the trilogy on government financial policy prepared for the lay public by the Brookings Institution.

Mayo, Elton, The Human Problems of an Industrial Civilization. New York: The Viking Press, 1933. B-G-O-M (5+3=8) Mayo's first reflections upon the Hawthorne experiments created a landmark book for the Human Relations movement. Mayo was suspicious of purely scientific studies, and the best chapters in this book deal with general theories of government and the new industrial order, the problem of anomie, and Mayo's hope that a new administrative elite could be discovered who would create the security and community of agrarian society within the factories of industrial civilization. In addition, the first five chapters on fatigue, monotony, and morale provide short summaries of some of the Hawthorne experiments and studies leading up to them.

Meltsner, Arnold J., Policy Analysts in the Bureaucracy. Berkeley: University of California Press, 1976. B-P-G (0+6=6) Most books on policy analysis focus on how-to-do-it. This book explains what it is like to do it: the social psychology of being a policy analyst. Meltsner examines the roles that analysts play (technician, politician, entrepreneur) and the type of work that they do, from fighting fires to writing elaborate studies. The essence of their job, Meltsner says, is "either getting ready to give advice or . . . giving it." The book outlines the factors that shape the relationship between the policy analyst and "the client." It describes how policy analysts are formally organized into the bureaucracy and how this affects their work. It describes how problems get selected for analysis and cut down to size so they can be analyzed. Meltsner emphasizes how powerfully the method used to communicate any study affects the reception given the results and concludes with a chapter on predicaments that analysts find themselves in. The book is full of examples, essentially from federal programs; officially the book is based on 116 interviews of leading policy analysts.

Merewitz, Leonard, and Stephen H. Sosnick, The Budget's New Clothes. Chicago: Markham Publishing Co., 1971. G-F-B-M (0+10=10) An in-depth but readable analysis of how PPB was supposed to work under the Office of Management and Budget directive of 1965. The authors maintain that PPB required agencies to institute five major reforms: program accounting, multi-year costing, detailed description of alternatives, zero-base budgeting, and benefit-cost analysis. A chapter on each of these elements follows. The authors then turn to an explanation of how to handle special problems of analysis, including discounting, estimating benefits, dealing with multiple objectives, and calculating costs. They conclude with two case studies showing how benefit-cost analysis was applied to the California Water Project and the U.S. supersonic transport decision. The book is considered balanced, in the sense that Merewitz and Sosnick concentrate on the overall objectives of PPB and are willing to discount the hysteria of universal reform that accompanied early promotional efforts.

Merton, Robert K., et al., eds., Reader in Bureaucracy. New York: The Free Press, 1952. C-G-O-M-T-U-B (11+3=14) The best early collection of articles and essays, some fifty in all, on the importance of bureaucracy in the Western world as a social phenomenon. Merton begins with discussions of Weber's theory of bureaucracy and the reasons for the rise of the bureaucratic form. The contributors review the ways in which bureaucratic organizations increase their power and examine the much publicized thesis that this tends to produce a shift in the locus of control from the owners of organizations to professional managers. Sections follow on the exercise of authority within bureaucracies, the fight for status, conflict between bureaucracies, and the way in which bureaucrats climb the career ladder. Two major sections examine the personality of the bureaucrat and the pathological behavior that tends to appear in highly bureaucratic organizations. Here one can find Merton's classic 1940 article on "Bureaucratic Structure and Personality" in which he suggests that attempts to install Weber's "ideal type" organization will produce

bureaucratic dysfunctions such as goal displacement.   The
final section takes up methodological issues.

Merton, Robert K., Social Theory and Social Structure.   New
York: The   Free   Press,   1949.   Subsequent   ed.
O-T-B-M-F-C-G   (8+5=13) Merton has proved to be one of
the most influential sociologists of the 20th century, a
result not only of his intellect but also of his decision to
deal with the sociology of the "middle range:" problems
like bureaucracy, anomie, propoganda, and the role of
intellectuals in society. This book provides a collection of
his work, twenty-one pieces in all, on a wide range of
topics.   The pieces are arranged into four sections.   The
first, on issues of sociological theory, is often skipped by
students of public administration.   The second, on "social
and cultural structure," deals extensively with bureaucracy,
with the way in which people behave in response to it, and
the forces that cause them to do so.   Here one can find
Merton's famous work on cosmopolitans and locals, his suggestion that anomie is a product of social structure, and
his much quoted work on the dysfunctions of bureaucracy.
Section three deals with mass communications and the
"sociology of knowledge;" while section four takes up the
relationship between science, the economy and supporting
beliefs such as faith in democracy and the Protestant
Ethic.   Unlike so many pieces in sociology, Merton's work
is beautifully written, free of jargon, yet at the same time
profound.

Meyerson, Martin, and Edward C. Banfield, Politics, Planning,
and the Public Interest.   New York: The Free Press, 1955.
U-O-P-G-B   (4+3=7) A sumptuous book-length case study on
politics and city planning written at a time when the case
approach was a dominant force in public administration.
The case tells the story of the political controversy surrounding the first large, federally-financed public housing
construction project in the city of Chicago.   In particular,
it is a story of the politics of site selection: the question,
set against a background of racial segregation, of whether
Chicago would disperse its public housing units or concentrate them in existing slums. (The eventual outcome was
concentration on Chicago's blighted South Side.)   The
authors skillfully describe the influence of personality upon
political decisions, giving the book the flavor of an expose.

As a study of the elements of decision making, the book is especially hard on the representatives of urban rationality: the planners and staff of the Chicago Housing Authority. In addition to the case chronology itself, there are chapters on politicians, neighborhood opinion, the public administration of public housing, politics, planning, and the public interest.

Mooney, James D., The Principles of Organization. New York: Harper and Brothers, 1939. (7+1=8) M-G. Onward Industry (with Allen C. Reiley). New York: Harper and Brothers, 1931. O-M-B-G (2+2=4) A total of twelve citations were given to what is essentially the same book under different titles. Both deal with the same subject, with much of the same language: the spread of orthodox principles of administration through Western civilization. Like principles of physics, recently discovered but present since time immortal, Mooney tries to show that the recently discovered principles of administration have been operating since ancient times. He discusses four principles: coordination, the scalar principle, the functional principle, and staff. These principles are revealed through studies of state, church, military and industrial organization from Greece and Rome through the Middle Ages, in the Catholic Church, in the rise of nationalism, and in the industrial revolution. The 1931 edition (586 pages) contains more detail and historical examples than the 1939 version (235 pages), along with a lengthy history of the industrial revolution that largely disappeared in later editions to be replaced with a discussion of the administrative problems of modern industry.

Mosher, Frederick C., ed., Governmental Reorganizations. Indianapolis, IN: The Bobbs-Merrill Co., 1967. O-G-U-P (4+3=7) One of the last great collections of case studies put out under the auspices of the famous Inter-University Case Program, the great collector and publisher of case studies in public administration. By 1967 (the date of publication), criticism of the case method for its disinclination toward proposition-testing had mounted. In this collection of twelve reorganization case studies, Mosher attempts to meet that criticism. In a lengthy analysis of the twelve cases, he comments on the purpose and methods of reorganization. Most of the reorganizations took place incrementally. Most were undertaken to promote changes in the "image," policy, or programs of the agency. Few were undertaken for the purpose of promoting economy and efficiency. The cases examined do not support the proposition that the effectiveness of a reorganization will be enhanced if employees are allowed to participate in it. State and local reorganizations, and California in particular, are emphasized in the selections.

Mosher, Frederick C., Democracy and the Public Service. New York: Oxford University Press, 1968. M-O-P-U-C-G (6+15=21) One of the most readable introductions to the field of personnel administration, written with a historical perspective. Mosher considers the issues involved in relating a non-elected public service to the democratic process so that "a highly differentiated body of public employees will act in the interests of all the people." He begins by explaining the way in which the educational system shapes the structure of the public service -- first in the creation of the administrative class systems of Europe and then in the more egalitarian American experience. The heart of the book follows. Mosher reviews the evolution of the American civil service since 1789 by describing the values it has sought to represent: guardianship, the common man, good government, efficiency, administrative management, and science with its commensurate emphasis upon professionalism in the public service. (Government employs three times as many professionals in proportion to its share of the work force than the private sector.) Mosher explains the tendency of professionals to seek autonomy from political interference and the impact that this has had on control of government agencies. He concludes with a discussion of the career systems in government and challenges to them, the impact of unionization on the public service, and some final thoughts on the moral implications of the movement toward the "professional" management of public affairs.

Moynihan, Daniel P., Maximum Feasible Misunderstanding: Community Action in the War on Poverty. New York: The Free Press, 1969. G-U-P (7+4=11) What happens when social scientists attempt to translate their theories into government policy? In one of the best essays on the new policy orientation in the social sciences, Moynihan traces the history of the War on Poverty from its academic inception to the administrative requirement that local programs provide for the "maximum feasible participation" of the poor. Along the way, he shows how administrative institutions like the Ford Foundation and special commissions such as the President's Committee on Juvenile Delinquency translate social theory into social policy. Moynihan criticizes social scientists for not doing their homework before advancing the theory that poverty was a result of "powerlessness" and public officials for not checking it out. He insists that the only forecast which they could verify was the proposition that such a theory would produce high levels of conflict among the government sponsored community action programs. Evidence for Moynihan's thesis comes from a fascinating case study of anti-poverty efforts in New York City. The central chapters of the book provide a historic account of the federally sponsored War on Poverty from idea to implementation. Other chapters deal with the intellectual origins of the idea that America was suffering from a loss of community, the willingness of governmental and professional organizations to move into the business of social reform, and an essay on the role of social science in formulating social policy. Moynihan concludes that social scientists make poor social policy and urges them to confine themselves to the more manageable task of measuring its results.

Musgrave, Richard A., and Peggy B. Musgrave, Public Finance in Theory and Practice. New York: McGraw-Hill, 1973. Subsequent eds. P-F-M (0+6=6) The two Musgraves (both economists) have written a highly sophisticated textbook on public sector economics. At the core of the book rests the traditional subject matter of public finance: taxes. The Musgraves describe personal income, corporate income, sales, property, wealth, and payroll taxes, the issues surrounding their use, and the people who bear their burden. This 250 page section -- one-third of the book -- would be a textbook in itself, were it not for the insistance of the Musgraves that taxing decisions be studied within the context of fiscal policy and economic theory. Thus the reader is treated to a tour through fiscal institutions, fiscal politics, theories of social goods and optimal distribution, principles of expenditure decisions, excess burden, the impact of taxes and expenditures on employment, productivity and inflation, welfare policy, environmental policy, and the operation of public finance through the federal system, internationally, and in developing countries. The text is thick reading, with graphs and formulas, but rich in content.

Nathan, Richard P., Allen D. Manuel and Susannah E. Calkins, Monitoring Revenue Sharing. Washington, DC: The Brookings Institution, 1975. U-F-M-G (0+7=7) The first product of a five year study of the general revenue sharing program, enacted by Congress in 1972. Both this, and the second book by Nathan, Revenue Sharing: The Second Round, examine whether the program met the goals of its framers. This is made obviously difficult by the fact that in order to enact the program, the framers had to embrace goals that were plainly contradictory. Some framers, for example, wanted states and cities to use revenue sharing, which was underwritten by the progressive federal income tax, to ease reliance on the more regressive system of state and local taxes. Others thought that revenue sharing would encourage states to spend money on public needs they could otherwise not afford to meet. State and local governments obliged by doing both. Some used revenue sharing for tax relief, while most used at least some of the money for new spending. Thirty-eight thousand units of government received revenue sharing funds, producing so much diversity in response that even contradictory goals could be met. The authors analyze the distributional effects of the legislative formula for allocating funds, the fiscal effects on taxing and spending, and the political anticipation that revenue sharing would promote decentralization of power. The authors conclude, over a mass of detail, that revenue sharing contained "something for everyone," and thus fell short of the more radical goals of redistributing funds between rich and poor localities or decidedly changing the nature of political participation within participating governments.

Neustadt, Richard, Presidential Power. New York: John Wiley & Sons, 1960. P-B-F-O-G (5+5=10) A 20th century Machiavelli wrote this book to warn President Kennedy of the difficulties of maintaining Presidential power. Neustadt advances the thesis that a President must persuade powerful people to do what he wants of them not because

he wants it but because it is in their own best interest as
they perceive it.   The President can maintain this power
to persuade through professional reputation and public
prestige.   The advice is developed through case studies
from the Truman and Eisenhower administrations.   The
book was received famously after the Silent Fifties; it fell
into disfavor when Lyndon Johnson and Richard Nixon
showed political scientists what a President with power
could really do.

Nigro, Felix A., and Lloyd G. Nigro, Modern Public Administration.   New York: Harper & Row, 1965.   Subsequent
eds.   G-M   (3+4=7) A practical, current issues textbook on
American public administration, combining a number of
perspectives on the field.   The traditional concerns of
public administration -- people and money -- are emphasized in large sections on personnel and financial administration.   The text, first issued in the 1960s when the
behavioral movement was at its height, takes a number of
topics from organization and management theory and
relates them to current practices: organization structure,
decision making, communications, leadership, and informal
organization.   Especially in later editions, the authors discuss a number of forces that shape administrative procedures, including approaches to policy making, value conflicts, ethics, and different cultural norms.   There are also
short sections on administrative responsibility, dealing primarily with personal abuse of power, and the personal
hardships incurred by public servants overseas administering
international programs.

Niskanen, William A., Bureaucracy and Representative Government.   Chicago: Aldine Publishing Co., 1971.   G-B-O-F
(0+6=6) Along with the books by Gordon Tullock and James
Buchanan, this is one of the gospels of the public choice
school in public administration.   Niskanen treats the role
of bureaucracy in government as a problem in markets.
The bureau is supplying a service, in exchange for which it
receives a budget.   Fundamentally, the relationship can be
described as a bilateral monopoly.   The bureau is the
exclusive supplier of the service; its budget is supplied by
politicians who are the sole specialists in the same area.
For a variety of reasons (having to do with the self interest of bureaucrats), the bureaucrat will seek to maximize

his or her budget. By plugging in a series of assumptions and carrying the reader through a difficult series of proofs, Niskanen generates eleven hypotheses on behavior within bureaus. In essence, they provide a theoretical explanation for the tendency of public bureaucracies to grow faster and be less willing to adopt cost-saving measures than competitive industries. Niskanen suggests that the existing budget review process will not produce the optimal level of services and size of government based on public preferences. He attempts to demonstrate this through more proofs, then considers a variety of reforms that might provide a more optimal level of public services, including competition between bureaus, more control by the executive and the senior civil service, and changes in the structure of the tax system. Although criticized for placing too little blame on Congress for the growth of government, the book continued to provide ideological fire for conservative efforts to cut back the bureaucracy.

Novick, David, ed. Program Budgeting. Cambridge: Harvard University Press, 1965. G-U-P-M-F-T-B (9+8=17) One of the first guides to the installment of program budgeting in the federal government published shortly after President Johnson's 1965 Executive Order requiring all agencies to use PPB. The book contains 12 papers. Part I reviews the process of administrative control as it is exercised through the federal budget, PPB, and cost-benefit analysis. Program budgeting is applied to six policy areas from national defense to natural resource management in part II. In part III the authors consider the risks and problems of implementation and contrast them to the benefits received from PPB.

Olson, Mancur, Jr., The Logic of Collective Action: Public Goods and the Theory of Groups. Cambridge: Harvard University Press, 1965. G-O-B-P (5+3=8) An economic analysis of group dynamics that explicitly questions the assumption made by authors from Karl Marx to David Truman that individuals with common interests will join together to further common goals. Olson's analysis is based on the logic of economic payoffs, and is more persuasive for large groups than small ones. In a review of labor unions, Marx's theory of classes, and pressure group theory from political science, Olson suggests that large

economic groups "have had to develop special institutions
to solve the membership problem posed by the large scale
of their objectives." He offers an alternative explanation
of group solidarity which shows how group leaders are
obliged to use special incentives -- mainly coercion and
private benefits -- in order to insure group loyalty. The
book was a seminal work in the application of economic
theory to public policy and the rise of the "public choice"
school that followed, inasmuch as public choice advocates
also sought to question the pluralistic assumption that
group activity supports representative government.

Ostrom, Vincent, The Intellectual Crises in American Public
Administration. University, AL: University of Alabama
Press, 1973. Subsequent eds. G-O-C-M (0+8=8) One of
the major challenges to the intellectual framework of
public administration issued at a time when the field
seemed to be searching for a new center. Ostrom is an
advocate of the "public choice" approach, which is rooted
in the study of economics and is a major influence among
policy analysts. In the book, Ostrom argues that public
administration has been led down the wrong path, reluc-
tantly accepting the Wilsonian-Weberian model of a well-
ordered professional bureaucratic state because it saw no
viable alternative. Ostrom offers the theory of public
choice as an alternative, tracing its roots not only to contemporary political economists but back to the democratic
principles upon which the United States was founded. The
book opens with an intellectual discourse on the "crises of
confidence" in American public administration and the various streams of thought that have led toward it. After
reviewing the work of contemporary political economists
and the ideas of the founders, he lays out the general
principles upon which a new paradigm of public administration could be based. Ostrom's critique of modern public
administration was very well received; his "alternative
future" failed to achieve dominance.

Ott, David J., and Attiat F. Ott, Federal Budget Policy.
Washington, DC: The Brookings Institution, 1965. Subsequent eds. F-G (4+7=11) An introduction to the economic
aspects of public budgeting. When the first edition
appeared, it signaled the accumulating influence of economists on the study of governmental budgeting and financial

management. The text moves quickly through basic budget concepts and the budget preparation and review process, the primary concern of administrative specialists. This is followed by a discussion of the history of federal expenditures, taxes, and debt; an explanation of the effect of aggregate spending and government debt on employment, prices, and other economic activities; and a short analysis of economic considerations in determining the level of spending for major federal functions.

Parkinson, C. Northcote, Parkinson's Law and Other Studies in Administration. Boston: Houghton-Mifflin Co., 1957. O-M-B-G (5+3=8) "Work expands so as to fill the time available for its completion." Dismissing books on the science of administration as "fiction placed between the novels of Rider Haggard and H. G. Wells," Parkinson gives us a glimpse of real operations in the bureaucratic form of organization. Although the essays are satirical, they offer unique insights into the pathologies present in modern-day organizations. Parkinson's first law is quoted above; nine essays follow on subjects such as corporate decision making, committees, personnel selection, stagnant bureaucracies, status in organizations, and retirement systems.

Pechman, Joseph A., Federal Tax Policy. Washington, DC: The Brookings Institution, 1966. Subsequent eds. F-G (2+8=10) A fairly complex book on the different considerations, both empirical and social, that must be taken into account when revising federal tax policy. Pechman is a policy activist in Washington, D.C., and an early proponent of achieving the goal of full employment through tax policy. He is committed to the pursuit of equity in tax burden decisions, to the use of tax structure as "a major instrument of social and economic policy," and suggests, at least in the early editions, that Americans could afford to pay more taxes. Thus warned, the reader is launched into intricate explanations of stabilization and growth policies, the structural and economic effects of the major federal taxes, the methods by which tax reforms become law, and an added chapter indicting state and local taxes for "regressivity and sluggish response to income growth."

Perrow, Charles, Complex Organizations: Glenview, IL: Scott Foresman & Co., 1972. Subsequent eds. O-G-B (0+7=7)

The most hard-nosed defense of bureaucracy that one is likely to find in a leading organization theory text. "Bureaucracy," Perrow says, "is a form of organization superior to all others we know or can hope to afford in the near and middle future." It purges particularism and restrains the abuse of executive power. Hierarchy promotes accountability and the alternatives to an organization based on rules are either more demeaning than bureaucracy or are outlandishly expensive. Perrow takes on the critics of bureaucracy, from the Hawthorne studies to Warren Bennis, and attempts to debunk their theories. He then summarizes what he considers to be the most promising efforts to extend the institutional school of organization thought, including the work of James March, Herbert Simon, and Philip Selznick. Even people who disagree with Perrow's conclusions find this short book to be an excellent summary of a half century of organizational theory.

Pfiffner, John M., and Frank P. Sherwood, <u>Administrative Organization</u>. Englewood Cliffs, NJ: Prentice-Hall, 1960. O-M-G-T-U-B (9+3=12) Textbooks on management are generally written by professors of business administration. Here is a text with a management emphasis written by two professors of public administration. They profess, in their preface, that "there is a large common ground inbetween" business and public administration and, thus motivated, proceed to discard the traditional preoccupation of public administration with process (budgetary and personnel) and focus instead on issues of organization structure and behavior. There are 24 chapters under five headings. The authors introduce organization theory and the role of organizations in society; consider traditional problems of organization structure such as specialization, coordination, staff work, and decentralization; describe the impact of "modifying systems" such as culture, status, communication networks, power, and leadership; contrast the Argyris and Simon models of organization; and discuss normative issues (what is the "good" organization?) and future trends.

Pressman, Jeffrey L., and Aaron B. Wildavsky, <u>Implementation</u>. Berkeley: University of California Press, 1973. Subsequent ed. P-U-F-B-M-G (0+14=14) The book that helped to launch the interest in implementation studies among policy analysts. On the surface, it applies a conventional method to a standard public administration problem, being a detailed case study of the obstacles encountered by the U.S. Economic Development Administration in its efforts to head off urban unrest in Oakland by providing financial assistance for public works and business development. What sets the book apart is the unwillingness of the authors to get bogged down in discussions of administrative technique. They study, instead, the conspiracy of delay inherent in the premise underlying creative federalism, namely that all participating groups had to agree on more than a score of administrative decisions in order for implementation to proceed. Public officials, the authors maintain, pay too little attention to the implementation process. The authors also suggest that the program itself, announced by press conference, was ill-conceived. In addition to the case study, which fills the heart of the book, the authors offer advice on administrative strategies, program planning, the capabilities of government, and the study of implementation by social scientists.

Presthus, Robert, The Organizational Society. New York: Alfred A. Knopf, 1962. Subsequent ed. M-G-O-T-B-P (9+4=13) A general essay on the development of the bureaucratic society and its impact on the individuals who must reside within it. Presthus relies heavily upon psychological studies of anxiety and neurosis and the elite theories of C. Wright Mills. The book is dark and pessimistic in tone; Presthus views individuals in the organizational society as victims of a system that manipulates and dehumanizes them. He describes three general patterns by which individuals accommodate themselves to organizational anxiety pressures: upward mobile striving, indifference, and ambivalence. Other chapters discuss the bureaucratic model, the evolution of the organizational society, the way in which the organizational personality is formed through the socialization process, the way in which organizations use anxiety and approval to promote conformance, and a final chapter on the future of organizations that sees bureaucracy as the fate of our times.

Pyhrr, Peter A., Zero-Base Budgeting. New York: John Wiley & Sons, 1973. M-G-F (0+9=9) A "how to do it" textbook by the person who helped develop zero-base budgeting at

Texas Instruments and institute it in the State of Georgia under then-governor Jimmy Carter. Pyhrr details the elements of the zero-base budgeting process: the development of decision packages, the information they should contain, the procedures for ranking the decision packages and subjecting them to top management review, administrative problems and scheduling, and the use of the computer to improve the process. He anticipates a number of problems that would emerge in the installation of ZBB in the federal government: its relationship to the planning process, its interface with PPB, and its use in reprogramming, supplemental appropriations, and other "last-minute" alterations. The chapters sound like a viewgraph-driven management training seminar, emphasizing the mechanics and objectives of the system, with the result that the reader does not get the opportunity to view ZBB in relation to the historic stream of budgetary reforms and the possibilities they pose for progress and disappointment.

Quade, E. S., Analysis for Public Decisions. New York: Elsevier Science Publishing Co., 1975. Subsequent ed. G-P (0+6=6) A very well written, non-technical introduction to what policy analysts can do to help improve the performance of government. Policy analysts can clarify and help measure the attainment of objectives, examine alternatives, identify costs, construct models, engage in quantitative analysis, use computers to carry out simulations, employ nonquantitative methods and gaming techniques, manipulate criteria used to judge alternatives, evaluate programs and conduct experiments, make forecasts and participate in planning. Quade devotes one-half of the book to explaining these processes and illustrating how they can be fit together and carried out. He then offers, in gradually increasing complexity, three chapter-length illustrations of policy analysis. Beginning with the problems involved in purchasing a car, he moves on to the complexities of improving fire company response time and the analysis of ways to prevent deaths from heart attacks. Along the way he discusses the special challenges facing policy analysts: the effect that uncertainty and lack of information have on policy analysis, the limitations of quantitative analysis, the difference between good analysis and the forces that govern the acceptance of analysis, problems of implementation, the importance of judgement and intuition in successful analysis, the pitfalls that analysts create for themselves, and the role of ethics and politics. Although Quade is cautious and realistic, he remains an advocate. "The purpose of this book," he says, "is to advocate. . . analytic methods." He believes that current decision techniques are responsible for ineffective policy plus wasted funds and believes that analysis could improve the situation if it was appropriately employed. Having stated his bias, he spends the first five chapters of the book laying out the need for analysis and explaining how to initiate it.

Raiffa, Howard, Decision Analysis. Reading, MA: Addison-Wesley, 1968. M-T-B-P-G (2+5=7) This book is designed to teach readers the mathematics of decision making, a process that is central to the fields of policy analysis and management science. The method embraces real life situations, where the decision-maker is confronted with multiple objectives and multiple courses of action and is uncertain about whether or not certain courses of action will lead to a desired result. Decision analysis provides a formal, mathematical strategy for selecting the best course of action under these conditions. To perform the analysis, the decision-maker must draw a decision tree that graphically replicates the various courses of action, scale the consequences at the end of each limb of the decision tree with what are called utility values and, where results are uncertain, decide the probability that they will occur. Most of the book explains how this is laid out and the calculations performed; a final chapter on "the art of implementation" attempts to show readers how to apply the model to large, complex, messy decision problems.

Raphaeli, Nimrod, ed., Readings in Comparative Public Administration. Boston: Allyn and Bacon, 1967. G-O-C-M (4+3=7) Many of the most important contributions that led to the blossoming of comparative public administration in the sixties appeared as articles or papers, and this is one of the best collections. Reflecting the preoccupation of that time, the book emphasizes the lessons to be learned from public administration in developing countries. The collection opens with an overview of the field and the problems of model-building. The second section focuses on civil service systems in different countries, both ancient and modern, communist and western. The problems and processes of administrative modernization in the less-developed countries begin to be examined in the third section, which carries a practical tone and includes references to particular countries. This constitutes an introduction to the model-building that goes on in section four, where papers focus on the way in which bureaucracies develop (or fail to develop) under the various conditions of modernization.

Reagan, Michael D. & John G. Sanzone, The New Federalism. New York: Oxford University Press, 1972. Subsequent ed. P-U-M-G (0+8=8) Six essays that summarize the current understanding of the practice of intergovernmental relations in America. The authors explain the extensive system of shared powers between the federal government and the states for the delivery of domestic programs, forwarding the argument that the federal government plays the dominant role. Five essays outline the transition from the old division of powers to the new system of shared powers, criticize taxing and spending policies for "giving the national government the affluence and the local government the effluents," show why categorical grants-in-aid remain the dominant instrument for intergovernmental relations, and explain what has been learned from the experience with general revenue sharing and block grants. A final chapter reviews the case for more local experimentation and less federal dominance. Scattered throughout the book are short summaries of the most important empirical studies and theoretical treatments of American federalism.

Redford, Emmette S., Democracy in the Administrative State. New York: Oxford University Press, 1969. M-G-O-U (5+5=10) Is an energetic public administration where decisions are made through administrative institutions compatible with the moral tenets of democracy? Redford suggests that it is, basing his argument upon the "extreme pluralism" of the national administrative-political system and the proposition that power tends to gravitate toward the most "comprehensive, democratic jurisdiction" whose institutional leaders know how to respond to the demands placed upon them. The heart of the book (chapters three through five) "analyze the great complexity of decision making in the national administrative-political system," debunking the old

myth of democratic representation through voting and
showing the many different ways by which interests gain
access to public policy. Redford then goes on to discuss
the many devices that allow individuals to influence policies and operations in the administrative state: both the
rights of individuals as citizens and the influence exercised
by individuals who work as employees within the system.
Around these chapters Redford dissects the tenants of
democratic morality, the characteristics of the administrative state and presents a theory of administrative realism
that he defines as a "workable democracy." The book, for
all of its difficulties in style and logic, represents the high
watermark of the administrative faith in pluralism. That
same year Theodore Lowi attacked pluralism with his End
of Liberalism, while the Buchanan-Tullock attack on the
unrepresentative character of bureaucratic government was
well underway.

Riggs, Fred W., Administration in Developing Countries: The
     Theory of Prismatic Society. Boston: Houghton-Mifflin
     Co., 1965. M-G-O-C-B (6+4=10) The prismatic model of
     administration in developing nations has been characterized
     by the observation that "things are not what they appear
     to be." The prismatic society is created when Western
     institutions and ideas about authority merge with tradi-
     tional values in a transitional society. The functions per-
     formed by structures in such a society -- structures such
     as administrative agencies -- become more specialized.
     Riggs uses the analogy of light passing through a prism to
     characterize the movement of structures from a "fused" to
     a "diffracted" situation. Since structures in the adminis-
     trative sector have not fully emerged from the prismatic
     experience, they tend to be called upon to perform all
     sorts of non-administrative functions associated with tradi-
     tional society: social, economic, political, and cultural
     functions. Riggs characterizes the resulting mix-up of
     administrative and social functions with a strange, new
     prismatic vocabulary. He introduces concepts such as
     overlapping and heterogeneity, bazaar-canteen economics,
     price indeterminacy, kaleidoscopic stratification of elites,
     poly-communalism, clects, poly-normativism, the status-
     contract nexus, double-talk, blocked throughputs, the
     dependency syndrome and the interference complex. Once
     the reader masters this alien vocabulary, it is possible to

understand the paradoxical nature of administrative arrangements in developing societies through a detailed "sala" model of bureaucratic behavior and strange mixing of modern form and social tradition which Riggs characterizes as formalism.

Rivlin, Alice M., <u>Systematic Thinking for Social Action</u>. Washington, DC: The Brookings Institution, 1971. G-M (0+8=8) A balanced, well received book on policy analysis by the person who went on to become the first director of the Congressional Budget Office. Using practical examples, Rivlin assesses the use of PPBS, benefit-cost analysis, performance measurement, program evaluation, survey research and systematic experimentation in analyzing social programs. She asks (and answers) how good a job we are doing in answering the following questions: where are the social problems and who suffers from them; who benefits from a particular program (and who pays for it); what types of programs do the most good; how can the relative effectiveness of similar programs be measured; and how can we hold bureaucrats accountable for producing better services and responding to the communities they serve? Rivlin gives policy analysts low marks for their answers to all but the first two questions, then goes on to explain the different ways that public officials can improve their understanding of social programs and build incentives into those programs to encourage effectiveness in their delivery. Her examples are based in the Johnson administration, but the insights she offers span decades.

Roethlisberger, F. J., and William J. Dickson, <u>Management and the Worker</u>. Cambridge: Harvard University Press, 1939. B-G-O-M-T (8+8=16) Here is the complete review of the research program conducted at the Western Electric Company's Hawthorne Works near Chicago that gave birth to the Human Relations movement. The book goes over the four key experiments which took place at the Hawthorne works. The illumination experiment, which began in 1924 and revealed the importance of "human factors" in establishing levels of productivity, is treated briefly as an introduction to the main human relations experiments. The relay assembly room experiment, which began in 1927, is presented in great detail. Again, factors such as the length of the work day, rest breaks and fatigue appeared to have little impact on productivity. The output of the women in the Relay Assembly Room gradually improved, irregardless of changes in physical conditions such as these. In hindsight, it seems clear that the women were responding to the participatory style of supervision utilized by the research team and their willingness to let the women develop as a group. Like the authors of a good detective story, Roethlisberger and Dickson only hint at "the stores of latent energy and productive cooperation" into which the research team had accidently tripped. The authors unfold this discovery through detailed descriptions of the interview program and the bank wiring observation room, the third and fourth important phases of the research program, which continued until 1932. The interview program was designed simply to inform the managers of the plant about working conditions; the researchers soon realized that they had tapped into complex sentiments about the social positions held by different workers throughout the plant. The Bank Wiring Observation Room experiment finally revealed those relationships in detail: the existance of informal groups and the power with which they could regulate the conduct of employees, especially in enforcing what was thought by group members to be a fair day's work. In a relatively short concluding session, the authors recount their discoveries and help to launch the behavioral approach.

Rourke, Francis E., ed., Bureaucratic Power in National Politics. Boston: Little, Brown & Co., 1965. Subsequent ed. O-P-G (2+9=11) A collection of some twenty-nine articles and excerpts from books by leading academics writing about the power that bureaucrats and administrative agencies exercise over public policy making. The selections begin by exploring the two major sources of power for administrative agencies: their ability to cultivate a constituency and their technical expertise. The struggle for political influence is examined, including the intramural conflicts between departments and their interaction with political appointees and elected politicians. This leads to questions of public control of bureaucratic power and to proposals to reorganize and reform public administration. The latter are treated with deference to the political realities involved, while the former steps up to the high plateau of constitutional debate and democratic goals. The

articles provide a rich source of lore about the functioning
of modern bureaucratic government, essentially at the
national level, but also containing commentaries on the
way in which cities have traded in popular government to
become bureaucratic city-states. The book is designed to
be used as a companion to Rourke's Bureaucracy, Politics,
and Public Policy, which was written four years later.

Rourke, Francis E., Bureaucracy, Politics, and Public Policy.
  Boston: Little, Brown & Co., 1969. Subsequent eds.
  M-G-O-P-B (6+16=22) A widely used primer on the politics
  of administration. Rourke examines "the belief that power
  in the modern state is now centered in the corridors of
  bureaucracy." He explains from where that power comes:
  from the rich technical expertise that allows administrative
  agencies to "formulate policy proposals in many areas long
  before the public is even aware that decisions need to be
  made;" from the ability of agencies to cultivate a clientele
  in a country where pressure groups play such a large role
  in national politics; from administrative skill in the use of
  ideology or a sense of mission to attract highly talented
  people to the agency itself; and from the imprint placed
  on the agency by the chieftains who lead it. Rourke uses
  these four sources of power to explain the skills of
  bureaucracy, their ability to mobilize political support, and
  differentials in agency power. That fills the first half of
  the book. In the second half he investigates the way in
  which large government bureaucracies make public policy.
  He shows how recruitment patterns, hierarchy, professionalism, and secrecy shape the policy making process within
  bureaucracies. He reviews the various techniques that
  elected and appointed officials use to improve the performance of sluggish bureaucracies: administrative reorganization, the quantification of decision making, and privatization (the shifting of bureaucratic functions toward the
  private sector or analogues of it). In the final chapter he
  confronts the belief that bureaucrats are becoming society's
  power elite, tries to demonstrate the fragmented nature of
  bureaucratic power, and warns of the difference between
  the importance of public control and the dangers of "poli-
  ticizing" the bureaucracy.

Sanford, Terry, Storm Over the States. New York: McGraw-
  Hill Book Co., 1967. U-P (3+4=7) A book that pleads the

case for giving the states a greater measure of responsibility over public affairs, written by a former governor of North Carolina who served at a time when the states were widely viewed as political and administrative anachronisms. The book is most famous for his critique of "picket fence federalism," a term which Sanford uses to describe the way in which people interested in narrowly specialized programs (members of subgovernments) use federal administrative requirements to build vertical ties from top to bottom in the federal system. These "pickets" in the federal fence weaken the power of administrative generalists like the governor who might want to broadly coordinate the otherwise narrowly constructed programs. As part of his plan to revitalize states, Sanford grabs the reformist standard of strong executive leadership, urging on the states virtually untouched the reforms that the Brownlow Commission pressed on the federal government in 1937. The book is based on anecdotes, insights and interviews, and was prepared more for public consumption than for an academic audience. Academics and administrative specialists, however, were impressed with his expose of the way in federal requirements were being used to shape state government.

Schein, Edgar H., Organizational Psychology. Englewood Cliffs, NJ: Prentice-Hall, 1965. Subsequent ed. O-T-M-G-C (4+4=8) A short, readable introduction to organization theory and behavior written by an author who seeks to move readers closer to the "open systems" approach supporting modern organization development. Schein discusses four general types of human problems that organizations confront: the initial recruitment and training of workers, the problems inherent in exercising managerial authority, the integration of informal groups with formal goals, and the process by which complex organizations seek to adapt to changes in the environment in which they operate. The book attempts to provide a framework for the reader to understand modern behavioral science findings and theories bearing on these problems; it is probably most famous for Schein's characterization of organization health and incapacity and for popularizing the concept of the "psychological contract" (matching the expectations of the worker to the expectations of the organization).

Schick, Allen, <u>Budget Innovation in the States</u>. Washington, DC: The Brookings Institution, 1971. G-F-B-M (0+11=11) Really three books in one, and not at all confined to the states. The first and last four chapters are devoted to an analysis of budgetary reform, based largely on the leadership of the national government with occasional references to the states. The central part of the book investigates the answer to a rather straightforward question: did twenty-four states which said that they were going to implement planning-programming-budgeting systems really do so? (Schick examines five in detail.) The answer is: not really, for the standard reasons of political and bureaucratic resistance. The third contribution of the book, spread throughout the volume, is an attempt to explain how real budgetary reform takes hold. This is done with reference to the three purposes of budgeting: the traditional emphasis upon managerial and financial control, the middle purpose of work load and performance measurement, and the newer thrust toward policy planning and program analysis. These are roughly synonymous in theory with line-item, performance, and program budgeting, but in practice most states adopted hybrid systems that combined the most acceptable elements of each style.

Schultze, Charles L. <u>The Politics and Economics of Public Spending</u>. Washington, DC: The Brookings Institution, 1968. G-F-P-M-B (7+7=14) The budget director for President Lyndon Johnson, who tried unsuccessfully to get all federal agencies to adopt program budgeting (PPB), asks whether PPB can be "effectively applied to governmental decisions that are reached through the essentially political process of advocacy, bargaining, and negotiated solutions." Schultze's description of the goals and methods of PPB is one of the best. He admits that PPB introduces values of utility and efficiency into the policy process, but suggests that executives will adopt PPB because it increases their staff and their power over the bureaus below them. He also states his hope that PPB will introduce "a new set of participants into the decision process," who he labels "partisan efficiency advocates," as a means of improving the quality of debate over different spending levels. In a final section he discusses another aim of systematic analysis: the discovery of incentives, such as graduated charges on industrial polluters based on the level of their discharge, that will allow government to decentralize its operating programs while at the same time assuring that public goals are met. The book is richly illustrated with examples from federal programs, primarily from the domestic sphere where PPB got such a cold reception.

Seidman, Harold, Politics, Position, and Power: The Dynamics of Federal Organization. New York: Oxford University Press, 1970. Subsequent eds. G-M-U-P-O (2+14=16) One of the richest, most comprehensive sources of information on the politics of administration in the federal government. Seidman emerged from the U.S. Office of Management and Budget, where he was Assistant Director for Management and Organization, to write a book on the forces shaping executive branch structure. The book begins with a review of Presidential study commissions on administrative organization, from the Brownlow Commission on down, whose orthodox views of management Seidman finds sorely out of touch with the reality of administrative pluralism in the federal government. Seidman then proceeds to examine in great detail the true determinants of executive structure: Congressional committees, interest groups, state and local agencies, the "culture and personality" inhabiting each agency, and the difficulties this creates for a President who thinks he is The Chief Executive. The book also contains a piercing analysis of the various organizational species inhabiting the federal forest, including government cooperations, coordinating groups, advisory commissions, intergovernmental agencies, and private firms operating under federal sponsorship.

Selznick, Philip, TVA and the Grass Roots. New York: Harper & Row, 1949. O-M-G-T-B (10+8=18) One of the best studies of political action in public administration. Selznick, a sociologist, sets out to write a case study of the formative years of that famous model of New Deal administration, the Tennessee Valley Authority. He reviews the ideological aims of the founders of the TVA -- democratic planning, decentralization, and grass roots administration -- then explains how this ideology became a resource in the struggle for power. He concludes that the TVA's commitment to radical agricultural policies such as rural land use planning was compromised because the TVA needed to win the support of established farming interests for its controversial public electric policies. Selznick calls this process "cooptation": an informal arrangement by which clientele groups are allowed to influence agency policy in return for which the clientele tacitly agree to support the general mission of the agency. His major theme has recently been re-interpreted (by those who view the TVA as an tool of the establishment) as a morally pessimistic theory of bureaucracy in the legacy of Robert Michels' "iron law of oligarchy."

Selznick, Philip, Leadership in Administration: A Sociological Interpretation. New York: Row, Peterson, 1957. O-M-G-T-B (10+4=14) A ground-breaking study that took much of what had been learned from organization theory and behavior and applied it to the practical problem of managing large institutions. Selznick begins by separating the concepts of organization and institution. An organization, he says, is something temporary, established for the task at hand. An institution is a responsive, adaptive social organism that will search for new tasks to accomplish so that the personal and group needs of its associates will continue to be satisfied. The job of the executive, says Selznick, is to identify the key values and distinctive competence of the institution and maintain them. This requires executives to perform certain key tasks: the definition of institutional mission, the embodiment of purpose in the social structure of the institution, the defense of institutional integrity against forces that would weaken it, and the setting of boundaries on permissible conflict. To accomplish these goals, Selznick paints a picture of an executive shaping the institution by altering the environment in which it operates, building an institutional core, defining new directions through recruitment and training, bargaining with power centers within the organization, and allowing institutional elites sufficient autonomy to maintain their distinctive identity. This little treatise is illustrated with examples of institutional leadership from around the world, including cases where executives have operated in ignorance of the "internal strivings and external pressures" that cause institutions to grow.

Shafritz, Jay M., ed., A New World: Readings on Modern Public Personnel Management. Chicago: International Personnel Management Association, 1975. G-M (0+6=6) A selection of some of the best articles from <u>Public</u> <u>Personnel</u> <u>Management</u>, the journal of the International Personnel Management Association. For many years, IPMA has worked to professionalize personnel administration. This collection is an effort to call attention to the new skills that personnel managers must possess in order to maintain professional proficiency: an understanding of labor relations, participatory management, motivation theory, organization development, management development, and job design. In addition, Shafritz presents new perspectives on old functions -- selection, training, classification and pay -- and a section on the changing roles of personnel managers. Some three dozen articles explore these regions, with short introductions to each section by editor Shafritz.

Sharkansky, Ira, <u>The</u> <u>Politics</u> <u>of</u> <u>Taxing</u> <u>and</u> <u>Spending</u>. Indianapolis: The Bobbs-Merrill Co., 1969. G-F-U-P (6+8=14) A short but very popular introduction to taxing and spending decisions in federal, state and local governments. Sharkansky summarizes the "economic environment of financial decisions:" the conflicting beliefs about the effect that taxing and spending policies, such as the balanced budget question, have on the economy. He identifies the principle institutions involved in taxing and spending decisions at the different levels of government and characterizes the processes that guide them. To complete the setting, he explains the historic factors -- such as war and the Great Depression -- that have shaped patterns of taxing and spending in the United States. He characterizes taxing and spending decisions as highly political, lacking objective standards, and emotionally charged. To make policy making manageable under such conditions, decision makers at the federal level adopt strategies that Sharkansky characterizes as "incremental" and "contained specialization." State officials, limited by weaker institutions and confronting less controllable economic conditions, adopt even simpler, more incremental decision rules. Sharkansky concludes with a statistical review of "the results of taxing and spending" which suggests that more taxing and spending by themselves will not produce better public services.

Siffin, William J., ed., <u>Toward</u> <u>the</u> <u>Comparative</u> <u>Study</u> <u>of</u> <u>Public</u> <u>Administration</u>. Bloomington, IN: The Department of

Government, Indiana University, 1957.   O-B-C-M   (4+3=7)
An early collection of papers that helped to define comparative public administration as an area of study and promote the ecological approach to interpreting administrative
and political change in developing countries.   The volume
consists of eight papers.   Siffin outlines the intellectual
development of the field and offers the argument that
administrative principles drawn from one distinct culture
are unlikely to pass unchanged into another culture.   In
one of the earliest presentations of his theory, Fred Riggs
describes the social systems that support administrative
behavior in two ideal type societies: agraria and industria.
Six papers follow on the evolution and social underpinnings
of public administration in Turkey, Egypt, France, Bolivia,
Thailand, and the Philippines.   They contain some of the
notable concepts (such as formalism, or the disjunction
between official form and internal behavior) that would
guide comparative public administration through the decade
in which it reached maturity.

Simon, Herbert A., <u>Administrative</u> <u>Behavior</u>.   New York: The
Free   Press,   1945.   Subsequent   eds.   O-B-P-M-U-T-G
(14+16=30)   Herbert Simon is one of the finest intellects
ever to apply his or her mind to the subject of public
administration.   Since the 1940s, Simon has held steadfast
to the idea that decision making ought to be the focus of
a new administrative science, a belief that has moved him
further and further away from the mainstream of the field.
This is his first book, a pioneering study in the behavioral
revolution, much of it developed while Simon was still a
doctoral student.   In it he criticizes the principles of
administration -- the first attempt to find scientific laws
underlying organizational efficiency -- for being nothing
more than untestable proverbs.   The science of administrative decisions for which he calls would subsequently take
off in two general directions.   One would be the science
of improving decision making in organizations through
operations research, game theory, and computer technology;
the other an attempt to understand the process by which
decisions are reached in administrative organizations.   It is
the latter that is the subject of this book.   In the original
version, Simon takes up the fact-value controversy, rationality in administrative behavior, the psychology of administrative decisions, the equilibrium of the organization, the

efficiency criterion, and the methods of achieving compliance with official objectives through authority, communication and organizational identification. The book is best remembered for its claim that facts and values can be separated for the purpose of scientific inquiry, a claim that drew a sharp rebuttal from Dwight Waldo; and Simon's argument that "it is impossible for the behavior of a single, isolated individual to reach any high degree of rationality" in making administrative decisions. Administrators, Simon said, "satisfice" rather than maximize in making choices. This argument would launch Simon into a stimulus-search-response theory of decision making that he would elaborate more fully in his 1958 book on Organizations, listed under the name of co-author James March, and eventually propel Simon into the world of artificial intelligence and computers.

Simon, Herbert A., Donald W. Smithburg, and Victor A. Thompson, Public Administration. New York: Alfred A. Knopf, 1950. G-M-O-P-U-B (7+5=12) Shortly after publishing Administrative Behavior, Simon decided to try his hand at writing a textbook on public administration. Simon and his collaborators set out to build a bridge between the three dominant concerns of public administration at that time: the traditional preoccupation with administrative processes in government agencies, the relatively new understanding of human behavior in organizations, and the rapidly expanding interest in the politics of administration. The result was an extensive textbook that introduced students in a more or less practical way to individual and small group behavior, specialization, authority and status, communication within organizations, centralization, intergroup relations, the personnel process, organizational equilibrium, political tactics for organizational survival, planning, organization change, compliance and control, the measurement of efficiency and methods for holding the bureaucracy accountable.

Simon, Herbert A., Models of Man: Social and Rational. New York: John Wiley & Sons, 1957. P-O-B-M-T-F-G (5+3=8) In Administrative Behavior, Simon called for a science of organizations built around unambiguous propositions whose validity could be tested as facts. In Models of Man, a book consisting of sixteen articles authored or coauthored

by Simon between 1947 and 1956, he shows how this can
be done. The articles are astonishingly wide-ranging, having been published in journals serving the disciplines of
sociology, psychology, economics, and political science. In
them Simon uses the language of mathematics to clarify
what is meant by various concepts and theories employed
in the social sciences. He asks, for example, what is
meant by the statement that "Peron holds a monopoly of
power in Argentina." "Prove it," he says, challenging himself to reformulate the proposition in a way that can be
measured. This part of the book -- the first half -- can
be read as a test of Simon's hope for a science of behavior founded on a separation of facts and values. Officially, these sections treat the nature of influence processes and group behavior in organizations. In the latter
part of the book, Simon applies this sort of analysis to the
theory of "economic man" and to his alternative theory of
"bounded rationality," which he offers as more appropriate
than the rational-comprehensive model for predicting the
behavior of people in organizational settings. The tests he
offers are often of the sort that tend to tease the mind,
attacking conventional assumptions with fairly straightforward situations that can be manipulated mathematically so
as to lend force to his argument. In these sections Simon
takes up a theory of the firm, an employment contract, a
method for scheduling production, a definition of rational
choice, and a funny little organism that runs around on a
flat plain in search of food, busily casting doubts on the
explanatory power of "rational man" theory as it tries to
survive. The articles often raise more questions than they
answer, but then they are not meant to be conclusive.
They are meant to show the possibility of establishing an
empirical science of administrative behavior based on
Simon's decision making theory.

Simon, Herbert A., The New Science of Management Decision.
New York: Harper & Row, 1960. Subsequent ed.
O-M-B-P-T (8+3=11) In 1960, two years after the publica-
tion of James March and Herbert Simon's Organizations,
Simon turned his interest in decision making toward the
world of computers. Much earlier, in Administrative
Behavior, he had identified "incompleteness of knowledge"
as the first limitation upon "rationality in actual behavior."
Now he was not so sure. It had become clear to him that

computers were producing an information rich world, a fact that appeared to be changing the techniques by which decisions were made. To explore this transition, he reviews in The New Science of Management Decision the various ways by which managers make decisions, ranging from habit and intuition to mathematical analysis. He observes that computers have already made possible great advances in programmed decision making (in areas such as operations research). As for unprogrammed decisions, he makes a most utopian forecast. This area of decision making, which heretofore had been the province of satisfiers and rules of thumb, is "beginning to undergo as fundamental a revolution as the one which is currently transforming programmed decision making in business organizations." Advances in the understanding of cognitive processes and computer programs will, in essence, produce computers that can automate the work of certain managers. Not surprisingly, those computers utilize search processes that replicate the type of decision making that Simon describes in some of his earlier work. The heart of this argument is contained in chapter two of the revised edition. (It the original version, this section made up practically the the whole book.) Simon uses the remainder of the book to give his views on a number of questions raised as a result of advances in computer technology. Will the corporation increasingly be managed by machines? (It will.) Will those machines and the new decision making technology associated with them dehumanize blue collar and clerical work? (Simon says no to this very controversial question.) How will the shape of organizations change as a result? (Simon believes that they will become more rationalized and professionalized and remain hierarchical.) Will computers encourage widespread unemployment and accelerated consumption of unrenewable resources so as to create limits on economic growth? (Simon argues that technology will save us.)

Stahl, O. Glenn, Public Personnel Administration. New York: Harper & Row, 1936. Subsequent eds. M-C-G (2+11=13) Originally published in 1936 by William Mosher and Donald Kingsley, the authorship of this basic textbook on public personnel administration eventually passed to O. Glenn Stahl. The original volumes celebrated the forward movement of the merit principle, heralded the acceptance of the civil service commission as a professional personnel agency, and focused on the functions needed to be performed following the professionalization of personnel administration: organization, selection, compensation, training, and terms of employment. Stahl retains the same basic, practical emphasis found in the early editions, dealing in detail with the fundamental functions of selection, classification, pay, separation, and the organization of the personnel system. At the same time, this is joined with new developments in motivation, training, unionization, and the spread of professional personnel administration around the world.

Stanley, David T., The Higher Civil Service. Washington, DC: The Brookings Institution, 1964. M-O-P-G-C (3+4=7) A general survey of the people who occupy the higher managerial and professional positions in the federal civil service and their attitudes toward the system under which they work. Gathering information from interviews, questionnaires, statistical profiles, and a search through relevant reports and books, Stanley attempts to characterize the 16,000 persons who work at the top and use this information to suggest needed reforms. He begins by describing the careers of top civil servants, drawing a picture of steady advancement without lateral mobility. In two chapters he summarizes the attitudes of persons at the top on issues such as pay, selection and assignment, job satisfaction, civil service regulations, and why they leave the service. This is followed by two chapters on possible reforms, including an embryonic proposal for what would fourteen years later grow into maturity as the Senior Executive Service.

Stieber, Jack, Public Employee Unionism. Washington, DC: The Brookings Institution, 1973. G-M (0+6=6) Half of all public employees in state and local government belong to unions or union-like employee associations; that is proportionately larger than in private industry. Stieber has prepared a descriptive reference guide to the structure, growth, and activities of public employee unions and associations. He focuses on emerging union activity among such groups as police, firefighters, sanitation workers and nurses, passing over teachers and transit workers who have a longer history of collective bargaining. The book proceeds to describe the myriad types of public employee organizations, detailing in turn the structure of each type and its leadership, staff, finances, and minority group participation. The second section describes union activities and behavior. It surveys the conflicts resulting from the efforts of different unions to organize and represent public employees, the occasional areas of cooperation, the drive toward wider use of collective bargaining, the increasing willingness of unions of public employees to resort to strikes, and the involvement of public employee associations in elections, fundraising, and political action. A final chapter summarizes emerging trends, foretelling an increased orientation toward union type activities as collective bargaining becomes more widespread. Based on primary sources and personal interviews, and covering so many types of government and employee associations, the book tends to take on the character of an encyclopedia.

Suchman, Edward A., Evaluative Research. New York: Russell Sage Foundation, 1967. M-P-B (0+6=6) A carefully written primer on the logic of evaluation research. Here that logic is grounded in the pure science of medical research, inasmuch as the author is a specialist in public health. There are plenty of illustrations from public health and medical research, exposing the reader who may be accustomed to pedestrian evaluation studies to the standards of proof in a field founded on science. At the same time, the book is not a polemic on behalf of pure research. (In fact, the complexities and quirks of public health, such as the "placebo" effect (cures without medicine), provide fine examples of the limits of scientific investigation.) The author treats the different uses to which evaluation studies are put with understanding (the tendency to appraise effort rather than effect, for example,) yet always keeps the criteria of scientific methodology as a base line. Ten chapters form three sections on the conceptual, methodological, and administrative aspects of evaluation, and include a comparison of different research designs.

Sundquist, James L., with the collaboration of David W. Davis, Making Federalism Work. Washington, DC: The Brookings Institution, 1969. M-G-U-P (6+7=13) Out of the theories of Morton Grodzins came the belief that a little chaos was healthy for the American federal system, inasmuch as it enforced an unshakable measure of decentralization on the conduct of domestic programs. Under the rapid expansion of domestic legislation during the early years of the administration of Lyndon Johnson, the chaos became a bit more chaotic. This is the problem that Sundquist and Davis attack: the demand for more forceful coordination of intergovernmental programs, especially at the state and local level, and the devises created to meet that demand. Based on interviews of more than 700 officials in 14 states, the authors explain the need for coordination, critique the two principal devices designed during the Johnson administration to attain it (Community Action Programs in the "War on Poverty" and Model Cities for the rehabilitation of urban centers), and describe five different approaches being used to coordinate intergovernmental programs in rural America. The authors then lay out the argument for multi-county coordinating structures for non-metropolitan areas and describe how the federal government can promote coordination at the local level. Although their favorite programs, such as Model Cities, largely withered away, the blast that Sundquist and Davis leveled at the problems of coordinating intergovernmental programs helped establish the commitment to search for new types of federalism to replace the mildly chaotic brand of "cooperative federalism" espoused by Grodzins.

Taylor, Frederick W., Scientific Management. New York: Harper & Brothers, 1947. B-G-O-M (6+6=12) Scientific management was one of the most important movements in the early study of administration. Taylor called it "a complete mental revolution" where management and workers would replace antagonism with cooperation in order to produce a surplus so large that it would be "unnecessary to quarrel over how it shall be divided." This new attitude toward management required all members of the firm to substitute scientific investigation for intuition and opinion. Taylor developed the system as an engineer in a steel works, scientifically planning the flow of work and using demonstrations rather than discipline to encourage workers to increase their output. That was 1890. Not until much later were his written theories solicited and published: a paper presented to the American Society of Mechanical Engineers in 1903; an essay which he published at his own expense in 1911; and an extraordinary question and answer session following testimony before a Congressional committee in 1912 investigating Taylor's misgivings about collective bargaining.

Taylor, Frederick W., The Principles of Scientific Management. New York: W. W. Norton & Co., 1911. O-T-P-G (3+6=9) The most famous of the three papers cited above is contained in this single volume. In two relatively short chapters, Taylor examines the causes of inefficiency in modern organizations (fear of unemployment, soldiering, and rule of thumb methods) and lays out the principles underlying his scientific approach to management. The "most prominent single element" in his approach, revolutionary in its day, was the use of experts to plan out in advance in great detail the tasks that workers were to perform. The paper contains the most famous illustrations of Taylorism: the art of cutting metals, the science of shovelling, the use of time and motion studies, and the famous dialogue with Schmidt who is described by Taylor as an ideal worker, "merely a man of the type of the ox, heavy both mentally and physically."

Thompson, Frank J., Personnel Policy in the City. Berkeley: University of California Press, 1975. G-M (0+6=6) This book is part of the Oakland Project, which produced among other books the classic study on Implementation by Pressman and Wildavsky. Here the subject is personnel policy or, more precisely, the "politics of jobs." The book describes strategies and processes that characterize the functioning of the merit civil service system in the city of Oakland. It characterizes personnel policy in much the same manner as Wildavsky -- under whom the author studied -- has described the politics of the budgetary process in the federal government. There are chapters on the politics of deciding how many positions different managers shall have to fill, the politics of settling salary and fringe benefit issues, and politics of publicizing job openings and selecting new employees, the politics of assuring adequate minority representation on the work force, the politics of removing personnel, and a final chapter on the problems of tempering civil service principles given the information and leverage actually available to city officials. The book is based largely on the experience gained by the author after working part time for two years for the Oakland personnel director and city manager.

Thompson, James D., Organizations in Action: The Social Science Bases of Administrative Theory. New York: McGraw-Hill, 1967.   O-G-T-U-B-P   (5+10=15)   Thompson attempts to construct a formal theory of organization based on the open systems approach that dominated efforts at theory building in the latter years of the behavioral revolution. His book is organized around the theme that "organizations abhor uncertainty" and seek to subject uncertainty to "norms of rationality." New technologies and changes in their environment, Thompson says, are "basic sources of uncertainty for organizations." He advances the idea that "organizations with similar technological and environmental problems" will tend to exhibit "similar behavior." This is followed by his famous three-part classification of technologies that organizations use: long linked, mediating, and intensive. Part one of the book consists of a series of propositions explaining how the dominant form of technology which an organization utilizes affects the process by which the organization goes about establishing its domain, designing the activities it will perform, building an appropriate structure, and selecting methods for assessing its operations. In part two, Thompson applies his theory to the people who work within organizations. He suggests, first of all, that the inducements which an organization uses to encourage individual participation will vary in relation to the type of technology within which an individual must work. Thompson is primarily concerned, in this section, with the way in which different individuals exercise discretion and how the organization tries to control them. He describes this as a problem of conflict and power, varying again in relation to with the complexity of the operation. He terms the old "command and control" style of administration outmoded and suggests that the high levels of technical achievement in modern societies are the result of organizational leaders who understand the various methods necessary to subject uncertainty and interdependence to norms of rationality in modern organizations.

Thompson, Victor A., Modern Organization. New York: Alfred A. Knopf, 1961.   C-G-O-B-M-P   (9+10=19)   A book on the various dysfunctions arising from the bureaucratic form of organization. Thompson argues that the merging forces of technology, rapid change, specialization, and hierarchy have conspired to give subordinates the skills needed to solve problems but left the power to command in the hands of their less competent superiors. This creates what Thompson calls "an imbalance between ability and authority." The most clever chapters are deductive essays on "Bureaupathology" and "Dramaturgy." In the former Thompson suggests that the ability of individuals to deal with organizational power is a function of their psychological maturity; in the latter he explores the need for persons to create images in order to ascend the career ladder. Thompson also discusses the meaning of bureaucracy, the drive toward specialization, the reenforcement of hierarchy, the assault on hierarchy by specialists, the use of ideology to reenforce hierarchy, and the various methods by which cooperation between specialists and those in command can be achieved. Thompson admits that modern management faces up to the conflict created by the imbalance between ability and authority by "reliance . . . upon the command power of the superior," and suggests some modest alternatives for bringing the two forces into balance.

Truman, David, The Governmental Process. New York: Alfred A. Knopf, 1951. M-O-G-P-F-U (10+5=15) This pioneering study on the role of pressure groups in American government helped to launch the policy orientation in political science. By focusing on the systematic interaction between groups and government, Truman helped to move the focus of political research away from the institutions of government and toward the policies it adopts. Part I deals with the role of interest groups in a complex society, drawing upon the sociology of large groups and the history of pressure groups in America. In part II Truman explores the internal dynamics of pressure groups: their structure, leadership, and struggle to preserve cohesion. Part III is a textbook of American government told through the eyes of interest groups and the influence that they possess over parties, elections, public opinion and the three branches of government. A concluding section tries to present an empirical answer to the normative question that asks whether pressure groups pose a danger to representative democracy.

Tullock, Gordon, The Politics of Bureaucracy. Washington, DC: Public Affairs Press, 1965. O-B-P-F-G (4+3=7) An early

contribution to the public choice approach to public
administration. This is not a book about the politics of
administration, a la Wildavsky, but a treatise on politics
within governmental administration, among bureaucrats and
executives. Through anecdotes and common sense (he was
a bureaucrat in the State Department for nine years), Tullock attempts to explain what happens when rational individuals pursue their self-interest through political strategies
in large public bureaucracies. In a lengthy discussion of
political regimes and management controls, Tullock tries to
show how large organizations become bogged down in
clumsy mechanisms of supervision and lose their ability to
effect public goals. His solution, solidly in the vein of the
public choice school, is to dismantle the giant units of the
administrative state and encourage a wider use of local
governments.

Van Riper, Paul P., History of the United States Civil Service.
Evanston, IL: Row, Peterson and Company, 1958.
O-M-C-G (2+7=9) An extensive analysis of the development of the federal civil service system, and the only
major administrative history to follow Leonard White's
chronicles into the twentieth century. Van Riper traces
the beginnings of an elite service under the Federalists and
Jeffersonians, describes the principle features of the Jacksonian spoils system, then turns to the major thrust of his
book: the extension of (and assaults on) civil service
reform. Alterations in the civil service system are linked
to politics, economics, and religious beliefs, marked in
large part by the passage of different presidential administrations. Van Riper is especially interested in the gradual
movement toward a representative bureaucracy in an army
of federal civil servants under the merit system that numbers 2.8 million strong.

Vroom, Victor H., Work and Motivation. New York: John
Wiley & Sons, 1964. O-M-G-B (3+4=7) A rich summary of
some 500 research studies, mainly from industry, on the
science of employee satisfaction and motivation. After
presenting a general overview of the elements of motivation, Vroom arranges the research into three general areas.
He summarizes then-existing research on how employees
choose occupations, on the determinants of job satisfaction,
and on factors that motivate employees to perform at

higher levels. Readers accustomed to one-dimensional theories of motivation will be surprised by the complexity of the research findings and the necessity to take a number of factors into account in order to predict satisfaction in a particular work situation. Regarding job satisfaction, he identifies six major environmental conditions creating a "satisfactory work role," including pay and participatory management, then unveils studies suggesting that certain personalities are satisfied or dissatisfied regardless of their work roles. Some widely accepted beliefs, such as the assumption that greater job satisfaction leads to higher productivity, are not supported by data.

Vroom, Victor H., ed., Methods of Organizational Research. Pittsburgh: University of Pittsburgh Press, 1967. G-O-M-T (3+4=7) Public administration operates through large, technologically complex organizations, yet the contributions of public administrators to the recent study of complex organizations is slight compared to the work of sociologists and psychologists. It was thus with much expectation that the small band of public administrators who study structure and behavior in complex organizations welcomed this book, a primer showing would-be researchers how to conduct scientific studies of complex organizations. For those who would work at home, there is a chapter on the conduct of organization research in the laboratory. For mathematical wizards, a chapter on computer simulation methods appears. Tom Burns explains the comparative study of organizations for those who want to know why similar organizations are different and there is a difficult chapter on conducting research on real organizations in the field. Each chapter is authored by a different individual, all of whom were brought together for a social science research seminar in 1964 from which this book emerged.

Waldo, Dwight, The Administrative State. New York: The Ronald Press, 1948. O-M-G-P-U-B (8+11=19) Waldo is the leading historian of the disciplined study of public administration. He wrote this book as an angry young graduate student at Yale University, aiming to destroy the dogmatic claim made by early administrative scientists that "they were concerned only with facts." Waldo describes what he takes to be the position of these administrative scientists on some of the most important questions of political phi-

losophy: what is the nature of the good life, what criteria
should be employed in making decisions, who should rule,
and how should government be organized, the latter primarily with reference to the doctrine of separation of
powers and the issue of centralization versus decentralization. Quoting extensively from the formative writings on
public administration, Waldo demonstrates conclusively that
supporters of the supposedly "value free" administrative
science movement possess definite views on these value-
loaded issues. He exposes those views in detail, principally
the faith in progress and science and the gospel of efficiency. Having placed the movement in its philosophic
context, Waldo goes on to consider "the virtues and vices
of the theories which it accepts as its own." He contrasts
the world-view of administrative science with other systems of belief, such as the medieval trust in faith and the
eighteenth century worship of reason, revealing the point
at which concepts like efficiency cease to be objective and
become matters for philosophic debate.

Waldo, Dwight, The Study of Public Administration. New
York: Random House, 1955. O-M-G (3+5=8) In 1955,
Waldo wrote this overview of the development of public
administration and the search for doctrines to guide the
field. He sought to define the meaning of public administration, map out the principle "schools of thought",
describe the contributions of other fields and disciplines,
and describe how MPA programs were organized at that
time. These sections of the book are often read in conjunction with his article on "Public Administration" in the
International Encyclopedia of the Social Sciences (1968),
especially as the encyclopedia article updates his descriptions of the schools of thought. Overall, the book is principally remembered for Waldo's efforts to force the field
away from its growing attachment to logical positivism.
Waldo traces the transformation of public administration
from a premature science based on the orthodox pursuit of
economy and efficiency to the efforts of Herbert Simon
and others to make it a real science based on the separation of facts and values. Waldo outlines the weaknesses of
logical positivism and pleas for a politically conscious study
of public administration, one that recognizes the role that
values play in any publicly-based system of rational cooperation.

Waldo, Dwight, ed., <u>Public</u> <u>Administration</u> <u>in</u> <u>a</u> <u>Time</u> <u>of</u> <u>Turbulence</u>. Scranton, PA.: Chandler Publishing Co., 1971. G-C-B-M-U-O (0+8=8) Considered by many to be the second step in the movement toward a "new" public administration. (For the first, see the anthology by Frank Marini.) One year after the Minnowbrook conference, Waldo assembled another group of young professionals to discuss new directions in public administration, this time at the annual convention of the American Political Science Association. Seven of the fourteen papers in the volume deal with ideological issues underlying the new P.A.: radical politics, moral purpose, liberalism, participation, community, and the challenge to traditional values embedded in science, consensus politics, and capitalism. Four of the papers deal with administrative change in the areas of science, information technology, environmental quality, and government regulation. Waldo adds a paper on the major discontinuities afflicting public administration and calls on two representatives from the "older" public administration for papers they had previously written on the movement toward representativeness and away from bureaucracy in the public service.

Weber, Max, translated, edited, and with an introduction by H. H. Gerth and C. Wright Mills, <u>From</u> <u>Max</u> <u>Weber</u>: <u>Essays</u> <u>in</u> <u>Sociology</u>. New York: Oxford University Press, 1946. O-M-G-B-P (7+8=15) Fourteen selections from Max Weber's books, essays, and lectures. They include Weber's famous essay in which he identifies the major characteristics of an ideal-type bureaucracy: fixed authority, a hierarchy of offices, impersonality, a career service, and the principle of rules. This "Essay on Bureaucracy" is mainly concerned with the causes and effects of bureaucratic development, with Weber stressing factors such as the presence of a money economy, rational authority and the rise of mass democracy. The other selections deal with science and politics, imperialism, social groups, charismatic authority, the sociology of discipline, religion, rural life in Germany, the landed aristocracy, castes in India, and the Chinese intellectual ruling class. The editors begin the book with a very readable introduction to Weber's life and ideas.

Weber, Max, <u>The</u> <u>Theory</u> <u>of</u> <u>Social</u> <u>and</u> <u>Economic</u> <u>Organization</u>, 1915 apx.; translated by A. M. Henderson and Talcott Par-

sons. New York: Oxford University Press, 1947.
G-O-T-B-M (8+4=12) Weber's most complete work, an
enormously complex statement of his theory of social
structure and social action in modern Western civilization.
It strongly influenced the branch of American sociology
from which organization theory emerged. Readers will
easily recognize Weber's typology of authority: legal-ra-
tional, the basis of bureaucratic organization; traditional,
associated with older forms of organization founded on
ethics; and charismatic, an unstable revolutionary force
which if successful undergoes a metamorphosis to become
routine administration. This is preceded by Weber's difficult ideal-type theory of sociology and economic action
based upon the rationalization of human affairs. Weber's
life and work are reviewed again in an extensive introduction by Talcott Parsons.

Weiss, Carol H., Evaluation Research. Englewood Cliffs, NJ:
Prentice-Hall, 1972. G-M-P (0+12=12) A short but comprehensive introduction to a variety of methodological and
practical issues involved in the evaluation of social programs. The author, an evaluator and consultant herself,
recommends strategies designed to enhance the use of
evaluation reports. The strategies sometimes require the
evaluator to compromise the purely scientific method, for
"evaluation uses the methods and tools of social research
but applies them in an action context that is intrinsically
inhospitable to them." Weiss gives advice on the purpose
of evaluation, on defining program objectives, on selecting
indicies that can be used to measure program results, on
choosing the appropriate type of evaluation study (a
research design problem), on avoiding conflict with the
agency personnel being evaluated, and on maximizing the
impact of the evaluation study.

White, Leonard D., Introduction to the Study of Public Administration. New York: Harper & Brothers, 1926. Subsequent eds. G-M-U (6+3=9) White is credited with writing
the first textbook on public administration, a text that set
a number of important precedents. It is a practical book,
introducing readers to the process of management in
governmental organizations, and as such helped to set the
precedent that the teaching of public administration would
be aimed at practitioners rather than scholars. The book

treats administration as a single process, universally the same throughout different levels of government and different policy areas. This set the precedent that textbooks of public administration would deal, in White's words, with "certain common underlying problems: organization, personnel, control, finance." Although White was a professor of political science, the book largely ignores politics, treating governmental management as a technical problem rather than as a problem in governing. This helped to strengthen the pervading politics-administration dichotomy. Finally, White emphasizes the growing influence of science and experts in the administration of government policy, professing his belief that administration could become one of the sciences. The two decades prior to the publication of the first edition had seen a marvelous expansion of the literature on "the business side of government" (White's own words), which he sought to pull together in chapters on centralization, integration, reorganization, personnel, morale, recruitment, salary standardization, promotion, discipline and removal, retirement systems, administrative rules, and the control of administration by the executive, the legislative branch, and the courts.

White, Leonard D., The Federalists, The Jeffersonians, The Jacksonians, and The Republican Era. New York: The Macmillan Company, 1948, 1951, 1954, 1958. O-G-M-P-U (8+4=12) An elegant administrative history of the federal government from 1789 to 1901, based on public reports, office memoranda, and private letters. Two major themes stand out: the continuity of administrative institutions in spite of political and economic convulsions, and the contest between Federalist and Jacksonian doctrines of administration. The Federalists, especially Hamilton, sought a stable, competent, politically neutral public service within a government acting as a positive force in society, administrative conditions which the Jeffersonians generally continued. The Jacksonians revolutionized this administrative system with democratic dogmas, the mass political party, and the rule of rotation. The Jacksonian system was tempered with Federalist doctrine during the Republican era that followed. Each book in the series takes up four major points of concern: the relationship between the executive and legislative branches in controlling administration; the operation of the departments; the personnel system; and the major administrative problems in each era.

Wholey, Joseph S., et al., Federal Evaluation Policy. Washington, DC: The Urban Institute, 1970. G-P-M (0+6=6) An early plea for effective program evaluation with lots of practical recommendations, focusing not on the methodological issues confronting evaluators but on the administrative problems encountered by public officials overseeing them. The authors base their recommendations on a study of evaluation procedures in federal agencies which administer domestic programs. The study, conducted by the Urban Institute, prompted important improvements in federal evaluation procedures. The book opens with a quick overview on the ability of federal agencies to "measure their successes and failures," titled "many programs, uncertain results." The authors then proceed to outline the four steps required to manage useful evaluation projects and review the most common pitfalls encountered in trying to complete them. Drawing on examples from their study, they recommend administrative procedures, staffing and funding levels and methods for coordinating the evaluation process among Congress, the executive, the agency, and participating state and local governments. Only one chapter deals specifically with methodological and technical issues, given that the bulk of the book is oriented toward the administrative side of evaluation. The authors conclude by summarizing the contributions that the various branches and levels of government should make in the evaluation process.

Wildavsky, Aaron, The Politics of the Budgetary Process. Boston: Little, Brown & Company, 1964. Subsequent eds. O-B-P-M-U-T-G-F (15+21=36) The best received book on the politics of administration, written at the end of the period of description. Wildavsky describes a dynamic budgetary game in which the actors play complementary roles: the agency (advocate), the Office of Management and Budget (defender of the President's program), the House Appropriations Committee (guardian of the purse), and the Senate Appropriations Committee (court of appeals). Wildavsky believes the process to be so complex that rational planning will fail where the unseen hand of incrementalism will succeed. He describes the budgetary process as specialized, incremental, fragmented, and sequential. The book is full of anecdotes suggesting strategies that agency heads use to beat the system. The final sections appraise proposals for budgetary reform, where Wildavsky earns his reputation as a critic of program budgeting and other efforts to "rationalize" the budgetary process. The section on budgetary reforms has expanded from two chapters in the first edition to five in the fourth, as Wildavsky has been obliged to apply his skepticism to PPB, ZBB, and the new Congressional budget process. For all that, he does not remain a skeptic forever, turning advocate when confronted with uncontrollable federal spending. He presses for a reform known as "reconciliation." The reconciliation process would force legislators to set a ceiling on total government expenditures (Wildavksy would do this through a constitutional amendment), aggregate cuts in governmental programs and vote on them in total. Only in this way, he says, can the bias toward big government inherent in the currently fragmented budgetary process be controlled.

Wilensky, Harold L., Organizational Intelligence: Knowledge and Policy in Government and Industry. New York: Basic Books Inc., 1968.   B-O-T-M-P-F-U-G (6+10=16) How do public officials locate the information they need to make decisions, especially when the stakes are high and the right decision must be made? In this pioneering work, Wilensky seeks to identify factors that contribute to intelligence coups and failures. He begins by identifying the situations in government and business when knowing the facts really count and showing how preconceived stereotypes and slogans persist even when evidence shows them to be wrong. Persistently, Wilensky analyzes the factors "that maximize distortion and blockage": hierarchy, specialization, centralization, misguided doctrines of intelligence gathering, secrecy and its counterpart, excessive publicity. If this were not enough, Wilensky goes on to show how different political, economic and organizational systems affect the flow of information. His many remedies are as diverse as the causes of failure, although he generally favors advocacy systems that allow executives "to break through the wall of conventional wisdom" and allow specialists "to effect the general tone of policy discourse." The insights are generously illustrated with scandalous examples of intelligence failures, a few successes, and a chapter length study on the U.S. Council of Economic Advisers. The book deals mainly with intelligence gathering in government, making references to corporate practices where relevant.

IV

The Knowledge Base of Public Administration: 1200 Books in Thirty-three Categories

Part IV contains a list of those books that are important enough to be cited at least two or three times by experts working in the various areas that support the study and practice of public administration. It is here the diversity of the field is fully revealed. There are books from economics, sociology, psychology, business administration, labor and industrial relations, political science, social psychology, philosophy, history, law, mathematics, computer science, education and -- of course -- a large group from people who specialize in public administration. People have been conducting systematic studies of public administration for some one hundred years and borrowing ideas from other fields and disciplines for just as long. Many books produced twenty to even fifty years ago remain relevant, not just the classics that have shaped the field, but books that have made valuable contributions to specific areas of study and are considered essential reading today.

Some 1200 books appear, including the most frequently cited works from Part III. They are arranged into thirty-three categories. These categories constitute the principal specializations within public administration, drawn from the major schools of thought and the areas of application where knowledge is put into operation by people who practice the business of public affairs. The thirty-three categories in turn are assembled into ten general groups. The group of books and the specializations they contain are outlined below.

General public administration, a grouping which stretches from the politics of administration and the problems of implementing public programs to attempts to utilize management principles (including many drawn from the business world) in the public sector;

Values, ethics, and the development of public administration, a grouping which takes up administrative ethics, political theory, the history of public administration, and the broad trends in society that shape government and the way in which it is administered;

The behavioral approach, where specialists investigate human problems of administration such as supervision and motivation and attempt to locate patterns in the operation of organizations and the behavior of people within them;

The systems approach, an offshoot of the rational school that is concerned with the impact of computers and high technology on management and the creation of a science of management that will improve decision making;

The study of bureaucracy, the principal form of government organization in the 20th century, which includes efforts to understand why bureaucratic organizations grow large and inflexible and what can be done to counteract this;

The policy approach, a large grouping that includes instruction in the specifics of program evaluation and policy analysis, explanations about how government policy gets made (such as incremental theory and the public choice approach), some books about specific types of policies (domestic, regulatory, national security, and science policy), and general works on politics and American government.

State and local administration, which incorporates intergovernmental relations, the administration of state government, city management, and the social setting within which urban administration takes place;

Comparative public administration, beginning with an analysis of the practical problems encountered when administering programs in developing countries, then moving to the more ethereal attempts to understand the different ways in which countries develop administratively and modernize their public sectors;

Public personnel administration, which emphasizes the development and operation of the merit system in government and the perplexing challenge of labor relations in the public sector;

Budgeting and finance, a grouping of books generally concerned with the way in which government raises money and decides upon the scope of public expenditures and specifically concerned with the problems of organizing a budget process that can be used as a tool for planning, evaluating, and controlling public programs.

An understanding of the development of public administration, as presented in Part II, will prove helpful in using and interpreting this section. Someone looking for books on policy analysis, for example, is assisted by knowing that policy analysis links up with management science in its effort to develop analytic techniques such as cost benefit analysis. Likewise, the user of books scanning the category titled "Administering Public Programs" in the section on general public administration should know how easily these books blend into the study of "Politics and Administration." Since each book is listed only once, under the primary category from which it comes, users are wise to consult two or more categories in what might be called associated groups to find the most important books on a subject. These sorts of relationships are explained in the essay in Part II of this guide.

Once again, the more frequently a book is cited, the less likely that it belongs exclusively to the single category in which it appears. The author may have written it for that specialization, but its popularity has caused it to be cited by persons representing many areas of interest. Frederick Mosher's Democracy and the Public Service is a good example. It can be used as a general introduction to public personnel administration, but the lessons it contains go considerably beyond that specialization. This is revealed by the code letters that follow the Mosher citation: M-O-P-U-G-C. The letters reveal that persons studying public management and personnel administration (M) are not alone in using and citing the book, but are joined by people interested in organization theory and behavior (O), policy analysis (P), state and local public administration (U), comparative public administration (C), and overviews of the field (G). Conversely, people engaged in the study of bureaucracy (B), management science (T), and budgeting and finance (F) have not -- at least not the ones who put together the eighty-one lists used in the construction of this bibliography. The method used to assign the letter codes is explained in the introduction to Part III.

To gain entrance to this section, a book needed to be cited on at least three of the eighty-one lists or -- for newly published or recognized works -- on at least two of the lists. The exact number of times that a book is cited is given by the numbers that follow each letter code. The first number gives the citation frequency from the first ranking (out of forty possible); the second number gives the frequency with which the book is cited on more recent lists (out of forty-one). Although a total score of eighty-one is possible, the highest rated book (Aaron Wildavsky's Politics of the Budgetary Process) received a score of thirty-six. The average score for a typical book is between four and five. It is rare for a book to receive a combined score of ten or more citations. A book receiving such a score would place in the top eight percent of the titles based on the combined citation frequency.

The large number of books with what appear to be low scores is in part a reflection of the diversity of the field. A field that depended upon a single discipline for its knowledge would exhibit more agreement on its basic sources. Public administration is not such a field. By necessity it must draw upon a variety of sources, some apparently unconnected, for the knowledge needed to improve administration in modern government. This section provides a detailed examination of those sources and the more important books that are to be found within them.

GENERAL PUBLIC ADMINISTRATION

The Administrative Science Movement

Copley, Frank B., Frederick W. Taylor. Two volumes. New York: Harper and Brothers, 1923. G-O-M (3+0=3)

Fayol, Henri, General and Industrial Management. New York: Pitman Publishing Corporation, 1949. G-O-M-T (5+2=7)

Goodnow, Frank J., Politics and Administration. New York: Russell and Russell, 1900. G-O-M (4+3=7)

Gulick, Luther, and L. Urwick, eds., Papers on the Science of Administration. New York: Augustus M. Kelley Publishers, 1937. G-O-M-P-B-F (11+15=26)

Karl, Barry Dean, Executive Reorganization and Reform in the New Deal: The Genesis of Administrative Management, 1900-1939. Cambridge: Harvard University Press, 1963. G-O (0+2=2)

Landis, James M., The Administrative Process. New Haven: Yale University Press, 1938. G-P-M (3+2=5)

Mooney, James D., and Allen C. Reiley, Onward Industry. New York: Harper & Row, 1931. M-G (2+2=4)

Mooney, James D., The Principles of Organization. New York: Harper and Row, 1939. O-M-B-G (7+1=8)

Polenberg, Richard, Reorganizing Roosevelt's Government. Cambridge: Harvard University Press, 1960. O-P-G (2+1=3)

Sheldon, Oliver, The Philosophy of Management. New York: Sir Isaac Pitman & Sons, 1930. M (3+1=4)

Taylor, Frederick W., The Principles of Scientific Management. New York: W. W. Norton & Company, 1911. O-T-P-G (3+6=9)

Taylor, Frederick W., Scientific Management. New York: Harper and Brothers, 1947. G-O-M-B (6+6=12)

Urwick, Lyndall, The Elements of Administration. New York: Harper and Brothers, 1943. M-O (3+0=3)

Wallace, Schuyler, Federal Departmentalization. New York: Columbia University Press, 1941. M-P-U-B (5+1=6)

Politics and Administration

Allison, Graham T., Essence of Decision: Explaining the Cuban Missile Crisis. Boston: Little, Brown and Company, 1971. G-P-M-T-O (0+8=8)

Altshuler, Alan A., The Politics of the Federal Bureaucracy. New York: Dodd, Mead & Company, 1968. Subsequent eds. B-U-P-G-O (3+4=7)

Appleby, Paul H., Big Democracy. New York: Alfred A. Knopf, Inc., 1945. M-O-P-U (6+0=6)

Appleby, Paul H., Policy and Administration. University, AL: University of Alabama Press, 1949. O-G-M-P-B-C (6+4=10)

Bent, Alan Edward, The Politics of Law Enforcement. Lexington, MA: D. C. Heath & Co., 1974. U (0+2=2)

Bernstein, Marver H., The Job of the Federal Executive. Washington, DC: The Brookings Institution, 1958. O-G-B-M-P (8+2=10)

Bernstein, Marver H., Regulating Business by Independent Commission. Princeton: Princeton University Press, 1955. P-G (3+5=8)

Caro, Robert A., The Power Broker: Robert Moses and the Fall of New York. New York: Vintage Books, 1974 U-G-P (0+5=5)

Cater, Douglas, Power in Washington. New York: Random House, 1964. B-P (3+1=4)

Fritschler, A. Lee, Smoking and Politics: Policymaking and the Federal Bureaucracy. Englewood Cliffs, NJ: Prentice Hall, 1969. Subsequent eds. T-U-P-G (4+6=10)

Gaus, John, Reflections on Public Administration. University, AL: University of Alabama Press, 1947. O-M-P-B-C-G (4+2=6)

Harris, Joseph P., Congressional Control of Administration. Washington, DC: The Brookings Institution, 1964. G-M-F-P-O-U (6+6=12)

Hawley, Claude E., and Ruth Weintraub, eds., Administrative Questions and Political Answers. Princeton, NJ: D. Van Nostrand Co., 1966. G-M (2+1=3)

Herring, E. Pendleton, Public Administration and the Public Interest. New York: Russell & Russell, 1936. P-O-M-G (5+2=7)

Holtzman, Abraham, Legislative Liaison: Executive Leadership in Congress. Chicago: Rand McNally, 1970. G-P (0+2=2)

Kaufman, Herbert, The Forest Ranger. Baltimore: Johns Hopkins University Press, 1960. O-G-P-M-T-B (7+9=16)

Maass, Arthur, Muddy Waters. Cambridge: Harvard University Press, 1951. O-G-P (4+0=4)

Martin, Roscoe C., ed. Public Administration and Democracy. Syracuse: Syracuse University Press, 1965. G-C-O-F-P-M (6+5=11)

Meyerson, Martin, and Edward C. Banfield, Politics, Planning and the Public Interest: The Case of Public Housing in Chicago. New York: The Free Press, 1955. G-B-U-O-P (4+3=7)

Millett, John D., Management in the Public Service. New York: McGraw-Hill, 1954. O-M (4+0=4)

Morstein Marx, Fritz, ed., Elements of Public Administration. Englewood Cliffs, NJ: Prentice-Hall, 1946. Subsequent ed. M-B-P-C (5+2=7)

Mosher, Frederick C., Governmental Reorganizations. Indianapolis, IN: The Bobbs-Merrill Company, 1967. O-G-U-P (4+3=7)

Nigro, Felix A., ed., Public Administration: Readings and Documents. New York: Rinehart, 1951. M (3+0=3)

Rourke, Francis E., Bureaucracy, Politics and Public Policy. Boston: Little, Brown & Company, 1969. Subsequent eds. G-O-P-M-B (6+16=22)

Rourke, Francis E., ed., Bureaucratic Power in National Politics. Boston: Little, Brown & Company, 1964. Subsequent ed. O-P-G (2+9=11)

Rourke, Francis E. Secrecy and Publicity. Baltimore: The Johns Hopkins University Press, 1961. G-M (0+3=3)

Selznick, Philip, TVA and the Grass Roots. New York: Harper & Row, 1949. O-M-G-T-B (10+8=18)

Stave, Bruce M., ed., Urban Bosses, Machines, and Progressive Reformers. Lexington, MA: D. C. Heath & Co., 1972. M (0+2=2)

Stein, Harold, ed., American Civil-Military Decisions: A Book of Case Studies. University, AL: University of Alabama Press, 1963. M-P-B (4+0=4)

Stein, Harold, ed., Public Administration and Policy Development: A Casebook. New York: Harcourt, Brace & Company, 1952. M-G-O-P-B-C (7+2=9)

Yarwood, Dean L., ed., The National Administrative System. New York: John Wiley and Sons, 1971. G (0+2=2)

Administering Public Programs

Allensworth, Don, Public Administration: The Execution of
Public Policy. Philadelphia, PA: J. P. Lippincott Company, 1973. G (0+2=2)

Bailey, Stephen K., and Edith K. Mosher, ESEA: The Office of
Education Administers a Law. Syracuse: Syracuse University Press, 1968. O-P-M (5+3=8)

Bardach, Eugene, The Implementation Game. Cambridge, MA:
MIT Press, 1977. P-G (0+5=5)

Barton, Weldon V., Interstate Compacts in the Political Process. Chapel Hill: University of North Carolina Press,
1967. G-U (0+2=2)

Benveniste, Guy, The Politics of Expertise. Berkeley: Glendessary Press, 1972. Subsequent ed. G-B-M (0+7=7)

Buechner, John C., Public Administration. Belmont, CA:
Dickenson Publishing Company, 1968. M (2+2=4)

Caiden, Gerald E., Administrative Reform. Chicago: Aldine
Publishing Company, 1969. O-G-U-C (3+2=5)

Davidson, Roger H., The Politics of Comprehensive Manpower
Legislation. Baltimore: Johns Hopkins University Press,
1972. P-U-M (0+3=3)

Derthick, Martha, The Influence of Federal Grants: Public
Assistance in Massachusetts. Cambridge: Harvard University Press, 1970. U-F-P-M-G (2+5=7)

Derthick, Martha, New Towns In-Town. Washington, DC: The
Urban Institute, 1972. P-U (0+4=4)

Dodd, Lawrence, and R. L. Schott, Congress and Administrative
State. New York: John Wiley & Sons, 1979. G (0+2=2)

Donovan, John C., The Politics of Poverty. Indianapolis, IN:
Pegasus, 1967. Subsequent eds. P-U (0+2=2)

Flash, Edward S., Jr., Economic Advice and Presidential Leadership. New York: Columbia University Press, 1965. P-F (5+0=5)

Freeman, J. Leiper, The Political Process: Executive Bureau-Legislative Committee Relations. New York: Random House, 1965. O-G-P-U (6+2=8)

Frieden, Bernard J., and Marshall Kaplan, The Politics of Neglect: Urban Aid From Model Cities to Revenue Sharing. Cambridge, MA: MIT Press, 1975. U-P (0+4=4)

Gawthrop, Louis C., Administrative Politics and Social Change. New York: St. Martin's Press, 1971. G-O (0+2=2)

Guttman, Daniel, and Barry Willner, The Shadow Government: The Government's Multi-Billion-Dollar Giveaway of Its Decision-Making Powers to Private Management Consultants, "Experts," and Think Tanks. New York: Pantheon, 1976. P-M (0+2=2)

Hargrove, Erwin C., The Missing Link: The Study of the Implementation of Social Policy. Washington, DC: The Urban Institute, 1975. P (0+3=3)

Jacob, Charles E., Policy and Bureaucracy. Princeton, NJ: D. Van Nostrand Company, 1966. G-O-P (4+0=4)

Kaufman, Herbert, Are Government Organizations Immortal? Washington, DC: The Brookings Institution, 1976. P-G-B (0+4=4)

Levine, Charles H., Managing Fiscal Stress: The Crisis in the Public Sector. Chatham, NJ: Chatham House Publishers, 1980. U-F (0+2=2)

Levine, Robert A., Public Planning: Failure and Redirection. New York: Basic Books, 1972. P-G-B (0+5=5)

Levitan, Sara and Joyce K. Zickler, The Quest for a Federal Manpower Partnership. Cambridge, MA: Harvard University Press, 1974. U-M (0+3=3)

Mainzer, Lewis C., Political Bureaucracy.   Glenview, IL:
    Scott, Foresman and Co., 1973. G-C-B-M   (0+8=8)

Millett, John D., Organization for the Public Service.   Prince-
    ton, NJ: D. Van Nostrand Company, Inc., 1966.   G-U-P
    (3+1=4)

Mirengoff, William, and Lester Rundler, The Comprehensive
    Employment and Training Act. Washington, DC: National
    Academy of Sciences, 1976. P-U-M (0+3=3)

Mosher, Frederick C., and John E. Harr, Programming Systems
    and Foreign Affairs Leadership. New York: Oxford Univ-
    ersity Press, 1970. G-O-F-T (0+4=4)

Moynihan, Daniel P., Maximum Feasible Misunderstanding:
    Community Action in the War on Poverty.   New York:
    The Free Press, 1969. G-U-P (7+4=11)

Nathan, Richard P., The Plot That Failed: Nixon and the
    Administrative Presidency.   New York: John Wiley and
    Sons, 1975. U-G (0+3=3)

Pressman, Jeffrey L., and Aaron B. Wildavsky, Implementation.
    Berkeley: University   of   California   Press,   1973.
    P-U-F-B-M-G (0+14=14)

Redford, Emmette S., Democracy in the Administrative State.
    New York: Oxford University Press, 1969.   G-O-U-M
    (5+5=10)

Ripley, Randall B., and Grace A. Franklin, Congress, the
    Bureaucracy, and Public Policy. Homewood, IL: Dorsey
    Press, 1976. Subsequent eds. G-M-P (0+4=4)

Seidman, Harold, Politics, Position & Power: The Dynamics of
    Federal Organization. New York: Oxford University Press,
    1970. Subsequent eds. G-M-U-P-O (2+14=16)

Shapiro, Martin, The Supreme Court and Administrative Agen-
    cies. New York: The Free Press, 1965. G-M (0+2=2)

Sharkansky, Ira, Whither the State? Politics and Public Enter-
    prise in Three Countries. Chatham, NJ: Chatham, 1979.
    G-C (0+2=2)

Shipman, George A., Designing Program Action--Against Urban Poverty. University, AL: University of Alabama Press, 1971. U-G (0+2=2)

Smith, Bruce L. R., and D. C. Hague, eds., The Dilemma of Accountability in Modern Government. New York: St. Martin's Press, 1971. G (0+4=4)

Sundquist, James L., Making Federalism Work. Washington, DC: The Brookings Institution, 1969. G-U-P-M (6+7=13)

Walsh, Annmarie H. The Public's Business: The Politics and Practices of Government Corporations. Cambridge, MA: MIT Press, 1978. G (0+2=2)

Wamsley, Gary L., and Mayer M. Zald, The Political Economy of Public Organizations. Lexington, MA: Lexington Books, 1973. G-C (0+3=3)

Wilensky, Harold L., Organizational Intelligence: Knowledge and Policy in Govenment and Industry. New York: Basic Books, Inc., 1968. B-O-T-M-P-F-U-G (6+10=16)

Williams, Walter, and Richard Elmore, eds., Social Program Implementation. New York: Academic Press, 1976. P-F (0+3=3)

Wolfe, Tom, Radical Chic and Mau-Mauing The Flak Catchers. New York: Farrar, Straus and Giroux, 1970. T-M (0+2=2)

General Management

Albers, Henry H., Principles of Management. New York: John Wiley and Sons, 1969. M-T-U (2+1=3)

Allen, L. A., Management and Organization. New York: McGraw-Hill, 1958. M-U-T (3+0=3)

Anderson, Harold H., ed., Creativity and Its Cultivation. New York: Harper & Row, 1959. M-P-G (2+1=3)

Ansoff, H. Igor, Corporate Strategy. New York: McGraw-Hill, 1965. T-M (2+1=3)

Bross, Irwin D. J., ed., Design for Decision. New York: The Macmillan Company, 1953. M-P-G-B (2+3=5)

Chandler, Alfred D., Strategy and Structure: Chapters in the History of the Industrial Empire. Cambridge: MIT Press, 1962. G-T (0+2=2)

Cleveland, Harlan, The Future Executive: A Guide for Tomorrow's Managers. New York: Harper and Row, 1972. G-M (0+6=6)

Dale, Ernest, Management: Theory and Practice. New York: McGraw-Hill, 1969. G-U-M-T (5+0=5)

Dale, Ernest, Planning and Developing the Company Organization Structure. New York: American Management Association, 1952. M-T-O-G (4+1=5)

Davis, Keith, and Robert L. Blomstrom, Business and Its Environment. New York: McGraw-Hill Book Company, 1966. T-M (3+0=3)

Davis, Kenneth C. Administrative Law and Government. St. Paul, MN: West Publishing Company, 1960. Subsequent eds. G-M (0+2=2)

Dimock, Marshall E., The Executive in Action. New York: Harper & Brothers, 1945. M (2+1=3)

Donabedian, Avedis, Aspects of Medical Care Administration. Cambridge, MA: Harvard University Press, 1974. U (0=2=2)

Dowling, William F., Jr., and Leonard R. Sayles, How Managers Motivate: The Imperatives of Supervision. New York: McGraw-Hill, 1978. M (0+2=2)

Drucker, Peter, The Concept of the Corporation. Boston: Beacon Press, 1960. B-O-G-M (5+0=5)

Drucker, Peter, The Effective Executive. New York: Harper & Row, 1967. O-G (3+3=6)

Drucker, Peter, Management: Tasks, Responsibilities and Practices. New York: Harper & Row, 1973. U-M (0+2=2)

Drucker, Peter, The Practice of Management. New York: Harper & Row, 1954. M-T-U-G (7+2=9)

Emery, James C., Organizational Planning and Control Systems. New York: The Macmillan Company, 1969. M-O-G (2+2=4)

Ewing, D. W., ed., Long-Range Planning for Management. New York: Harper & Brothers, 1960. M-G (4+1=5)

Gellhorn, Ernest, Administrative Law and Process in a Nutshell. St. Paul, MN: West Publishing Company, 1972. G-M (0+2=2)

Glover, J. D., and R. M. Hower, The Administrator: Cases on Human Relations in Business. Homewood, IL: Richard D. Irwin, 1949. Subsequent eds. M-B (4+0=4)

Goetz, Billy E., Quantitative Methods. New York: McGraw-Hill Book Company, 1965. G-M (3+0=3)

Golembiewski, Robert T., Frank Gibson and Geoffrey Y. Cornog, eds., Public Administration: Readings in Institutions, Processes, Behavior, Policy. Chicago: Rand-McNally, 1966. G-U (3+5=8)

Golembiewski, Robert T., and Michael White, Cases in Public Management. Chicago: Rand McNally, 1973. Subsequent eds. G-M (0+3=3)

Golembiewski, Robert T., ed., Perspectives on Public Management: Cases and Learning Designs. Itasca, IL: F. E. Peacock, 1967. O-G (2+4=6)

Gordon, Robert A., Business Leadership in Large Corporations. Berkeley: University of California Press, 1961. B-G-M-U (5+0=5)

Granick, David, Management of the Industrial Firm in the USSR. New York: Columbia University Press, 1954. M-O-F-B (3+2=5)

Granick, David, The Red Executive. New York: Doubleday/Anchor, 1961. O-M-B (4+1=5)

Harbison, Frederick, and C. A. Myers, Management in the Industrial World: An International Analysis. New York: McGraw-Hill, 1959. M (3+0=3)

Holden, P. E., L. S. Fish and H. L. Smith, Top Management Organization and Control. New York: McGraw-Hill, 1951. M-T-G (4+1=5)

Humble, John W., MBO in Action. Maidenhead, Berkshire, England: McGraw-Hill, 1970. M-G (0+2=2)

Koontz, Harold, and Cyril O'Donnell, Principles of Management. New York: McGraw-Hill Book Company, 1955. Subsequent eds. O-M-T-U-B (10+1=11)

Koontz, Harold, ed., Toward a Unified Theory of Management. New York: McGraw-Hill, 1964. T-M (2+1=3)

Le Breton, Preston P., and Dale A. Henning, Planning Theory. Englewood Cliffs, NJ: Prentice-Hall, 1961. M-T (5+0=5)

Lepawsky, Albert, Administration. New York: Alfred A. Knopf, 1949. M-B (4+1=5)

Levey, Samuel, and N. Paul Loomba. Health Care Administration. Philadelphia: Lippencott, 1973. T (0+2=2)

Lipset, Seymour, et al. Union Democracy: The Internal Politics of the International Typographical Union. Glencoe, IL: Free Press, 1956. F-M (0+2=2)

Longenecker, Justin G., Principles of Management and Organizational Behavior. Columbus, OH: Charles E. Merrill Books, 1964. M-T (2+1=3)

Mason, Edward S., ed. The Corporation in Modern Society. Cambridge: Harvard University Press, 1959. T-M (4+0=4)

McConkey, Dale D., MBO for Nonprofit Organizations. New
    York: American Management Association, 1975. M
    (0+2=2)

Medeiros, James A., and David E. Schmitt. Public Bureauc-
    racy: Values and Perspectives. North Scituate, MA: Dux-
    bury Press, 1977. C-M (0+2=2)

Miller, George A., Eugene Galanter and Karl H. Pribram, Plans
    and the Structure of Behavior. New York: Holt, Rinehart
    & Winston, 1960. T-M-G (2+1=3)

Morrisey, George L., Management by Objectives and Results in
    the Public Sector. Reading, MA: Addison-Wesley, 1970.
    Subsequent eds. M-F (0+2=2)

Newman, William H., Administrative Action. Englewood Cliffs,
    NJ: Prentice-Hall, 1951. Subsequent ed. M-O-U (5+0=5)

Newman, William H., Charles E. Summer and E. Kirby Warren,
    The Process of Management. Englewood Cliffs, NJ: Pren-
    tice-Hall, 1961. Subsequent eds. T-M-U (7+0=7)

Normanton, E. L., The Accountability and Audit of Govern-
    ments. New York: Praeger, 1966. G (0+2=2)

Odiorne, George S., Management by Objectives. New York:
    Pitman Publishing Corporation, 1965. O-T-G (2+2=4)

Odiorne, George S., Management Decisions by Objectives.
    Englewood Cliffs, NJ: Prentice-Hall, 1969. M (0+2=2)

Petersen, E., and E. G. Plowman, Business Organization and
    Management. Homewood, IL: Richard D. Irwin, 1941.
    Subsequent eds. M-O-U (4+0=4)

Pfiffner, John M., and Frank P. Sherwood, Administrative
    Organization. Englewood Cliffs, NJ: Prentice-Hall, 1960.
    O-M-G-T-U-B (9+3=12)

Richards, Max D., and William A. Nielander, Readings in Man-
    agement. Cincinnati, OH: South-Western Publishing Com-
    pany, 1958. Subsequent eds. M-U-T (3+0=3)

Rose, Richard, Managing Presidential Objectives. New York:
Free Press, 1976. M-F (0+2=2)

Rosenbloom, Richard S., and John R. Russell, New Tools for
Urban Management: Studies in Systems and Organizational
Analysis. Boston: Harvard Business School, 1971. U-F
(0+2=2)

Rowat, Donald C., ed., Basic Issues in Public Administration.
New York: The Macmillan Company, 1961. U-M (3+0=3)

Rowland, Virgil K., Managerial Performance Standards. New
York: American Management Association, 1960. M-G
(2+1=3)

Schon, Donald A., Beyond the Stable State. New York: Random House, 1971. P-O-M (0+3=3)

Seckler-Hudson, Catheryn, Organization and Management. Mt.
Airy, MD: Lomond Publications, 1955. G-M (5+0=5)

Sherman, Harvey, It All Depends: A Pragmatic Approach to
Organization. University, AL: University of Alabama
Press, 1966. O-P-M-G (3+3=6)

Sigband, Norman B., Communication for Management and Business. Glenview, IL: Scott, Foresman & Co., 1969. Subsequent ed. G-M (0+2=2)

Steiner, George A., ed., Managerial Long-Range Planning. New
York: McGraw-Hill, 1963. M-T-G (2+1=3)

Steiner, George A., ed., Top Management Planning. New York:
The Macmillan Company, 1969. T-M (0+2=2)

Tosi, Henry L., and W. Clay Hamner, eds., Organizational
Behavior and Management: A Contingency Approach.
Chicago: St. Clair Press, 1977. G (0+2=2)

Townsend, Robert, Up the Organization. Greenwich, CT:
Fawcett Crest Books, 1970. M (0+5=5)

Villiers, Raymond, The Dynamics of Industrial Management.
New York: Funk & Wagnalls, 1954. M-O (3+0=3)

Warren, E. Kirby, Long-Range Planning. Englewood Cliffs, NJ: Prentice-Hall, 1966. T-M-G (3+1=4)

Textbooks on General Public Administration

Berkley, George E., The Craft of Public Administration. Boston: Allyn and Bacon, 1975. Subsequent ed. G (0+2=2)

Caiden, Gerald E., The Dynamics of Public Administration. New York: Holt, Rinehart and Winston, 1971. G-O-M (0+5=5)

Davis, James W., Jr., An Introduction to Public Administration: Politics, Policy, and Bureaucracy. New York: The Free Press, 1974. C-G (0+3=3)

Dimock, Marshall E., and Gladys Ogden Dimock, Public Administration. New York: Holt, Rinehart, and Winston, 1952. Subsequent eds. G-M-T (6+2=8)

Gortner, Harold F., Administration in the Public Sector. New York: John Wiley and Sons, 1977. (0+2=2)

Henry, Nicholas, Public Administration and Public Affairs. Englewood Cliffs, NJ: Prentice-Hall, 1975. Subsequent ed. C-G-M (0+5=5)

Lutrin, Carl E., and Allen K. Settle, American Public Administration: Concepts and Cases. Palo Alto, CA: Mayfield Publishing Company, 1976. Subsequent ed. G (0+2=2)

McCurdy, Howard E., Public Administration: A Synthesis. Menlo Park, CA: Benjamin Cummings, 1977. G (0+2=2)

Morrow, William L., Public Administration: Politics, Policy, and the Political System. New York: Random House, 1975. Subsequent eds. G-M (0+4=4)

Nigro, Felix A., and Lloyd G. Nigro. Modern Public Administration. New York: Harper & Row, 1965. Subsequent eds. G-M (3+4=7)

Pfiffner, John M., and Robert V. Presthus, Public
    Administration. New York: The Ronald Press, 1935.
    Subsequent eds. O-M-G-T-U-B (6+2=8)

Rehfuss, John, Public Administration as Political Process. New
    York: Charles Scribner and Sons, 1973. C-G-M (0+5=5)

Richardson, Ivan L., and Sidney Baldwin, Public Administration:
    Government in Action. Columbus, OH: Merrill Publishing
    Company, 1976. G (0+2=2)

Sharkansky, Ira, Public Administration: Policy Making in
    Government Agencies. Chicago: Rand-McNally, 1970.
    Subsequent eds. G-M (0+4=4)

Simon, Herbert A., D. W. Smithburg, V. A. Thompson, Public
    Administration. New York: Alfred A. Knopf, 1950.
    M-O-P-U-B-G (7+5=12)

Simmons, Robert H., and Eugene P. Dvorin, Public Administra-
    tion: Values, Policy and Change. Port Washington, NY:
    Alfred Publishing Company, 1977. G (0+2=2)

Stillman, Richard J., ed., Public Administration: Concepts and
    Cases. Boston: Houghton-Mifflin, 1976. Subsequent ed.
    G (0+2=2)

Uveges, Joseph A., Jr., The Dimensions of Public Administra-
    tion. Boston: Holbrook Press, 1971. Subsequent eds. G
    (0+2=2)

Waldo, Dwight, ed., Ideas and Issues in Public Administration.
    New York: McGraw-Hill, 1953. M (3+1=4)

White, Leonard D., Introduction to the Study of Public Admin-
    istration. New York: Harper & Brothers, 1926. Subseq-
    uent eds. G-M-U (6+3=9)

VALUES, ETHICS, AND THE DEVELOPMENT OF PUBLIC ADMINISTRATION

Political Theory and Administrative Ethics

Appleby, Paul H., Morality and Administration in Democratic Government. Baton Rouge: Louisiana State University Press, 1952. O-M-B-G (3+5=8)

Arendt, Hannah, Crises of the Republic. New York: Harcourt, Brace Jovanovich, 1972. M-O (0+2=2)

Davis, Kenneth Culp, Discretionary Justice. Baton Rouge: Louisiana State University Press, 1969. M-P-B-G (3+5=8)

Devine, Donald J., The Political Culture of the United States. Boston: Little, Brown & Company, 1972. U-M (0+2=2)

Dewey, John, The Public and Its Problems. New York: Holt, 1927. G-O (0+2=2)

Friedrich, Carl J., ed., Nomos Vol. 5 (The Public Interest). New York: Atherton Press, 1962. P-M-B-G (3+2=5)

Friedrich, Carl J., The Pathology of Politics. New York: Harper and Row, 1972. B-M (0+2=2)

Gawthrop, Louis C., ed., The Administrative Process and Democratic Theory. Boston: Houghton-Mifflin, 1970. G-O (0+2=2)

Golembiewski, Robert T., Men, Management and Morality: Toward a New Organizational Ethic. New York: McGraw-Hill, 1965. O-T-P-G (3+3=6)

Hayek, Friedrich A., The Road to Serfdom. Chicago: University of Chicago Press, 1944. B-P-M (0+3=3)

Leys, Wayne A. R., Ethics for Policy Decisions. Englewood Cliffs, NJ: Prentice-Hall, 1952. M-P (2+1=3)

Lowi, Theodore J., The End of Liberalism. New York: W. W. Norton and Company, 1969. O-P-U-G-M (3+8=11)

Machiavelli, Niccolo, The Prince and the Discourses. New York: Modern Library, 1513. O-M (4+1=5)

MacIver, Robert M., The Web of Government. New York: Macmillan Company, 1947. Subsequent ed. M-G (2+1=3)

McConnell, Grant, Private Power and American Democracy. New York: Alfred A. Knopf, 1966. P-U-G (3+4=7)

Nader, Ralph, et al., Whistle Blowing. New York: Grossman, 1972. B-M (0+3=3)

Okun, Arthur M., Equality and Efficiency: The Big Tradeoff. Washington, DC: The Brookings Institution, 1975. P-M (0+2=2)

Rawls, John, A Theory of Justice. Cambridge, MA: Belknap, 1971. G (0+2=2)

Redford, Emmette S., Ideal and Practice in Public Administration. University, AL: University of Alabama Press, 1958. G (0+2=2)

Rohr, John A., Ethics for Bureaucrats. New York: Marcel Dekker, 1978. G-M (0+2=2)

Schubert, Glendon A., The Public Interest. New York: Free Press, 1960. B-O-M-G (5+1=6)

Speer, Albert, Inside the Third Reich. New York: Macmillan, 1970. G-M (0+2=2)

Thayer, Frederick C., An End To Hierarchy! An End To Competition! New York: New Viewpoints, 1973. Subsequent ed. G-O-C-M (0+5=5)

Tugwell, Rexford, A Model Constitution for a United Republics of America. Santa Barbara, CA: Center for the Study of Democratic Institutions and James E. Freel and Associates, 1970. G-U (0+2=2)

Waldo, Dwight, The Administrative State. New York: Ronald Press, 1948. O-M-G-P-U-B (8+11=19)

Weisband, Edward, and Thomas M. Franck, Resignation in Protest. New York: Grossman Publishers, 1975. G-M (0+3=3)

Wildavsky, Aaron, How to Limit Government Spending. Berkeley: University of California Press, 1980. G-F (0+2=2)

Wise, David, The Politics of Lying: Government, Deception, Secrecy, and Power. New York: Random House, 1973. M (0+2=2)

Wolin, Sheldon S., Politics and Vision: Continuity and Innovation in Western Political Thought. Boston: Little, Brown & Company, 1960. O-M (2+1=3)

The Evolution and Study of Public Administration

Barker, Ernest, The Development of Public Services in Western Europe, 1660-1930. New York: Oxford University Press, 1944. O-M-C (3+0=3)

Caldwell, Lynton K., The Administrative Theories of Hamilton and Jefferson. Chicago: University of Chicago Press, 1944. M-O-U-G (5+1=6)

Chapman, Richard L., and Frederic N. Cleaveland, Meeting the Needs of Tomorrow's Public Service: Guidelines for Professional Education in Public Administration. Washington, DC: National Academy of Public Administration, 1973. G-M (0+2=2)

Charlesworth, James C., ed., Theory and Practice of Public Administration: Scope, Objectives, and Methods, Monograph 8. Philadelphia: American Academy of Political and Social Sciences, 1968. G-C (0+2=2)

George, Claude S., Jr., The History of Management Thought. Englewood Cliffs, NJ: Prentice-Hall, 1968. Subsequent ed. G-B (0+2=2)

Gladden, E. N., A History of Public Administration, 2 Vols. London: Frank Cass, 1972. C-M (0+3=3)

Marini, Frank, ed., Toward a New Public Administration. Scranton, PA: Chandler Publishing Company, 1971. G-M-O-C-B (2+12=14)

Mosher, Frederick C., American Public Administration: Past, Present, and Future. University, AL: University of Alabama Press, 1975. G-O-M (0+4=4)

Ostrom, Vincent, The Intellectual Crisis in American Public Administration. University, AL: University of Alabama Press, 1973. Subsequent ed. G-O-C-M (0+8=8)

Thompson, Victor Alexander, Without Sympathy or Enthusiasm: The Problem of Administrative Compassion. University, AL: University of Alabama Press, 1975. G (0+3=3)

Waldo, Dwight, Perspectives on Administration. University, AL: University of Alabama Press, 1956. M-O-P-G (3+2=5)

Waldo, Dwight, ed., Public Administration in a Time of Turbulence. Scranton, PA: Chandler Publishing Company, 1971. G-C-B-M-U-O (0+8=8)

Waldo, Dwight, The Study of Public Administration. Garden City, NY: Doubleday and Company, 1955. O-M-G (3+5=8)

White, Leonard D., The Federalists, the Jeffersonians, the Jacksonians, and the Republican Era, 4 vol. series. New York: The Macmillan Company, 1948, 1951, 1954, 1958. O-G-M-P-U (8+4=12)

Wittfogel, Karl A., Oriental Despotism. New Haven: Yale University Press, 1957. B-M-C (3+2=5)

Wren, Daniel A., The Evolution of Management Thought. New York: Ronald Press, 1972. Subsequent ed. (0+2=2)

The Changing Context of Public Administration

Barnet, Richard J., and Ronald E. Muller, <u>Global</u> <u>Reach</u>: <u>The</u> <u>Power</u> <u>of</u> <u>the</u> <u>Multinational</u> <u>Corporations</u>. New York: Simon & Schuster, 1974. G-B (0+2=2)

Bell, Daniel, <u>The</u> <u>Coming</u> <u>of</u> <u>Post-Industrial</u> <u>Society</u>: <u>A</u> <u>Venture</u> <u>in</u> <u>Social</u> <u>Forecasting</u>. New York: Basic Books, 1973. G-C-T-M-B (0+5=5)

Boulding, Kenneth E., <u>The</u> <u>Organizational</u> <u>Revolution</u>. New York: Harper and Brothers, 1953. O-M-T-G (5+1=6)

Burnham, James, <u>The</u> <u>Managerial</u> <u>Revolution</u>. Westport, CT: Greenwood Press, 1941. O-M-G (4+3=7)

Drucker, Peter F., <u>The</u> <u>Age</u> <u>of</u> <u>Discontinuity</u>. New York: Harper & Row, 1968. G-O-T-P (5+1=6)

Drucker, Peter F., <u>The</u> <u>New</u> <u>Society</u>. New York: Harper & Row, 1962. B-M-U (3+0=3)

Ellul, Jacques, <u>The</u> <u>Technological</u> <u>Society</u>. Translated by John Wilkinson. New York: Alfred A. Knopf, 1964. G-M (0+3=3)

Galbraith, John Kenneth, <u>The</u> <u>Affluent</u> <u>Society</u>. Boston: Houghton Mifflin Company, 1958. Subsequent eds. M-P-F-G (4+3=7)

Galbraith, John Kenneth, <u>The</u> <u>New</u> <u>Industrial</u> <u>State</u>. Boston: Houghton Mifflin Company, 1967. T-P-M-B (6+3=9)

Gardner, John W., <u>Self-Renewal</u>: <u>The</u> <u>Individual</u> <u>and</u> <u>the</u> <u>Inno-</u> <u>vative</u> <u>Society</u>. New York: Harper & Row, 1964. O-T-B-M (5+0=5)

Heilbroner, Robert L., <u>An</u> <u>Inquiry</u> <u>into</u> <u>the</u> <u>Human</u> <u>Prospect</u>. New York: W. W. Norton & Company, 1974. G-B (0+2=2)

Milgram, Stanley, <u>Obedience</u> <u>to</u> <u>Authority</u>: <u>An</u> <u>Experimental</u> <u>View</u>. New York: Harper & Row, 1973. M (0+2=2)

Mumford, Lewis, The Myth of the Machine: The Pentagon of
   Power. New York: Harcourt Brace Jovanovich, 1970.
   T-M (2+1=3)

Riesman, David, with Nathan Glazer and Reuel Denney, The
   Lonely Crowd. New Haven: Yale University Press, 1950.
   O-M-T (4+0=4)

Roszak, Theodore, Where the Wasteland Ends: Politics and
   Transcendence in Post-Industrial Society. Garden City, NY:
   Doubleday & Co., 1972. G-M (0+2=2)

Schumacher, E. F., Small is Beautiful: Economics as if People
   Mattered. New York: Harper & Row, 1973. B-O (0+2=2)

Schumpeter, Joseph A., Capitalism, Socialism and Democracy.
   New York: Harper and Brothers, 1942. Subsequent eds.
   B-F (0+2=2)

Shonfield, Andrew, Modern Capitalism: The Changing Balance
   of Public and Private Power. New York: Oxford University Press, 1965. G-B (0+2=2)

Scott, William G., and David K. Hart, Organizational America.
   Boston: Houghton Miffin, 1979. G-M (0+2=2)

Toffler, Alvin, Future Shock. New York: Random House,
   1970. G-B-M (0+4=4)

Tugwell, Franklin, ed., Search for Alternatives: Public Policy
   and the Study of the Future. Cambridge, MA: Winthrop
   Publishers, 1973. P-M (0+2=2)

Vickers, Geoffrey, Value Systems and Social Process. New
   York: Basic Books, 1968. G (0+2=2)

Weber, Max, The Protestant Ethic and the Spirit of Capitalism,
   1904-5. Translated by Talcott Parsons. New York:
   Charles Scribner's Sons, 1958. C-T-O-M-F (5+1=6)

Weidenbaum, Murray L., The Modern Public Sector. New York:
   Basic Books, 1969. M-G (0+2=2)

Whyte, William H., _The Organization Man_. New York: Dou-
    bleday Anchor, 1957. O-M-T-B-P-G (6+2=8)

THE BEHAVIORAL APPROACH

Human Relations

Bakke, E. Wight, Bonds of Organization. New York: Harper & Brothers, 1950. Subsequent ed. G-O (0+2=2)

Blumberg, Paul, Industrial Democracy: The Sociology of Participation. New York: Schocken Books, 1968. B-M-O (0+4=4)

Davis, Keith, and William G. Scott, eds., Readings in Human Relations. New York: McGraw-Hill, 1959. C-M (3=0=3)

Follett, Mary Parker, Creative Experience. New York: Longmans, Green and Company, 1924. O-M-G (3+3=6)

Follett, Mary Parker, Dynamic Administration: The Collected Papers of Mary Parker Follett, edited by Elliot M. Fox and L. Urwick. New York: Hippocrene Books, 1940. G-M-P-B-O (9+4=13)

Gardner, Burleigh B., and David G. Moore, Human Relations in Industry. Homewood, IL: Richard D. Irwin, 1964. O-M (4+0=4)

Gellerman, Saul W., Motivation and Productivity. New York: American Management Association, 1963. T-M-G (2+2=4)

Haire, Mason, Psychology in Management. New York: McGraw-Hill, 1964. O-T-M (5+0=5)

Lansberger, Henry, Hawthorne Revisited. Ithaca, NY: Cornell University Press, 1958. M-B-G (2+2=4)

Maier, Norman R. F., Principles of Human Relations. New York: John Wiley & Sons, 1952. M-O (3+0=3)

Mayo, Elton, The Human Problems of an Industrial Civilization. New York: The Viking Press, 1933. G-O-M-B (5+3=8)

Mayo, Elton, The Social Problems of an Industrial Civilization. New York: Viking Press, 1945. O-M-G-F (5+1=6)

Redfield, Charles E., Communication in Management. Chicago: University of Chicago Press, 1958. M-G (2+1=3)

Roethlisberger, F. J., Man-in-Organization. Cambridge: Harvard University Press, 1968. G-O-T (3+0=3)

Roethlisberger, F. J., Management and Morale. Cambridge: Harvard University Press, 1941. M-O-F (3+2=5)

Roethlisberger, F. J., and William J. Dickson, Management and the Worker. Cambridge: Harvard University Press, 1939. G-O-M-T-B (8+8=16)

Tead, Ordway, Human Nature and Management. New York: McGraw-Hill, 1929. O (2+1=3)

Walker, Charles R., and Robert H. Guest, The Man on the Assembly Line. Cambridge: Harvard University Press, 1952. T-O-G (3+1=4)

Organization Theory

Arrow, Kenneth J., The Limits of Organization. New York: W. W. Norton & Co., 1974. B-O (0+2=2)

Barnard, Chester I., The Functions of the Executive. Cambridge: Harvard University Press, 1938. G-O-M-T-U-B-P (13+17=30)

Becker, Selwyn W., and Duncan Neuhauser, The Efficient Organization. New York: American Elsevier Publishing Company, 1975. G-B (0+4=4)

Black, Max, The Social Theories of Talcott Parsons. Englewood Cliffs, NJ: Prentice-Hall, 1962. B-T-G (2+1=3)

Carzo, Rocco, Jr., and John N. Yanouzas, Formal Organization. Homewood, IL: Irwin Dorsey Press, 1967. O-G-T-M (6+1=7)

Cyert, Richard M., and James G. March, A Behavioral Theory of the Firm. Englewood Cliffs, NJ: Prentice-Hall, 1963. O-T-B-M (8+4=12)

Etzioni, Amitai, A Comparative Analysis of Complex Organizations. New York: The Free Press, 1961. G-O-T-B-M (9+2=11)

Etzioni, Amitai, ed., Complex Organizations: A Sociological Reader. New York: Holt, Rinehart & Winston, 1961. Subsequent eds. O-M-B-T-C (7+2=9)

Etzioni, Amitai, Modern Organizations. Englewood Cliffs, NJ: Prentice-Hall, 1964. O-T-B-M-P-G (4+9=13)

Eyan, William M., ed., Organizational Experiments: Laboratory and Field Research. New York: Harper & Row, 1971. O-G (0+2=2)

Gawthrop, Louis C., Bureaucratic Behavior in the Executive Branch. New York: The Free Press, 1969. G-O-P-F-M (5+2=7)

Golembiewski, Robert T., Organizing Men and Power. Chicago: Rand McNally, 1967. O-C-G (2+1=3)

Gore, William J., Administrative Decision-Making: A Heuristic Model. New York: John Wiley & Sons, 1965. O-T-G-B-P (5+2=7)

Gore, William J., and J. W. Dyson, eds., The Making of Decisions: A Reader in Administrative Behavior. New York: The Free Press, 1964. O-P-M (4+0=4)

Gross, Bertram M., The Managing of Organizations: The Administrative Struggle, 2 Vols. New York: The Free Press, 1964. O-G-B-M-P (8+4=12)

Gross, Bertram M., Organizations and Their Managing. New York: The Free Press, 1968. G-T-M (3+1=4)

Guetznow, Harold, ed., Simulation in Social Science. Englewood Cliffs, NJ: Prentice-Hall, 1962. O-P (2+1=3)

Haire, Mason, ed. Modern Organization Theory. New York: John Wiley & Sons, 1959. O-M-T-B (10+0=10)

Hall, Richard D., Organizations: Structure and Process. Englewood Cliffs, NJ: Prentice-Hall, 1972. P-G (0+2=2)

Hill, Walter A., and Douglas Egan, Readings in Organization Theory. Boston: Allyn and Bacon, 1967. O-M-T (3+0=3)

Hirschman, Albert O., Exit, Voice, and Loyalty: Responses to Decline in Firms, Organizations, and States. Cambridge: Harvard University Press, 1970. P-G-B-O (0+5=5)

Katz, Daniel, Barbara Gutek, Robert L. Kahn, and E. Barton, Bureaucratic Encounters: A Pilot Study in the Evaluation of Government Services. Ann Arbor: University of Michigan Survey Research Center, 1975. G-B (0+2=2)

Katz, Daniel, and Robert L. Kahn, The Social Psychology of Organizations. New York: John Wiley & Sons, 1966. Subsequent ed. O-G-P-M-T-C-B (8+13=21)

Kaufman, Herbert, Administrative Feedback. Washington, DC: The Brookings Institution, 1973. G-O-B-M (0+7=7)

Kaufman, Herbert, The Limits of Organizational Change. University, AL: University of Alabama Press, 1971. M-O-G (0+3=3)

Krupp, Sherman, Pattern in Organization Analysis. New York: Holt, Rinehart and Winston, 1961. U-O-B-T-G (4+2=6)

LaPorte, Todd R., ed., Organized Social Complexity. Princeton, NJ: Princeton University Press, 1975. B-O-G (0+3=3)

Lawrence, Paul R., and Jay W. Lorsch, Organization and Environment. Homewood, IL: Richard D. Irwin, 1969. O-T-M-B-P (3+5=8)

Leavitt, Harold J., William R. Dill, and Henry B. Eyring, The Organizational World. New York: Harcourt Brace Jovanovich, Inc., 1973. M-O (0+2=2)

Leavitt, Harold J., ed., The Social Science of Organizations. Englewood Cliffs, NJ: Prentice-Hall, 1963. O-T (5+0=5)

Litterer, Joseph A., The Analysis of Organizations. New York: John Wiley & Sons, 1965. O-T-M (2+2=4)

Luce, R. Duncan, and Howard Raiffa, Games and Decisions. New York: John Wiley & Sons, 1957. T-O-M-P-G-B (6+3=9)

Lyden, Fremont J., George A. Shipman, and Morton Kroll, Policies, Decisions and Organizations. New York: Appleton-Century-Crofts, 1969. G-M (0+2=2)

Mailick, Sidney, and Edward H. Van Ness, eds., Concepts and Issues in Administrative Behavior. Englewood Cliffs, NJ: Prentice-Hall, 1962. G-O-T-U-M (5+3=8)

March, James G., and Johan P. Olsen, Ambiguity and Choice in Organization. Bergen, Norway: Universititatesforlagek, 1976. P-G (0+2=2)

March, James G., ed. Handbook of Organizations. Chicago: Rand McNally & Co., 1965. G-O-T-U-P (14+8=22)

March, James G., and Herbert A. Simon, Organizations. New York: John Wiley & Sons, 1958. G-O-M-T-P-B-F (14+17=31)

Merton, Robert K., et al., eds., Sociology Today. New York: Basic Books, 1959. O-M-T (3+1=4)

Mouzelis, Nicos P., Organization and Bureaucracy: An Analysis of Modern Theories. Chicago: Aldine Publishing Co., 1968. M-O-G (2+4=6)

Parsons, Talcott, The Social System. New York: The Free Press, 1951. T-O-M-G (3+3=6)

Parsons, Talcott, Structure and Process in Modern Societies. New York: The Free Press, 1960. T-O-M-B (4+1=5)

Parsons, Talcott, and Edward A. Shils, eds., Toward a General Theory of Action. Cambridge: Harvard University Press, 1951. T-M-B-G (3+2=5)

Parsons, Talcott, Working Papers in the Theory of Action. Glencoe, IL: The Free Press, 1953. G-B (0+2=2)

Peabody, Robert, Organizational Authority. New York: Atherton Press, 1964. O-M-G (2+3=5)

Perrow, Charles, Organizational Analysis. Belmont, CA: Wadsworth Publishing Company, 1970. O-T-M-G (2+2=4)

Price, James L., Organizational Effectiveness. Homewood, IL: Richard D. Irwin, 1967. G-O-T-M (4+1=5)

Rapoport, Anatol, Fights, Games, and Debates. Ann Arbor: University of Michigan Press, 1960. O-P-G (2+1=3)

Rubenstein, Albert H., and Chadwick J. Haberstroh, eds., Some Theories of Organization. Homewood, IL: Dorsey Irwin Press, 1960. Subsequent ed. G-O-M-T-U-B-P (12+0=12)

Schuman, David, Bureaucracies, Organizations, and Administration: A Political Primer. New York: Macmillan Publishing Company, 1976. C (0+2=2)

Scott, William G., The Management of Conflict: Appeals Systems in Organizations. Homewood, IL: Richard D. Irwin, 1967. O-T-M-G (3+1=4)

Seashore, Stanley E., and David G. Bowers, Changing the Structure and Functioning of an Organization. Ann Arbor: Institute for Social Research, University of Michigan, 1963. O-M (3+0=3)

Seiler, J. A., Systems Analysis in Organizational Behavior. Homewood, IL: Irwin Dorsey Press, 1967. O-T-M (3+0=3)

Silverman, David, The Theory of Organizations: A Sociological Framework. New York: Basic Books, 1971. O-G-B (0+3=3)

Simon, Herbert A., Administrative Behavior. New York: The Free Press, 1945. Subsequent eds. G-O-M-T-U-B-P (14+16=30)

Simon, Herbert A., Models of Man. New York: John Wiley and Sons, 1957. P-O-B-M-T-F-G (5+3=8)

Thayer, Lee, Communication and Communication Systems: In Organizations, Management, and Interpersonal Relations. Homewood, IL: Richard D. Irwin, 1968. G-M (0+2=2)

Thompson, James D., ed., Approaches to Organizational Design. Pittsburgh: University of Pittsburgh Press, 1966. G-O-T (4+2=6)

Thompson, James D., et al., eds., Comparative Studies in Administration. Pittsburgh: University of Pittsburgh Press, 1959. O-T-C-M-B-G (5+2=7)

Thompson, James D., Organizations in Action. New York: McGraw-Hill, Inc., 1967. O-G-T-B-P-U (5+10=15)

Thompson, Victor A., The Regulatory Process in OPA Rationing. New York: King's Crown, 1950. O-B (0+2=2)

Von Neuman, John, and O. Morgenstern, Theory of Games and Economic Behavior. Princeton, NJ: Princeton University Press, 1944. Subsequent eds. O-M-T-B (2+2=4)

Vroom, Victor H., ed., Methods of Organizational Research. Pittsburgh: University of Pittsburgh Press, 1967. G-O-M-T (3+4=7)

Weber, Max, The Theory of Social and Economic Organization, 1915 apx. Translated by A. M. Henderson and Talcott Parsons. New York: Oxford University Press, 1947. G-O-T-B-M (8+4=12)

Woodward, Joan, Industrial Organization: Theory and Practice. London: Oxford University Press, 1965. M-O-G (0+3=3)

Zaltman, Gerald, Robert Duncan and Jonny Halbek, Innovations and Organizations. New York: John Wiley & Sons, 1973. B-G (0+2=2)

Organizational Behavior

Abegglen, James C., The Japanese Factory. New York: The Free Press, 1958. O-C-G-M (4+0=4)

Adams, Richard N., and Jack J. Preiss, eds., Human Organization Research. Homewood, IL: Dorsey Press, 1960. O-M (3+0=3)

Applewhite, Philip B., Organizational Behavior. Englewood Cliffs, NJ: Prentice-Hall, 1965. G-O-M (3+0=3)

Asch, Solomon E., Social Psychology. Englewood Cliffs, NJ: Prentice-Hall, 1952. O-T (3+0=3)

Bass, Bernard M., Leadership, Psychology and Organizational Behavior. New York: Harper & Brothers, 1960. O-M-G (5+0=5)

Berelson, Bernard, and Garry A. Steiner, Human Behavior: An Inventory of Scientific Findings. New York: Harcourt, Brace & World, 1964. O-T-M-G (5+1=6)

Cartwright, Dorwin, and Alvin Zander, eds., Group Dynamics Research and Theory. New York: Harper & Row, 1953. Subsequent eds. O-T-G-M-P-B (16+5=21)

Davies, James C., Human Nature In Politics. New York: John Wiley and Sons, 1963. B-M (0+2=2)

Dubin, Robert, ed., Human Relations in Administration. Englewood Cliffs, NJ: Prentice-Hall, 1951. Subsequent ed. M-O-T-B (7+1=8)

Dubin, Robert, et al., Leadership and Productivity: Some Facts of Industrial Life. San Francisco: Chandler, 1965. M-G (0+2=2)

Elbing, Alvar O., Behavioral Decisions in Organizations. Glenview, IL: Scott, Foresman & Co., 1970. Subsequent ed. G-M (0+2=2)

Fiedler, Fred E., A Theory of Leadership Effectiveness. New York: McGraw-Hill, 1967. G-O-T-M (5+2=7)

Goffman, Erving, Relations in Public: Microstudies of the Public Order. New York: Basic Books, 1971. O-M (0+2=2)

Gouldner, Alvin, ed., Studies in Leadership. New York: Harper & Brothers, 1950. O-G-M (4+0=4)

Hare, Paul A., Edgar F. Borgatta and Robert F. Bales, eds., Small Groups. New York: Alfred A. Knopf, 1955. O-M-B (2+1=3)

Hersey, Paul, and Ken Blanchard, Management of Organization Behavior. Chicago: St. Claire Press, 1969. Subsequent eds. O-G-M (0+4=4)

Homans, George C., The Human Group. New York: Harcourt, Brace and Company, 1950. O-T-B-G-M (10+2=12)

Katz, Daniel, et al., Productivity, Supervision and Morale Among Railroad Workers. Ann Arbor: Survey Research Center, University of Michigan, 1951. O-G (3+0=3)

Lawrence, Paul R., The Changing of Organizational Behavior Patterns. Cambridge: Harvard University Press, 1958. M-O (3+0=3)

Leighton, Alexander, The Governing of Men. Princeton, NJ: Princeton University Press, 1945. M-G-P (3+0=3)

Levinson, Harry, The Great Jackass Fallacy. Boston: Division of Research, Harvard Business School, 1973. M (0+2=2)

McClelland, David C., et al., The Achievement Motive. New York: Appleton-Century-Crofts, 1953. O-T-M-G (3+1=4)

Marwick, Dwaine, Career Perspectives in a Bureaucratic Society. Ann Arbor: University of Michigan Press, 1954. M-O (3+0=3)

Presthus, Robert, Behavioral Approaches to Public Administration. University, AL: University of Alabama Press, 1965. G-O (3+1=4)

Sayles, Leonard R., Behavior of Industrial Work Groups. New York: John Wiley & Sons, 1958. O-B-G-M (6+0=6)

Sayles, Leonard R., and George Strauss, Human Behavior in Organizations. Englewood Cliffs, NJ: Prentice-Hall, 1966. O-T-M-G (5+1=6)

Sayles, Leonard R., Individualism and Big Business. New York: McGraw-Hill, 1963. T-M (3+0=3)

Sayles, Leonard R., and George Strauss, The Local Union. New York: Harcourt, Brace & World, 1953. O-M (3+0=3)

Sayles, Leonard R., Managerial Behavior. New York: McGraw-Hill, 1965. O-T-M-G (6+1=7)

Scott, William G., Organizational Theory. Homewood, IL: Richard D. Irwin, 1967. T-P-G-B (2+3=5)

Seashore, S. E., Group Cohesiveness in the Industrial Work Group. Ann Arbor: Survey Research Center, University of Michigan, 1954. O-G-T (4+0=4)

Selznick, Philip, Leadership in Administration. New York: Row, Peterson, 1957. O-M-G-T-B (10+4=14)

Shartle, Carroll, Executive Performance and Leadership. Englewood Cliffs, NJ: Prentice-Hall, 1956. O-M (3+0=3)

Stogdill, Ralph M., Handbook of Leadership: A Survey of Theory & Research. New York: Free Press, 1974. G (0=2=2)

Swanson, G. W., J. M. Newcomb and E. L. Hartley, eds., Readings in Social Psychology. New York: Holt, Rinehart & Winston, 1952. O-G-P (3+1=4)

Thibaut, John W., and Harold H. Kelley, The Social Psychology of Groups. New York: John Wiley & Sons, 1959. O-G (3+0=3)

Viteles, Morris S., Motivation and Morale in Industry. New York: W. W. Norton and Company, 1953. O-M (5+0=5)

Vroom, Victor H., and Philip Yetton, <u>Leadership</u> <u>and</u>
   <u>Decision-Making.</u>   Pittsburgh: University of Pittsburgh
   Press, 1973. T-M (0+2=2)

Vroom, Victor H., and Edward L., Deci, eds., <u>Management</u> <u>and</u>
   <u>Motivation.</u>   New York: Penguin Books, 1971.   M-G
   <u>(0+2=2)</u>

Vroom, Victor H., <u>Some</u> <u>Personality</u> <u>Determinants</u> <u>of</u> <u>the</u>
   <u>Effects</u> <u>of</u> <u>Participation.</u>   Englewood Cliffs, NJ: Prentice-
   Hall, 1960.   O-B   (2+1=3)

Vroom, Victor H., <u>Work</u> <u>and</u> <u>Motivation.</u>   New York: John
   Wiley & Sons, 1964.   O-M-G-B (3+4=7)

Volmer, Howard M., and Donald L. Mills, eds., <u>Professionaliza-</u>
   <u>tion.</u>   Englewood Cliffs, NJ: Prentice-Hall, 1966.   O-T-G
   <u>(2+1=3)</u>

Whyte, William F., <u>Men</u> <u>at</u> <u>Work.</u>   Homewood, IL: Dorsey
   Press, 1961. O-T-G (3+0=3)

Whyte, William F., <u>Money</u> <u>and</u> <u>Motivation.</u>   New York: Harper
   & Brothers, 1955.   O-M-T   (5+0=5)

Organization Development

Argyris, Chris, <u>Integrating</u> <u>the</u> <u>Individual</u> <u>and</u> <u>the</u> <u>Organization.</u>
   New York: John Wiley & Sons, 1964.   G-O-T-M-B
   (8+5=13)

Argyris, Chris, <u>Interpersonal</u> <u>Competence</u> <u>and</u> <u>Organizational</u>
   <u>Effectiveness.</u>   Homewood, IL: Richard D. Irwin, 1962.
   O-M-T-G   (7+5=12)

Argyris, Chris, <u>Intervention</u> <u>Theory</u> <u>and</u> <u>Method:</u>   <u>A</u> <u>Behavioral</u>
   <u>Science</u> <u>View.</u>   Reading, MA: Addison-Wesley, 1970.
   B-O-G (0+3=3)

Argyris, Chris, <u>Management</u> <u>and</u> <u>Organizational</u> <u>Development.</u>
   New York: McGraw-Hill, 1971.   M-O-G   (0+3=3)

Argyris, Chris, Organization and Innovation. Homewood, IL: Dorsey Press, 1965. T-P-G (2+2=4)

Argyris, Chris, Personality and Organization. New York: Harper & Row, 1957. O-M-G (7+2=9)

Argyris, Chris, Understanding Organizational Behavior. Homewood, IL: Dorsey Press, 1960. O-M-U-P-B (8+0=8)

Beckhard, Richard, Organization Development: Strategies and Models. Reading, MA: Addison-Wesley, 1969. O-M-T-B (3+2=5)

Bennis, Warren G., Beyond Bureaucracy: Essays on the Development and Evolution of Human Organizations. New York: McGraw-Hill, 1973. G-O (0+2=2)

Bennis, Warren, Changing Organizations. New York: McGraw-Hill, 1966. G-O-T-P-M (10+7=17)

Bennis, Warren G., Organization Development. Reading, MA: Addison-Wesley Publishing Co., 1969. O-G-M-T (4+5=9)

Bennis, Warren G., Kenneth D. Benne and Robert Chine, eds., The Planning of Change. New York: Holt, Rinehart & Winston, 1961. T-M-O-C-P-B-G (9+7=16)

Bennis, Warren G., and Philip E. Slater, The Temporary Society. New York: Harper & Row, 1968. O-M-B-G (2+5=7)

Berelson, Bernard, ed., The Behavioral Sciences Today. New York: Basic Books, 1963. O-T-M (3+0=3)

Berne, Eric, Games People Play: The Psychology of Human Relationships. New York: Grove Press, 1964. B-M (0+2=2)

Berne, Eric, What Do You Say After You Say Hello? New York: Grove Press, 1972. G-B (0+2=2)

Bion, W. R., Experiences in Groups. New York: Basic Books, 1959. G-O (0+2=2)

Blake, Robert R., and Jane S. Mouton, Building a Dynamic Corporation Through Grid Organization Development. Reading, MA: Addison-Wesley, 1969. O-G-T (3+2=5)

Blake, Robert R., and Jane S. Mouton, Corporate Excellence Through Grid Organization Development. Houston: Gulf Publishing Company, 1968. O-T-M (6+1=7)

Blake, Robert R., and Jane S. Mouton, The Managerial Grid. Houston: Gulf Publishing Company, 1964. O-T-B (4+2=6)

Blake, Robert R., H. A. Shepard, Jane S. Mouton, Managing Intergroup Conflicts in Industry. Houston: Gulf Publishing Company, 1965. B-O (0+2=2)

Blumberg, Arthur, and Robert R. Golembiewski, eds., Learning and Change in Groups. London: Penguin, 1976. O-G (0+2=2)

Bradford, Leland P., Jack R. Gibb, and Kenneth D. Benne, eds., T-Group Theory and Laboratory Method. New York: John Wiley & Sons, 1964. O-P (6+3=9)

Burke, W. Warner, ed., Contemporary Organization Development: Conceptual Orientations and Interventions. Washington, DC: NTL Institute, 1972. B-O (0+2=2)

Burke, W. Warner, and H. A. Hornstein, The Social Technology of Organization Development. Fairfax, VA: Learning Resources Corporation, 1972. B-O-G (0+3=3)

Burns, Tom, and G. M. Stalker, The Management of Innovation. London: Tavistock Publications, 1961. O-T-P-G (6+4=10)

Filley, Alan C., and Robert J. House, Managerial Process and Organization Behavior. Glenview, IL: Scott Foresman and Company, 1969. O-T (2+1=3)

Ford, Robert N., Motivation Through the Work Itself. New York: American Management Association, 1969. O-M-G (0+3=3)

Fordyee, Jack K., and Raymond Weil, Managing With People: A Manager's Handbook of Organization Development Meth-

ods. Reading, MA: Addison-Wesley, 1971. O-B-G-M
(0+4=4)

French, Wendell L., and Cecil H. Bell, Jr., Organization Development: Behavioral Science Interventions for Organization Improvement. Englewood Cliffs, NJ: Prentice-Hall, 1973. O-B-M-G (0+5=5)

Gailbraith, Jay, Designing Complex Organizations, Reading, MA: Addison-Wesley, 1973. O-G (0+2=2)

Ginzberg, Eli, and E. W. Reilley, Effecting Change in Large Organizations. New York: Columbia University Press, 1957. M-O (2+1=3)

Golembiewski, Robert T., Renewing Organizations: The Laboratory Approach to Planned Change. Itasca, IL: F. E. Peacock Publishers, 1972. B-O-G (0+5=5)

Golembiewski, Robert T., and Arthur Blumberg, ed., Sensitivity Training and the Laboratory Approach. Itasca, IL: F. E. Peacock, 1970. Subsequent eds. O-G-M (0+4=4)

Guest, Robert H., Organizational Changes: The Effect of Successful Leadership. New York: Richard D. Irwin, 1962. O-T-M-G (6+1=7)

Hampton, David R., Charles E. Summer and Ross A. Webber, Organizational Behavior and the Practice of Management. Chicago: Scott, Foresman & Company, 1968. O-T-M (5+2=7)

Herzberg, Frederick, Bernard Mausner and Barbara Snyderman, The Motivation to Work. New York: John Wiley & Sons, 1959. O-T-M-G (5+5=10)

Herzberg, Frederick, Work and the Nature of Man. New York: Thomas Y. Crowell Company, 1966. O-T-M-G (2+5=7)

Huse, Edgar F., Organization Development and Change. St. Paul, MN: West Publishing Company, 1975. O (0+2=2)

Jaques, Elliott, The Changing Culture of a Factory. New York: The Dryden Press, 1952. O-T (5+0=5)

Jun, Jong S., and William B. Storm, eds., Tomorrow's
    Organizations. Glenview, IL: Scott, Foresman and Com-
    pany, 1973. O-B-M (0+3=3)

Lawrence, Paul R., and Jay W. Lorsch, Developing Organiza-
    tions: Diagnosis and Action. Reading, MA: Addison-Wes-
    ley Publishing Company, 1969. M-T-O (3+1=4)

Lesieur, Frederick G., ed., The Scanlon Plan. Cambridge: The
    Technology Press of MIT, 1958. B-M (0+2=2)

Lewin, Kurt, A Dynamic Theory of Personality. New York:
    McGraw-Hill, 1945. O-M-T (4+0=4)

Lewin, Kurt, Field Theory in Social Science. New York: Har-
    per & Row, 1951. O-T (4+0=4)

Likert, Rensis, The Human Organization. New York:
    McGraw-Hill, 1967. G-O-T-B-M (8+9=17)

Likert, Rensis, New Patterns of Management. New York:
    McGraw-Hill, 1961. O-T-M-P-G-U (10+7=17)

Lippitt, G. L., Organizational Renewal. New York: Appleton-
    Century-Crofts, 1969. B-M (0+2=2)

Lippitt, Ronald, Jeanne Watson and Bruce Westley, The
    Dynamics of Planned Change. New York: Harcourt,
    Brace, 1958. O-M-P (6+2=8)

Litwin, George H., and Robert A. Stringer, Jr., Motivation and
    Organizational Climate. Boston: Harvard Business School,
    1968. T-O (2+2=4)

Maher, J. R., New Perspectives in Job Enrichment. New York:
    Van Nostrand Reinhold, 1971. B-M (0+2=2)

Mann, Floyd C., Bernard P. Indik and Victor H. Vroom, The
    Productivity of Work Groups. Ann Arbor: Institute for
    Social Research, University of Michigan, 1963. O-T
    (3+0=3)

Margulies, Newton, and John Wallace, Organizational Change:
    Techniques and Applications. Glenview, IL: Scott, Fores-
    man & Company, 1973. O (0+2=2)

Marrow, Alfred J., Behind the Executive Mask. New York:
American Management Association, 1964. O-M (3+1=4)

Marrow, Alfred J., David G. Bowers and Stanley E. Seashore,
Management by Participation. New York: Harper & Row,
1967. G-O-T-B (3+6=9)

Maslow, Abraham H., Eupsychian Management. Homewood, IL:
Irwin-Dorsey Press, 1965. O-M-G (3+3=6)

Maslow, Abraham H., Motivation and Personality. New York:
Harper & Row, 1954. O-T-M-G (6+6=12)

Maslow, Abraham H., Toward a Psychology of Being. Princeton: Van Nostrand Reinhold Company, 1962. Subsequent
ed. O-G (2+1=3)

McGregor, Douglas, The Human Side of Enterprise. New York:
McGraw-Hill, 1960. G-O-T-M-P-B (12+12=24)

McGregor, Douglas, Leadership and Motivation. Cambridge:
MIT Press, 1966. O-M-G (2+1=3)

McGregor, Douglas, The Professional Manager. New York:
McGraw-Hill, 1967. O-T-M-G-B (6+3=9)

Miles, Matthew B., Learning to Work in Groups. New York:
Horace Mann Institute of School Experimentation, Columbia
University, 1959. O-M (3+0=3)

Miller, E. J., and A. K. Rice, Systems of Organization: The
Control of Task and Sentient Boundaries. London: Tavistock Publications, 1967. O-T (2+1=3)

Myers, M. Scott, Every Employee a Manager: More Meaningful
Work Through Job Enrichment. New York: McGraw-Hill,
1970. G-M (0+3=3)

O'Connell, Jeremiah J., Managing Organizational Innovation.
Homewood, IL: Richard D. Irwin, 1968. T-M-O (3+0=3)

Porter, Lyman W., and Edward E. Lawler, Managerial Attitudes
and Performance. Homewood, IL: Richard D. Irwin, 1968.
M-O-T-G (3+1=4)

Press, Charles, and Alan Arian, eds., Empathy and Ideology: Aspects of Administrative Innovation. Chicago: Rand McNally, 1966. O-U-M-C (4+1=5)

Rice, A. K., Productivity and Social Organization: The Anmedabad Experiment. London: Tavistock Publications, 1958. T-O (3+0=3)

Rogers, Carl R., Client-Centered Therapy. Boston: Houghton Mifflin Company, 1951. O-M (3+0=3)

Rush, Harold M. F., Behavioral Science Concepts and Management Application. New York: National Industrial Conference Board, Studies in Personnel Policy, No. 216, 1969. C-M (0+2=2)

Schein, Edgar H., Organizational Psychology. Englewood Cliffs, NJ: Prentice-Hall, 1965. O-T-M-G-C (4+4=8)

Schein, Edgar H., and Warren G. Bennis, Personal and Organizational Change Through Group Methods. New York: John Wiley & Sons, 1965. O-T-P (9+1=10)

Schein, Edgar H., Process Consultation. Reading, MA: Addison-Wesley, 1969. O-G-M (0+4=4)

Schmidt, Warren H., Organizational Frontiers and Human Values. Belmont, CA: Wadsworth Publishing Company, 1970. M-O (0+3=3)

Schmuck, R. A., et al., Handbook of Organization Development in Schools. Palo Alto, CA: National Press Books, 1972. B-O-M (0+3=3)

Schultz, William, FIRO: A Three Dimensional Theory of Interpersonal Behavior. New York: Holt, Rinehart, 1958. Later published as The Interpersonal Underworld. G-O (0+2=2)

Seashore, Stanley E., Assessing Organizational Performance With Behavioral Measurements. Ann Arbor, MI: Foundation for Research on Human Behavior Publications Department, 1962. O-G (2+1=3)

Sofer, Cyril, The Organization from Within. Chicago: Quadrangle Books, 1961. O-T (2=1=3)

Steiner, Gary A., ed., The Creative Organization. Chicago: University of Chicago Press, 1964. O-T (4+0=4)

Tannenbaum, Arnold S., Control in Organizations. New York: McGraw-Hill, 1968. O-T-G (2+1=3)

Tannenbaum, Arnold S., Social Psychology of the Work Organization. Belmont, CA: Wadsworth Publishing Company, 1966. O-T (3+0=3)

Tannenbaum, Robert, et al., Leadership and Organization. New York: McGraw-Hill, 1961. (6+0=6)

Thomas, John M., and Warren G. Bennis, eds., The Management of Change and Conflict. New York: Penguin Books, 1972. G (0+2=2)

Trist, E. L., et al., Organizational Choices. London: Tavistock Publications, 1963. O-T (3+0=3)

Wadia, Maneck S., Management and the Behavioral Sciences. Boston: Allyn and Bacon, 1968. G-O-T (3+0=3)

Walton, Richard E., Interpersonal Peacemaking: Confrontations and Third Party Interventions. Reading, MA: Addison-Wesley, 1969. O (0+2=2)

Zaleznik, Abraham, C. R. Christensen and F. J. Roethlisberger, The Motivation, Productivity and Satisfaction of Workers. Boston: Harvard Business School, 1958. O-T-M (4+0=4)

Psychology, Anthropology, and Perceptions

Barnett, Homer G., Anthropology in Administration. New York: Row, Peterson, 1956. O-M (3+0=3)

Bass, Bernard M., Organizational Psychology. Boston: Allyn and Bacon, 1965. M-O-T (4+0=4)

Boulding, Kenneth E., The Image. Ann Arbor: University of Michigan Press, 1956. T-B (3+0=3)

Brown, Ray E., Judgement in Administration. New York: McGraw-Hill, 1966. O-T-M (2+1=3)

Bruner, Jerome S., Jacqueline J. Goodnow and George A. Austin, A Study of Thinking. New York: John Wiley & Sons, 1956. T-O-M-P (4+0=4)

Costello, Timothy W., and Sheldon S. Zalkind, Psychology in Administration. Englewood Cliffs, NJ: Prentice-Hall, 1963. O-T-M (5+1=6)

Festinger, Leon, A Theory of Cognitive Dissonance. Stanford: Stanford University Press, 1957. O-P-T (6+1=7)

Goffman, Erving, Asylums: Essays on the Social Situation of Mental Patients and Other Inmates. Garden City, NY: Doubleday Anchor, 1961. O-B (2+2=4)

Hayakawa, Samuel I., Language in Thought and Action. New York: Harcourt, Brace and Jovanovich, 1939. Subsequent eds. P-M (0+2=2)

Homans, George C., Social Behavior: Its Elementary Form. New York: Harcourt, Brace and World, 1961. G-B (0+2=2)

Hull, Clark L., A Behavior System. New Haven: Yale University Press, 1952. O-T (3+0=3)

Johnson, Donald M., The Psychology of Thought and Judgement. New York: Harper & Brothers, 1955. M-P (3+0=3)

Kahn, Robert L., et al., Organizational Stress: Studies in Role Conflict and Ambiguity. New York: John Wiley & Sons, 1965. G-O-T (5+4=9)

Kaplan, Abraham, The Conduct of Inquiry. San Francisco: Chandler Publishing Company, 1964. B-M (2+1=3)

Kuhn, Thomas S., The Structure of Scientific Revolutions. Chicago: University of Chicago Press, 1968. T-M-G-C (2+2=4)

Leavitt, Harold J., Managerial Psychology. Chicago: University of Chicago Press, 1964. O-G-T-M-P (10+1=11)

Leavitt, Harold J., and Louis R. Pondy, eds., Readings in Managerial Psychology. Chicago: University of Chicago Press, 1965. O-T-M (4+0=4)

Levinson, Harry, The Exceptional Executive. Cambridge: Harvard University Press, 1968. G-O-M (3+3=6)

Levinson, Harry, et al., Men, Management and Mental Health. Cambridge: Harvard University Press, 1962. G-O-M (3+0=3)

Linton, Ralph, The Study of Man. New York: Appleton-Century-Crofts, 1936. T-O-M (3+0=3)

Marrow, Alfred J., Making Management Human. New York: McGraw-Hill, 1957. O-M (3+0=3)

Waldo, Dwight, The Novelist on Organization. Berkeley: Institute of Governmental Studies, University of California, 1968. G-O-M (2+1=3)

White, Leonard, ed., The State of the Social Sciences. Chicago: University of Chicago Press, 1956. M-P-B (3+0=3)

Power, Class, and Conflict

Bendix, Reinhard, and Seymour M. Lipset, eds., Class, Status and Power: A Reader in Social Stratification. New York: The Free Press, 1953. M-O-T (5+0=5)

Bendix, Reinhard, Work and Authority in Industry. New York: Chapman and Hall, 1965. O-M-T (5+1=6)

Blau, Peter M., Exchange and Power in Social Life. New York: John Wiley & Sons, 1964. G-B (0+2=2)

Boulding, Kenneth E., Conflict and Defense. New York: Harper & Row, 1963 B-P-T-G (3+2=5)

Cartwright, Dorwin, Studies in Social Power. Ann Arbor: University of Michigan Press, 1959. O-G-M-T (5+0=5)

Coser, Lewis A., The Functions of Social Conflict. New York: The Free Press, 1956. O-G-T-B-M (7+2=9)

Dalton, Melville, Men Who Manage. New York: John Wiley and Sons, 1959. O-G-T (6+0=6)

Dubin, Robert, The World of Work. Englewood Cliffs, NJ: Prentice-Hall, 1958. O-M-T-G (7+0=7)

Fried, Robert C., The Italian Prefects: A Study in Administrative Politics. New Haven: Yale University Press, 1963. O-B (2+1=3)

Jenkins, David, Job Power: Blue and White Collar Democracy. Garden City, NY: Doubleday & Co., 1973. O-M (2+0=2)

Korda, Michael, Power. New York: Random House, 1975. M (0+2=2)

Kornhauser, Arthur, R. Dubin, and A. M. Ross, eds., Industrial Conflict. New York: McGraw-Hill, 1954. M-O (4+0=4)

Mills, C. Wright, The Sociological Imagination. New York: Oxford Univesity Press, 1959. M-P (3+0=3)

Terkel, Studs, Working. New York: Avon Books, 1974. B-M (0+2=2)

THE SYSTEMS APPROACH

Management Science

Ackoff, Russell L., and Maurice W. Sasieni, Fundamentals of
   Operations Research. New York: John Wiley & Sons,
   1968. O-M-T-P (2+2=4)

Ackoff, Russell L., ed., Progress in Operations Research. New
   York: John Wiley & Sons, 1961 T-P (3+1=4)

Alexis, Marcus, and Charles Z. Wilson, Organizational Decision
   Making. Englewood Cliffs, NJ: Prentice-Hall, 1967. T-P
   (2+1=3)

Anthony, Robert N., Planning and Control Systems. Boston:
   Graduate School of Business Administration, Harvard University, 1965. G-T-M-P-F (5+5=10)

Baumol, William J., Economic Theory and Operations Analysis.
   Englewood Cliffs, NJ: Prentice-Hall, 1961. T-M-P
   (2+3=5)

Blumstein, Alfred, Murray Kamrass, and Armand Weiss, eds.,
   Systems Analysis for Social Problems. Washington, DC:
   Operations Research Council, 1970. P-F-T (0+3=3)

Bohigian, Haig, The Foundations and Mathematical Models of
   Operations Research with Extensions to the Criminal Justice System. Yonkers, NY: Gazette Press, 1971. P-T
   (0+2=2)

Brewer, Garry D., Politicians, Bureaucrats and the Consultant:
   A Critique of Urban Problem Solving. New York: Basic
   Books, 1973. U-B-P-T (0+5=5)

Byrd, Jack, Operations Research Models for Public Administration. Lexington, MA: Lexington Books, 1975. M-P (0+2=2)

Chartrand, Robert Lee, Systems Technology Applied to Social and Community Problems. New York: Spartan Books, 1971. M-T (0+2=2)

Churchman, C. West, Russell L. Ackoff and Leonard Ackoff, Introduction to Operations Research. New York: John Wiley & Sons, 1957. T-O-M (4+1=5)

Churchman, C. West, Prediction and Optimal Decision. Englewood Cliffs, NJ: Prentice-Hall, 1961. T-M-P (3+0=3)

Cleland, David, and William R. King, Systems Analysis and Project Management. New York: McGraw-Hill, 1968. T-M G (3+2=5)

Hillier, Frederick S., and Gerald J. Lieberman, Introduction to Operations Research. San Francisco: Holden-Day, 1974. P-T (0+2=2)

Dearden, John, and F. Warren McFarlan, Management Information Systems. Homewood, IL: Richard D. Irwin, 1966. M-G (0+2=2)

Drake, Alvin W., Ralph L. Keeney and Philip M. Morse, eds., Analysis of Public Systems. Cambridge: MIT Press, 1972. P-T (0+5=5)

Enke, Stephen, ed., Defense Management. Englewood Cliffs, NJ: Prentice-Hall, 1967. G-T-M-F-P (8+0=8)

Evarts, Harry F., Introduction to PERT. Boston: Allyn and Bacon, 1964. G-T (0+2=2)

Fishburn, Peter C., Decision and Value Theory. New York: John Wiley & Sons, 1964. B-T (0+2=2)

Gass, Saul I., Roger L. Sisson, eds., A Guide to Models in Governmental Planning and Operations. Potomac, MD: Sauger Books, 1975. G-P-T (0+3=3)

Goldman, Thomas A., ed., Cost-Effectiveness Analysis. New York: Frederick A. Praeger, 1967. T-P (2+1=3)

Hein, Leonard W., Quantitative Approach to Managerial Decisions. Englewood Cliffs, NJ: Prentice-Hall, 1967. T-P-G (2+2=4)

Hitch, Charles J., Decision-Making for Defense. Berkeley: University of California Press, 1965. G-T-P (5+2=7)

Hitch, Charles J., and Roland N. McKean, The Economics of Defense in the Nuclear Age. Cambridge: Harvard University Press, 1960. G-B-P-F (6+6=12)

Johnson, Richard A., Fremont E. Kast and James E. Rosenweig, The Theory and Management of Systems. New York: McGraw-Hill, 1963. G-T-M-P (9+2=11)

Kepner, Charles H., and Benjamin B. Tregoe, The Rational Manager. New York: McGraw-Hill, 1965. M-T-G (2+1=3)

Laidlaw, C., Linear Programming for Urban Development Plan Evaluation. New York: Praeger, 1972. P-T (0+2=2)

Larson, Richard C., Urban Police Patrol Analysis. Cambridge: MIT Press, 1972. U (0+2=2)

Levin, Richard, and Charles Kirkpatrick, Quantitative Approaches to Management. New York: McGraw-Hill, 1965. T-M (2+3=5)

Livingstone, John Leslie, and Sanford C. Gunn, eds., Accounting for Social Goals: Budgeting and the Analysis of Nonmarket Projects. New York: Harper & Row, 1974. T (0+2=2)

Mack, Ruth P., Planning on Uncertainty: Decision Making in Business and Government Administration. New York: Wiley-Interscience, 1971. P-F (0+2=2)

Miller, David W., and Martin Starr, Executive Decisions and Operations Research. Englewood Cliffs, NJ: Prentice-Hall, 1960. T-M-P-G (7+2=9)

Miller, David W., and Martin K. Starr, The Structure of Human Decisions. Englewood Cliffs, NJ: Prentice-Hall, 1967. O-T-U-G (2+2=4)

Morse, Philip M., and Laura W. Bacon, eds., Operations Research for Public Systems. Cambridge: MIT Press, 1967. T-M (0+2=2)

Neuschel, R. F., Management by System. New York: McGraw-Hill, 1960. M-T-G (2+1=3)

Quade, E. S., ed., Analysis for Military Decisions. Santa Monica, CA: The Rand Corporation, 1964. T-P-F (3+2=5)

Quade, E. S., and W. I. Boucher, eds., Systems Analysis and Policy Planning. New York: American Elsevier Publishing Company, 1968. M-T-G (2+1=3)

Raiffa, Howard, Decision Analysis. Reading, MA: Addison-Wesley, 1968. M-T-B-P-G (2+5=7)

Raser, John R., Simulation and Society: An Exploration of Scientific Gaming. Boston: Allyn and Bacon, 1969 M-T (0+3=3)

Reed, John, The Applications of Operations Research to Court Delay. New York: Praeger, 1973. P-T (0+2=2)

Richmond, Samuel, Operations Research for Management Decisions. New York: The Ronald Press, 1968. P-T (0+2=2)

Sayles, Leonard R., and Margaret K. Chandler, Managing Large Systems. New York: Harper & Row, 1971. O-M-G (0+3=3)

Schell, Erwin Haskell, Technique of Executive Control. New York: McGraw-Hill, 1950. G-T (2+1=3)

Sapolsky, Harvey M., The Polaris System Development: Bureaucratic and Programmatic Success in Government. Cambridge: Harvard University Press, 1972. G-O-F (0+4=4)

Starr, M. K., and D. W. Miller, Inventory Control: Theory and Practice. Englewood Cliffs, NJ: Prentice-Hall, 1962. P-T (0+2=2)

Thieranf, R. J., and Richard A. Grosse, Decision Making Through Operations Research. New York: John Wiley & Sons, 1970. Subsequent eds. F-P-T (0+3=3)

Wagner, Harvey M., Principles of Operations Research. Englewood Cliffs, NJ: Prentice-Hall, 1969. Subsequent eds. P-T (0+2=2)

Young, Stanley, Managment: A Systems Analysis. Chicago: Scott, Foresman and Company, 1966. T-M (3+0=3)

Science, Technology, Computers, and Administration

Anshen, Melvin, and George Leland Bach, eds., Management and Corporations, 1985. New York: McGraw-Hill, 1960. T-M-P (4+0=4)

Arnstein, Sherry, and Alexander Christakis, eds., Perspectives on Technology Assessment. Jerusalem: Science and Technology Publishers, 1975. G (0+2=2)

Boguslaw, Robert, The New Utopians. Englewood Cliffs, NJ: Prentice-Hall, 1965. O-T-P-B-G (4+4=8)

Bright, James R., Research Development and Technological Innovation. Homewood, IL: Richard D. Irwin, 1964. T-M (2+2=4)

Danhof, Clarence H., Government Contracting and Technological Change. Washington, DC: The Brookings Institution, 1968. G-O-T-P (5+0=5)

Diebold, John, Automation: The Advent of the Automatic Factory. New York: D. Van Nostrand Company, 1952. T-M-O (3+0=3)

Feigenbaum, Edward A., and Julian Feldman, eds., Computers and Thought. New York: McGraw-Hill, 1963. T (2+1=3)

Fuller, Richard Buckminster, An Operating Manual for Spaceship Earth. Carbondale, IL: Southern Illinois University Press, 1969. M (0+2=2)

Greenberg, Daniel S., The Politics of Pure Science. New York: New American Library, 1967. P-M (0+2=2)

Hahn, Walter A., and Kenneth F. Gordon, eds., Assessing the Future and Policy Planning. New York: Gordon and Breach Science Publishers, 1973. M (0+2=2)

Havelocks, Ronald G., Planning for Innovation Through Dissemination and Utilization of Knowledge. Ann Arbor: Institute for Social Research, University of Michigan, 1969. P-B (0+3=3)

Hower, Ralph, and Charles Orth, Managers and Scientists. Boston: Harvard Business School, 1963. T-M (3+0=3)

Jantsch, Erich, Technological Forecasting in Perspective. Paris: Organization for Economic Cooperation and Development, 1967. T (2+1=3)

Kahn, Herman, and Anthony J. Weiner, The Year 2000. New York: The Macmillan Company, 1967. P-T (2+1=3)

Kast, Fremont E., and James E. Rosenweig, eds., Science and Technology and Management. New York: McGraw-Hill, 1963. T-M (5+0=5)

Lakoff, Sanford A., ed., Knowledge and Power. New York: The Free Press, 1966. T-P (3+0=3)

Mann, Floyd C., and L. Richard Hoffman, Automation and the Worker. New York: Holt, Rinehart and Winston, 1960. T-O-G (3+1=4)

McMillan, Claude, Jr., Mathematical Programming: An Introduction to the Design and Applications of Optimal Decision Machines. New York: John Wiley & Sons, 1970. Subsequent ed. P-T (0+2=2)

Meadows, Donella H., Dennis L. Meadows, Jorgen Randers, and William W. Behrens, The Limits to Growth. New York: Universe Books, 1972. Subsequent eds. P-G-T-M (0+4=4)

Mesarovic, M., and E. Pestal, Mankind at the Turning Point: The Second Report of the Club of Rome. New York: E. P. Dutton, 1974. M-C (0+2=2)

Michael, Donald N., The Unprepared Society. New York: Basic Books, 1968. T-B-G (2+2=4)

Myers, Charles A., ed., The Impact of Computers on Management. Cambridge: MIT Press, 1966. G-T (2+1=3)

Nelson, Richard R., Merton J. Peck and Edward D. Kalacheck, Technology, Economic Growth and Public Policy. Washington, DC: The Brookings Institution, 1967. T-O-P (4+0=4)

Newell, Allen, and Herbert Simon, Human Problem Solving. New York: Prentice-Hall, 1972. P-T (0+2=2)

Orth, Charles D., Joseph C. Bailey and Francis W. Wolek, Administering Research and Development. Homewood, IL: Irwin, Dorsey Press, 1964. T-M (3+0=3)

Pelz, Donald C., and Frank M. Andrews, Scientists in Organizations. New York: John Wiley & Sons, 1966. O-T-P (5+1=6)

Roman, Daniel D., Research and Development Management. New York: Appleton-Century-Crofts, 1968. T-M (3+0=3)

Simon, Herbert A., The New Science of Management Decision. Englewood Cliffs, NJ: Prentice Hall, 1960. Subsequent ed. O-M-B-P-T (8+3=11)

Simon, Herbert A., The Sciences of the Artificial. Cambridge: Harvard University Press, 1969. O-T-G (4+0=4)

Simon, Herbert A., The Shape of Automation for Men and Management. New York: Harper & Row, 1965. G-M (3+1=4)

Systems Theory

Ashby, William Ross, An Introduction to Cybernetics. New York: Barnes & Noble, 1956. M-T-O (2+1=3)

Beer, Stafford, Cybernetics and Management. New York: John Wiley & Sons, 1959. G-P (2+1=3)

Beer, Stafford, Decision and Control. New York: John Wiley & Sons, 1966. M-P-T (2+2=4)

Brock, Bernard, et al., Public Policy Decision-Making: Systems Analysis and Comparative Advantages Debate. New York: Harper & Row, 1973. P-T (0+2=2)

Buckley, Walter, ed., Modern Systems Research for the Behavioral Scientist. Chicago: Aldine Publishing Company, 1968. T-M (3+1=4)

Buckley, Walter, Sociology and Modern Systems Theory. Englewood Cliffs, NJ: Prentice-Hall, 1967. O-G (2+2=4)

Chapple, Eliot D., and Leonard R. Sayles, The Measurement of Management. New York: The Macmillan Company, 1961. O-G-M-P-T (7+1=8)

Churchman, C. West, The Systems Approach. New York: Dell Publishing Company, 1968. G-M-P-B (2+3=5)

Cooper, William W., H. J. Leavitt, and M. W. Shelly, eds., New Perspectives in Organizational Research. New York: John Wiley & Sons, 1964. O-T-M-P (5+0=5)

Forrester, Jay W., Industrial Dynamics. Cambridge: MIT Press, 1961. G-T-M (4+0=4)

Forrester, Jay W., Urban Dynamics. Cambridge: MIT Press, 1969. T-G-U (3+2=5)

Forrester, Jay W., World Dynamics. Cambridge, MA: Wright-Allen, Inc., 1971. Subsequent ed. T (0+2=2)

Hitch, Charles J., On the Choice of Objectives in Systems Studies. Santa Monica, CA: The Rand Corporation, 1960. F-M (0+2=2)

Hoos, Ida R., Systems Analysis in Public Policy: A Critique. Berkeley: University of California Press, 1972. M-B-P-T-G (0+8=8)

Kast, Fremont E., and James E. Rosenweig, Organization and Management: A Systems Approach. New York: McGraw-Hill, 1970. G-T-M (3+2=5)

Kelleher, Grace J., ed., The Challenge to Systems Analysis: Public Policy and Social Change. New York: John Wiley & Sons, 1970. M-T (0+2=2)

Mesarvoic, Mihajlo D., Views on General Systems Theory. New York: John Wiley & Sons, 1964. M-P-T (3+0=3)

Optner, Stanford, Systems Analysis for Business Management. Englewood Cliffs, NJ: Prentice-Hall, 1968. M-P (3+0=3)

Pierce, J. R., Symbols, Signals and Noise: The Nature and Process of Communication. New York: Harper and Brothers, 1961. G-B (0+2=2)

Shannon, Claude E., and Warren Weaver, The Mathematical Theory of Communication. Urbana: University of Illinois Press, 1949. T-M (3+0=3)

Wiener, Norbert, Cybernetics. Cambridge: The MIT Press, 1948. O-M-B-G (2+2=4)

Wiener, Norbert, The Human Use of Human Beings. New York: Avon Books, 1950. G-T-M-P-O (6+1=7)

BUREAUCRACY

Bureaucratic Structure and Behavior

Bendix, Reinhard, Max Weber: An Intellectual Portrait. New York: Doubleday and Company, 1960. G-B (0+2=2)

Berkley, George E., The Administrative Revolution. Englewood Cliffs, NJ: Prentice-Hall, 1971. G-M (0+2=2)

Blau, Peter M., and Marshall W. Meyer, Bureaucracy in Modern Society. New York: Random House, 1956. Subsequent ed. M-G-T-B-P-C (5+5=10)

Blau, Peter, The Dynamics of Bureaucracy. Chicago: University of Chicago Press, 1955. O-B-M-P-G (9+3=12)

Blau, Peter, and W. Richard Scott, Formal Organizations: A Comparative Approach. San Francisco: Chandler Publishing Company, 1962. T-B-M-G (6+8=14)

Crozier, Michel, The Bureaucratic Phenomenon. Chicago: University of Chicago Press, 1964. O-C-G-T-B-P (8+13=21)

Crozier, Michel, La Societe' Bloque'e. Paris: Editions du Seuil, 1970. G-B (0+2=2)

Dalby, Michael T., and Michael S. Werthman, eds., Bureaucracy in Historical Perspective. Glenview, IL: Scott, Foresman & Co., 1971. M (0+2=2)

Downs, Anthony, Inside Bureaucracy. Boston: Little, Brown & Co., 1967. B-G-O-U-P-T-F (9+12=21)

238

Durkheim, Emile, The Division of Labor in Society. Translated by George Simpson. New York: The Free Press, 1893. B-O (2+2=4)

Dvorin, Eugene P., and Robert H. Simmons, From Amoral to Humane Bureaucracy. San Francisco: Canfield Press, 1972. U-G-O-M (0+10=10)

Gouldner, Alvin, Patterns of Industrial Bureaucracy. New York: The Free Press, 1954. T-B-O-G (9+4=13)

Hage, Jerald, and Michael Aiken, Social Change in Complex Organizations. New York: Random House, 1970. P-B (0+2=2)

Hill, Michael J., The Sociology of Public Administration. New York: Crane, Russak and Company, 1972. B (0+2=2)

Howton, William F., Funtionaries. Chicago: Quadrangle Books, 1969. B-M (0+2=2)

Jacoby, Henry, The Bureaucratization of the World. Berkeley: University of California Press, 1973. C-B (0+2=2)

Kaufman, Herbert, Red Tape: Its Origins, Uses and Abuses. Washington, DC: The Brookings Institution, 1977. G (0+2=2)

Merton, Robert K., et al., eds., Reader in Bureaucracy. New York: The Free Press, 1952. O-M-T-U-B-C-G (11+3=14)

Merton, Robert K., Social Theory and Social Structure. New York: The Free Press, 1949. Subsequent eds. O-T-B-M-F-C-G (8+5=13)

Michels, Robert K., Political Parties. Translated by Eden and Cedar Paul. New York: The Free Press, 1959. B-O-M (3+1=4)

Perrow, Charles, Complex Organizations. Glenview, IL: Scott, Foresman and Company, 1972. O-G-B (0+7=7)

Peter, Lawrence J., and Raymond Hull, The Peter Principle. New York: William Morrow, 1969. G-B-M (0+4=4)

Presthus, Robert, The Organizational Society. New York: Alfred A. Knopf, 1962. G-O-T-B-P-M (9+4=13)

Thompson, Victor A., Bureaucracy and Innovation. University, AL: University of Alabama Press, 1969. G-O-B (4+1=5)

Thompson, Victor A., Bureaucracy and the Modern World. Morristown: General Learning Press, 1976. O (0+2=2)

Thompson, Victor A., Modern Organization. New York: Alfred A. Knopf, 1961. G-O-B-M-P-C (9+10=19)

Weber, Max, From Max Weber: Essays in Sociology. Translated, edited and with an introduction by H. H. Gerth and C. Wright Mills. New York: Oxford University Press, 1946. O-M-B-G-P (7+8=15)

Bureaucratic Institutions

Anderson, Stanley V., ed., Ombudsman for American Government. Englewood Cliffs, NJ: Prentice-Hall, 1968. G-U-M-B (2+3=5)

Baum, Bernard H., Decentralization of Authority in a Bureaucracy. Englewood Cliffs, NJ: Prentice-Hall, 1961. M-B-U-T (3+1=4)

Berliner, Joseph S., Factory & Manager in the USSR. Cambridge: Harvard University Press, 1957. B-M-F (2+1=3)

Cohen, Stephen S., Modern Capitalist Planning: The French Model. Cambridge: Harvard University Press, 1969. B-F (0+2=2)

Friedrich, Carl J., and Taylor Cole, Responsible Bureaucracy. Cambridge: Harvard University Press, 1932. O-B-C (2+1=3)

Gellhorn, Walter, When Americans Complain. Cambridge: Harvard University Press, 1966. U-P-G (2+2=4)

Hackett, John, and Anne-Marie Hackett, Economic Planning in France. Cambridge: Harvard University Press, 1963. M-P-B (3+0=3)

Hyneman, Charles, Bureaucracy in a Democracy. New York: Harper & Brothers, 1950. O-M-P-B-G (7+2=9)

Jacob, Herbert, German Administration Since Bismark. New Haven: Yale University Press, 1963. O-C-B (3+1=4)

Mayntz, Renate, and Fritz W. Scharpf, Policy-Making in the German Federal Bureaucracy. Amsterdam: Elsevier, 1975. C-B (0+2=2)

Morstein Marx, Fritz, The Administrative State: An Introduction to Bureaucracy. Chicago: University of Chicago Press, 1957. O-P-B-M-C (3+2=5)

Parkinson, C. Northcote, The Law and the Profits. Boston: Houghton Mifflin, 1960. M-B-G (2+1=3)

Parkinson, C. Northcote, Parkinson's Law and Other Studies in Administration. Boston: Houghton Mifflin, 1957. O-M-B-G (5+3=8)

Powell, Norman John, Responsible Public Bureaucracy in the United States. Boston: Allyn and Bacon, 1967. (4+0=4)

Ridley, F., and J. Blondel, Public Administration in France. New York: Barnes & Noble, 1969. C-U (2+1=3)

Rowat, Donald C., ed., The Ombudsman: Citizen's Defender. Toronto: University of Toronto Press, 1968. P-O-C-U-B (4+1=5)

Rowat, Donald C., The Ombudsman Plan: Essays on the Worldwide Spread of an Idea. Toronto: McClelland and Stewart, 1973. C-G-M (0+3=3)

Suleiman, Ezra N., Politics, Power, and Bureaucracy in France: The Administrative Elite. Princeton: Princeton University Press, 1974. C-B (0+2=2)

Von Mises, Ludwig, Bureaucracy. New Haven: Yale University Press, 1944. O-B-M (5+1=6)

Warwick, Donald P., A Theory of Public Bureaucracy: Politics, Personality, and Organization in the State Department. Cambridge: Harvard University Press, 1975. O-B-C (0+3=3)

Weeks, Kent M., Ombudsmen Around the World. Berkeley: Institute of Government Studies, University of California, 1973. Subsequent eds. B-M (0+2=2)

Woll, Peter, American Bureaucracy. New York: W. W. Norton and Company, 1963. U-P-G (3+3=6)

Wynet, Alan J., ed., Executive Ombudsmen in the United States. Berkeley: Institute of Government Studies, University of California, Berkeley, 1973. G-B (0+2=2)

THE POLICY APPROACH

Program Evaluation and Policy Analysis

Abt, Clark, ed., The Evaluation of Social Programs. Beverly
Hills, CA: Sage Publications, 1976. P (0+2=2)

Bauer, Raymond A., ed., Social Indicators. Cambridge: MIT
Press, 1966. T-P-G (3+2=5)

Bennett, Carl A., and Arthur A. Lumsdaine, eds., Evaluation
and Experiment. New York: Academic Press, 1975. P
(0+2=2)

Blalock, Hubert M., Social Statistics. New York: McGraw-
Hill, 1960. Subsequent eds. P (0+2=2)

Campbell, Donald T., and Julian C. Stanley, Experimental and
Quasi-Experimental Designs for Research. Chicago: Rand
McNally and Company, 1963. P-G (0+2=2)

Caro, Francis G., ed., Readings in Evaluation Research. New
York: Russell Sage, 1971. Subsequent eds. G-B-P-M
(0+5=5)

Dolbeare, Kenneth M., ed., Public Policy Evaluation. Beverly
Hills, CA: Sage Publications, 1975. M-P (0+4=4)

Dorfman, Robert, ed., Measuring Benefits of Government
Investments. Washington, DC: The Brookings Institution,
1965. F-P-O-M (6+1=7)

Fairley, William B., and Frederick Mosteller, eds., Statistics
and Public Policy. Reading, MA: Addison-Wesley, 1977.
P (0+2=2)

243

Freeman, Howard, and Clarence Sherwood, Social Research and Social Policy. Englewood Cliffs, NJ: Prentice-Hall, 1970. P-M (0+2=2)

Guttentag, Maria, and Elmer L. Struening, eds., Handbook of Evaluation Research, Vols. 1 and 2. Beverly Hills, CA: Sage Publications, 1975. B-P (0+2=2)

Hatry, Harry P., and Donald M. Fisk, Improving Productivity and Productivity Measurements in Local Government. Washington, DC: National Commission on Productivity and Work Quality, 1971. U-M (0+3=3)

Hatry, Harry P., Richard E. Winnie, and Donald Fisk, Practical Program Evaluation for State and Local Governments. Washington, DC: The Urban Institute, 1973. U-M-P (0+5=5)

Hatry, Harry P., et al., Program Analysis for State and Local Government. Washington, DC: The Urban Institute, 1976. U-M-F-G (0+5=5)

Haveman, Robert H., and Julius Margolis, Public Expenditures and Policy Analysis. Chicago: Rand McNally Publishing Company, 1970. Subsequent eds. P-G-F-M (0+11=11)

Hinrichs, Harley H. and Graeme M. Taylor, Systematic Analysis: A Primer on Benefit Cost Analysis and Program Evaluation. Pacific Palisades, CA: Goodyear Publishing Company, 1972. P (0+2=2)

Hinrichs, Harley H., and Graeme M. Taylor, Program Budgeting and Benefit-cost Analysis. Pacific Palisades, CA: Goodyear Publishing Company, 1969. P-F-T-M (0+6=6)

Jones, Charles O., and Robert D. Thomas, eds., Public Policy Making in a Federal System. Vol. III, Sage Yearbooks in Politics and Public Policy. Beverly Hills, CA: Sage Publications, 1976. G-U (0+2=2)

McKean, Roland N., Efficiency in Government Through Systems Analysis. New York: John Wiley & Sons, 1958. O-B-M-P (4+5=9)

Meltsner, Arnold J., Policy Analysis in the Bureaucracy. Berkeley: University of California Press, 1976. B-P-G (0+6=6)

Mishan, E. J., Cost-Benefit Analysis: An Informal Introduction. New York: Praeger, 1971. Subsequent eds. P-G (0+3=3)

Mishan, E.J., Economics for Social Decisions: Elements of Cost Benefit Analysis. New York: Praeger Publishers, 1972. G-P-M (0+3=3)

North, Douglass, and Roger Leroy Miller, The Economics of Public Issues. New York: Harper & Row, 1976. P-F (0+2=2)

Ostrom, Elinor, ed., The Delivery of Urban Services: Outcomes of Change. Beverly Hills, CA: Sage Publications, 1976. M (0+2=2)

Quade, E. S., Analysis for Public Decisions. New York: Elsevier Science Publishing Company, 1975. Subsequent ed. G-P (0+6=6)

Riecken, Henry W., and Robert F. Boruch, eds., Social Experimentation: A Method for Planning and Evaluating Social Intervention. New York: Academic Press, 1974. P-G (0+4=4)

Rivlin, Alice M., and P. Michael Timpane, eds., Planned Variation in Education: Should We Give Up or Try Harder? Washington, DC: The Brookings Institution, 1975. P (0+2=2)

Rivlin, Alice M., Systematic Thinking for Social Action. Washington, DC: The Brookings Institution, 1971. G-M (0+8=8)

Ross, John, and Jesse Burkhead, Productivity in the Local Government Sector. Lexington, MA: Lexington Books, 1974. U-M-F-G (0+5=5)

Rossi, Peter H., and Walter Williams, eds., Evaluating Social Programs. New York: Seminar Press, 1972. G-P-F-B (0+5=5)

Rutman, Leonard, ed., Evaluation Research Methods: A Basic Guide. Beverly Hills, CA: Sage Publications, 1977. P-G (0+2=2)

Scioli, Frank P., Jr., and Thomas J. Cook, Methodologies for Analyzing Public Policies. Lexington, MA: Lexington Books, 1975. P-G (0+3=3)

Suchman, Edward A., Evaluative Research. New York: Russell Sage Foundation, 1967. M-P-B (0+6=6)

Tufte, Edward R., Data Analysis for Politics and Policy. Englewood Cliffs, NJ: Prentice-Hall, 1974. P (0+2=2)

Tufte, Edward R., The Quantitative Analysis of Social Problems. Reading, MA: Addison-Wesley Publishing Company, 1970. P (0+2=2)

Webb, Eugene J., et al., Unobtrusive Measures: Nonreactive Research in the Social Sciences. Chicago: Rand McNally and Company, 1966. P-O (0+2=2)

Weiss, Carol A., ed., Evaluating Action Programs. Boston: Allyn and Bacon, 1972. G-M-B (0+4=4)

Weiss, Carol A., Evaluation Research. Englewood Cliffs, NJ: Prentice-Hall, 1972. G-M-P (0+12=12)

Wholey, Joseph S., et al., Federal Evaluation Policy. Washington, DC: The Urban Institute, 1970. G-P-M (0+6=6)

Williams, Walter, Social Policy Research and Analysis: The Experience in the Federal Social Agencies. New York: American Elsevier Publishing Co., 1971. P-B-F-G (0+4=4)

Wilson, James Q., Varieties of Police Behavior: The Management of Law and Order in Eight Communities. Cambridge: Harvard University Press, 1968. U-M (0+2=2)

Zeckhauser, Richard, and Edith Stokey, A Primer for Policy Analysis. New York: W. W. Norton & Co., 1977. P-G (0+2=2)

General Models and Theories

Amacher, Ryan C., Robert D. Tollison and Thomas D. Willett, eds., The Economic Approach to Public Policy. Ithaca, NY: Cornell University Press, 1976. P (0+2=2)

Anderson, James E., Public Policy-making. New York: Holt, Rinehart & Winston, 1975. Subsequent eds. P-M-G-U (0+6=6)

Arrow, Kenneth J., Social Choice and Individual Values. New York: John Wiley & Sons, 1951. B-M-P (3+2=5)

Bauer, Raymond A. and Kenneth J. Gergen, eds., The Study of Policy Formulation. New York: The Free Press, 1968. O-P-T-F-G (5+5=10)

Bish, Robert L., The Public Economy of Metropolitan Areas. Chicago: Markham Publishing Company, 1971. G-F-U (0+3=3)

Bish, Robert L., and Vincent Ostrom, Understanding Urban Government: Metropolitan Reform Reconsidered. Washington, DC: American Enterprise Institute for Public Policy Research, 1973. U (0+2=2)

Borcherding, Thomas, ed., Budgets and Bureaucrats: The Sources of Government Growth. Durham, NC: Duke University Press, 1977. G-B-F (0+3=3)

Boyer, William W., Bureaucracy on Trial: Policy Making by Government Agencies. Indianapolis: Bobbs-Merrill Company, 1964. U-P (4+1=5)

Braybrooke, David, and Charles E. Lindblom, A Strategy of Decision: Policy Evaluation as a Social Process. New York: The Free Press, 1963. O-G-P-F-B (7+5=12)

Buchanan, James M., and Gordon Tullock, The Calculus of Consent. Ann Arbor: University of Michigan Press, 1962. B-P-F-G (3+6=9)

Dahl, Robert A., A Preface to Democracy Theory. Chicago: University of Chicago Press, 1956. B-P-F-G (3+2=5)

Dahl, Robert A., and Charles E. Lindblom, Politics, Economics and Welfare. New York: Harper & Brothers, 1953. O-M-T-P-F-G (8+2=10)

Dahl, Robert A., Who Governs? New Haven: Yale University Press, 1961. U-P-M (5+3=8)

Deutsch, Karl, The Nerves of Government. New York: The Free Press, 1963. P-M-C-G (5+2=7)

Domhoff, G. William, The Higher Circles: The Governing Class in America. New York: Random House, 1970. G-U (0+2=2)

Downs, Anthony, An Economic Theory of Democracy. New York: Harper and Row, 1957. O-P-B-F-G (5+3=8)

Dror, Yehezkel, Design for Policy Sciences. New York: American Elsevier Publishing Company, 1971. B-P-G (0+3=3)

Dror, Yehezkel, Public Policymaking Reexamined. San Francisco: Chandler Publishing Company, 1968. O-G-P-F-C-B-M (7+9=16)

Dror, Yehezkel, Ventures in Policy Sciences. New York: American Elsevier, 1971. G-B-P-M (0+4=4)

Dye, Thomas R., Politics, Economics and the Public. Chicago: Rand McNally Publishing Co., 1966. P-U-F-G (4+2=6)

Dye, Thomas R., Understanding Public Policy. Englewood Cliffs, NJ: Prentice-Hall, 1972. Subsequent eds. G-F-C-P-M (0+6=6)

Easton, David, A Framework for Political Analysis. Englewood Cliffs, NJ: Prentice-Hall, 1965. G (0+2=2)

Easton, David, The Political System. New York: Alfred A. Knopf, 1953. M-P (3+2=5)

Easton, David, A Systems Analysis of Political Life. New York: John Wiley & Sons, 1965. P-G (3+2=5)

Easton, David, ed., Varieties of Political Theory. Englewood
    Cliffs, NJ: Prentice-Hall, 1966. F (0+2=2)

Edelman, Murray, The Symbolic Uses of Politics. Urbana:
    University of Illinois Press, 1967. P-F-M-G (3+2=5)

Etzioni, Amitai, The Active Society: A Theory of Societal and
    Political Process. New York: The Free Press, 1968.
    O-G-P (5+0=5)

Gordon, Kermit, Agenda for the Nation. Washington, DC: The
    Brookings Institution, 1968. P-T-F (4+0=4)

Gregg, Phillip, ed., Problems of Theory in Policy Analysis.
    Lexington, MA: Lexington Books, 1976. P-G (0+2=2)

Greenberger, Martin, Matthew A. Crenson and Brian L. Crissey,
    Models in the Policy Process. New York: Russell Sage
    Foundation, 1976. P (0+3=3)

Gross, Bertram M., The State of the Nation: Social Systems
    Accounting. London: Tavistock Publications, 1966. T-P-C
    (2+1=3)

Hofferbert, Richard I., The Study of Public Policy. Indianapo-
    lis: Bobbs-Merrill, 1974. P (0+2=2)

Jones, Charles O., An Introduction to the Study of Public
    Policy. Belmont, CA: Duxbury Press, 1970. Subsequent
    ed. G-P (0+4=4)

Lasswell, Harold D., Politics: Who Gets What, When, How.
    Cleveland: Meridian Books, 1936. M-P (3+1=4)

Lasswell, Harold, A Pre-view of Policy Sciences. New York:
    American Elsevier Publishing Co., 1971. P-G (0+2=2)

Lerner, Daniel, and Harold D. Lasswell, eds., The Policy Sci-
    ences. Stanford: Stanford University Press, 1968. P-G
    (2+3=5)

Lindblom, Charles E., The Intelligence of Democracy: Decision
    Making Through Mutual Adjustment. New York: The Free
    Press, 1965. G-O-P-F-B (6+4=10)

Lindblom, Charles E., The Policy-Making Process. Englewood Cliffs, NJ: Prentice-Hall, 1968. Subsequent ed. P-F-M-G (5+10=15)

Lipset, Seymour, Political Man. Garden City, NY: Doubleday & Company, 1960. C-P-B (3+0=3)

Long, Norton E., The Polity. Edited and with an introduction by Charles Press. Chicago: Rand McNally, 1962. O-B-P-G (4+1=5)

Lowi, Theodore J., At the Pleasure of the Mayor. New York: Free Press of Glencoe, 1964. U-M (0+2=2)

Mills, C. Wright, The Power Elite. New York: Oxford University Press, 1956. M-U-T-P-G (5+2=7)

Mitchell, William C., The American Polity. New York: The Free Press, 1962. P-G (3+1=4)

Monsen, Joseph R., and Mark W. Cannon, The Makers of Public Policy: American Power Groups and Ideologies. New York: McGraw-Hill, 1965. G-T-P (4+0=4)

Nagel, Stuart, and Marian Neef, Legal Policy Analysis. Lexington, MA: Lexington Books, 1977. P (0+2=2)

Niskanen, William A., Bureaucracy and Representative Government. Chicago: Aldine Publishing Co., 1971. G-B-O-F (0+6=6)

Olson, Mancur, Jr., The Logic of Collective Action: Public Goods and the Theory of Groups. Cambridge: Harvard University Press, 1965. O-B-P-G (5+3=8)

Ranney, Austin, ed., Political Science and Public Policy. Chicago: Markham Publishing Company, 1968. P-G (0+3=3)

Riker, William H., The Theory of Political Coalitions. New Haven: Yale University Press, 1962. B-P-U (2+2=4)

Schattschneider, E. E., The Semi-Sovereign People. New York: Holt, Rinehart & Winston, 1960. M-P-U-G (2+3=5)

Schelling, Thomas C., The Strategy of Conflict. Cambridge: Harvard University Press, 1960. M-P-G (2+1=3)

Schultze, Charles L., The Public Use of Private Interest. Washington, DC: The Brookings Institution, 1977. P-F (0+2=2)

Sharkansky, Ira, ed., Policy Analysis in Political Science. Chicago: Markham Books, 1970. F-P-G (0+5=5)

Stigler, George J., The Theory of Price. New York: Macmillan Publishing Co., 1946. Subsequent eds. P (0+2=2)

Sundquist, James L., Politics and Policy: The Eisenhower, Kennedy and Johnson Years. Washington, DC: The Brookings Institution, 1968. P-F-U-G (3+3=6)

Truman, David, The Governmental Process. New York: Alfred A. Knopf, 1951. M-O-G-P-F-U (10+5=15)

Tullock, Gordon, The Politics of Bureaucracy. Washington, DC: Public Affairs Press, 1965. O-B-P-F-G (4+3=7)

Wade, L. L., and R. L. Curry, Jr., A Logic of Public Policy: Aspects of Political Economy. Belmont, CA: Wadsworth Publishing Company, 1970. G-P (0+3=3)

Wildavsky, Aaron, Speaking Truth to Power: The Art and Craft of Policy Analysis. Boston: Little, Brown & Co., 1979. G (0+2=2)

Wilson, Woodrow, Congressional Government. Cleveland: Meridian Books, 1885. P-M-G (2+1=3)

Wolfinger, Raymond E., The Politics of Progress. Englewood Cliffs, NJ: Prentice-Hall, 1974. U (0+2=2)

Zeigler, Harmon, Interest Groups in American Society. Englewood Cliffs, NJ: Prentice-Hall, 1964. M-P (3+0=3)

Policy and Administration:
Domestic Programs and Regulation

Bailey, Stephen, Congress Makes a Law. New York: Columbia
University Press, 1950. P-M-F (6+0=6)

Bauer, Raymond, Ithiel de Sola Pool and Lewis Dexter, American Business and Public Policy: The Politics of Foreign
Trade. New York: Atherton Press, 1963. P-M-F (3+2=5)

Cary, William L., Politics and the Regulatory Agencies. New
York: McGraw-Hill, 1967. G-P (3+0=3)

Coleman, James S., Equality of Educational Opportunity.
Washington, DC: Government Printing Office, 1966. P-T
(0+2=2)

Cushman, Robert E., The Independent Regulatory Commissions.
New York: Oxford University Press, 1941. M-P (3+0=3)

Eidenberg, E., and R. D. Morey, An Act of Congress: The
Legislative Process and the Making of Education Policy.
New York: Norton, 1969. P-M (0+2=2)

Glazer, Nathan, Affirmative Discrimination: Ethnic Inequality
and Public Policy. New York: Basic Books, 1975. M-G
(0+3=3)

Kohlmeier, Louis M., The Regulators: Watchdog Agencies and
the Public Interest. New York: Harper & Row, 1969. M
(0+2=2)

Krasnow, Erwin G., and L. D. Langley, The Politics of Broad-
casting Regulation. New York: St. Martin's Press, 1973.
Subsequent eds. G (0+2=2)

Krislov, Samuel, and Lloyd D. Musolf, eds., The Politics of
Regulation. Boston: Houghton Mifflin, 1964. P-F-G
(3+1=4)

Lawrence, Samuel A., United States Merchant Shipping Policies
and Politics. Washington, DC: The Brookings Institution,
1966. P (2+1=3)

Leiserson, Avery, Administrative Regulation. Chicago: University of Chicago Press, 1942. P (3+0=3)

Levitan, Sar A., The Great Society's Poor Law. Baltimore: Johns Hopkins University Press, 1969. P-U (3+1=4)

Mangum, Garth L., MDTA: Foundation of Federal Manpower Policy. Baltimore: Johns Hopkins University Press, 1967. M-U-P (3+1=4)

Mund, Vernon A., Government and Business. New York: Harper & Row, 1950. Subsequent eds. M-P (3+0=3)

Piven, Frances Fox, and Richard A. Cloward, Regulating the Poor: The Functions of Public Welfare. New York: Pantheon, 1971. U-G (0+2=2)

Schwartz, Bernard, The Professor and the Commissions. New York: Alfred A. Knopf, 1959. P-G (2+1=3)

Sheppard, Harold L., Bennett Harrison and William J. Spring, eds., The Political Economy of Public Service Employment. Lexington, MA: Lexington Books, 1972. M (0+2=2)

Wolman, Harold, Politics of Federal Housing. New York: Dodd, Mead & Company, 1971. G-P (0+2=2)

Steiner, Gilbert Y., Social Insecurity: The Politics of Welfare. Chicago: Rand McNally, 1966. P-U-M (5+1=6)

Policy and Administration:
International, Military, and Science Policy

Art, Robert J., The TFX Decision. Boston: Little, Brown & Co., 1968. P-G (2+1=3)

Brooks, Harvey, The Government of Science. Cambridge: MIT Press, 1968. T-P (3+0=3)

Clark, Keith C., and Laurence J. Legere, eds., The President and the Management of National Security. New York: Frederick A. Praeger, 1969. P-G (3+0=3)

Croly, Herbert, <u>The Promise of American Life</u>. New York:
Macmillan Publishing Co., 1909. U-M (0+2=2)

Davis, James W., and Kenneth M. Dolbeare, <u>Little Groups of
Neighbors: The Selective Service System</u>. Chicago:
Markham Publishing Company, 1968. P-G (4+1=5)

Dupre, J. Stefan, and Sanford A. Lakoff, <u>Science and the
Nation</u>. Englewood Cliffs, NJ: Prentice-Hall, 1962. T-P
(3+0=3)

Fann, K. T., and Donald C. Hodges, eds., <u>Readings in U.S.
Imperialism</u>. Boston: Porter Sargent, Inc., 1971. P
(2+1=3)

Gilpin, Robert, and Christopher Wright, eds., <u>Scientists and
National Policy-making</u>. New York: Columbia University
Press, 1964. T-P (3+0=3)

Jarrett, Henry, ed., <u>Environmental Quality in a Growing Econ-
omy</u>. Baltimore: Johns Hopkins University Press, 1966. T
(2+1=3)

Kahn, Herman, <u>On Thermonuclear War</u>. Princeton: Princeton
University Press, 1960. M-P (3+0=3)

Kennedy, Robert F., <u>Thirteen Days: A Memoir of the Cuban
Missle Crisis</u>. New York: W. W. Norton, 1969. G-P
(0+2=2)

Lyons, Gene M., and Louis Merton, <u>Schools for Strategy: Education and Research in National Security Affairs</u>. New
York: Frederick A. Praeger, 1965. P (3+0=3)

McNamara, Robert S., <u>The Essence of Security</u>. New York:
Harper & Row, 1968. M-P-T (2+1=3)

Peck, Merton J., and Frederick M. Scherer, <u>The Weapons
Acquisition Process</u>. Boston: Harvard Business School,
1962. M-P (4+0=4)

Price, Don K., <u>Government and Science</u>. New York: New
York University Press, 1954. T-P-M (5+0=5)

Price, Don K., The Scientific Estate. Cambridge: Harvard University Press, 1965. G-P (3+2=5)

Proxmire, William, Report from Wasteland: America's Military-Industrial Complex. New York: Frederick A. Praeger, 1970. T-P-M (2+1=3)

Skolnikoff, Eugene B., Science, Technology and American Foreign Policy. Cambridge: MIT Press, 1967. G-T (3+0=3)

Smith, Bruce L. R., The Rand Corporation. Cambridge: Harvard University Press, 1966. O-P (4+0=4)

Snow, C. P., Science and Government. Cambridge: Harvard University Press, 1961. G-T-P (3+2=5)

Policy and Administration:
American Government and Politics

Anderson, Patrick, The President's Men. Garden City, NY: Anchor Books, 1969. G-B (0+2=2)

Baldwin, Leland D., Reframing the Constitution. An Imperative for Modern America. Santa Barbara, CA: American Bibliographical Center, Clio Press, 1972. G-U (0+2=2)

Barber, James D., Power in Committees. Chicago: Rand McNally, 1966. O-P-F-G (2+2=4)

Barber, James D., The Presidential Character. Englewood Cliffs, NJ: Prentice-Hall, 1972. Subsequent ed. P (0+2=2)

Bryce, James, The American Commonwealth. New York: Macmillan Publishing Co., 1917. M-U (0+2=2)

Cronin, Thomas E., and Sanford D. Greenberg, eds., The Presidential Advisory System. New York: Harper & Row, 1969. G-P (2+2=4)

Domhoff, G. William, Who Rules America? Englewood Cliffs, NJ: Prentice-Hall, 1967. G-U (0+2=2)

Fenno, Richard, The President's Cabinet. Cambridge: Harvard University Press, 1959. P-G (3+2=5)

Greenstein, Fred I., The American Party System and the American People. Englewood Cliffs, NJ: Prentice-Hall, 1964. B-M (0+2=2)

Gross, Bertram, The Legislative Struggle. New York: McGraw-Hill, 1953. P-G (2+1=3)

Jewel, Malcolm, and Samuel Patterson, The Legislative Process in the United States. New York: Random House, 1966. P-F (2+1=3)

Keefe, William J., and Morris S. Ogul, The American Legislative Process. Englewood Cliffs, NJ: Prentice-Hall, 1964. P (2+1=3)

Key, V. O., Jr., Public Opinion and American Democracy. New York: Alfred A. Knopf, 1961. P-M (3+0=3)

King, Anthony, ed., The New American Political System. Washington, DC: American Enterprise Institute, 1978. P (0+2=2)

Koenig, Louis W., The Chief Executive. New York: Harcourt, Brace & World, 1968. Subsequent eds. G-P-M (4+2=6)

Mayhew, David R., Congress: The Electoral Connection. New Haven: Yale University Press, 1974. P (0+3=3)

Milbrath, Lester, Washington Lobbyists. Chicago: Rand McNally, 1963. P-G-M (2+3=5)

Neustadt, Richard, Presidential Power. New York: John Wiley & Sons, 1960. P-B-F-O-G (5+5=10)

Peabody, Robert, and Nelson Polsby, New Perspectives on the House of Representatives. Chicago: Rand McNally, 1963. P-G (2+1=3)

Redford, Emmette S., David B. Truman, Andrew Hacker, Alan
    F. Weston, and Robert C. Wood, Politics and Government
    in the United States. New York: Harcourt, Brace and
    World, 1965. P-F (0+2=2)

Rossiter, Clinton, The American Presidency. New York:
    Harcourt, Brace & World, 1956. Subsequent ed. P-G
    (2+2=4)

Schlesinger, Arthur, A Thousand Days. Boston: Houghton
    Mifflin, 1965. O-M (0+2=2)

Schlesinger, Joseph A., Ambition and Politics: Political
    Careers in the United States. Chicago: Rand McNally &
    Company, 1966. B-U (0+2=2)

Schubert, Glendon, Judicial Policy-Making. Chicago: Scott,
    Foresman & Company, 1965. P-U (2+1=3)

Sorensen, Theodore, Decision-Making in the White House. New
    York: Columbia University Press, 1963. P-B-F (5+1=6)

Truman, David, ed., The Congress and America's Future.
    Englewood Cliffs, NJ: Prentice-Hall, 1965. Subsequent
    eds. B-P (0+2=2)

Welch, Susan, and J. G. Peters, eds., Legislative Reform and
    Public Policy. New York: Praeger, 1977. P (0+2=2)

STATE AND LOCAL ADMINISTRATION

Intergovernmental Relations

Anderson, Martin, The Federal Bulldozer: A Critical Analysis of Urban Renewal. Cambridge: MIT Press, 1964. U-M (3=0=3)

Anderson, William, Intergovernmental Relations in Review. Minneapolis: University of Minnesota Press, 1960. U (2+2=4)

Anderson, William, The Nation and the States: Rivals or Partners? Minneapolis: University of Minnesota Press, 1957. U (2+1=3)

Aron, Joan B., The Quest for Regional Cooperation: A Study of the New York Metropolitan Regional Council. Berkeley: The University of California Press, 1969. U (3+0=3)

Bannett, Walter H., American Theories of Federalism. University, AL: University of Alabama Press, 1964. U (2+1=3)

Benson, George C. S., The Politics of Urbanism: The New Federalism. Woodbury, NY: Barron's Educational Series, 1972. U (0+2=2)

Bingham, Richard D., Public Housing and Urban Renewal: An Analysis of Federal-Local Relations. New York: Praeger Publishers, 1975. U (0+2=2)

Boyer, Brian D., Cities Destroyed for Cash: The FHA Scandal at HUD. Chicago: Follett Publishing Company, 1973. U-M (0+2=2)

Break, George F., Intergovernmental Fiscal Relations in the United States. Washington, DC: The Brookings Institution, 1967. U-F (3+2=5)

Carroll, James D., and Richard W. Campbell, eds., Intergovernmental Administration. Syracuse, NY: Maxwell School of Citizenship and Public Affairs, Syracuse University, 1976. G-U (0+2=2)

Caputo, David A., and Richard L. Cole, Revenue Sharing. Lexington, MA: D. C. Heath & Co., 1976. F-U (0+2=2)

Caputo, David A., and Richard L. Cole, Urban Politics and Decentralization. Lexington, MA: Lexington Books, 1974. U-M (0+3=3)

Cleaveland, Frederic N., et al., eds., Congress and Urban Problems. Washington, DC: The Brookings Institution, 1969. U-P (3+2=5)

Cole, Richard L., and David Caputo, Urban Politics and Decentralization: The Case of General Revenue-Sharing. Lexington, MA: Lexington Books, 1974. U (0+2=2)

Derthick, Martha, Between State and Nation. Washington, DC: The Urban Institute, 1972. B-U (0+2=2)

Dommel, Paul R., The Politics of Revenue Sharing. Bloomington: Indiana University Press, 1974. U (0+4=4)

Duchacek, Ivo D., Comparative Federalism. New York: Holt, Rinehart & Winston, 1970. U (0+2=2)

Elazar, Daniel J., American Federalism: A View from the States. New York: Thomas Y. Crowell, 1966. Subsequent eds. U-P-M-G (3+10=13)

Elazar, Daniel J., The American Partnership. Chicago: The University of Chicago Press, 1962. U (2+1=3)

Elazar, Daniel J., et al., eds., Cooperation and Conflict: Readings in American Federalism. Itasca, IL: F. E. Peacock Publishers, 1969. U (2+1=3)

Elazar, Daniel J., The Politics of American Federalism. Lexington, MA: D. C. Heath & Company, 1969. U (2+1=3)

Fesler, James W., Area and Administration. University, AL: University of Alabama Press, 1949. O-M-U-B-G (6+4=10)

Foss, Phillip O., Politics and Grass: The Administration of Grazing of the Public Domain. Seattle: University of Washington Press, 1960. U-P (2+1=3)

Glendening, Parris N., and Mavis Mann Reeves, Pragmatic Federalism. Pacific Palisades, CA: Palisades Publishers, 1977. U-G (0+4=4)

Goldwin, Robert, ed., A Nation of States. Chicago: Rand McNally & Company, 1961. G-U (2+2=4)

Graves, W. Brooke, American Intergovernmental Relations. New York: Charles Scribners's Sons, 1964. U-G (3+4=7)

Grodzins, Morton, The American System. Chicago: Rand McNally & Company, 1966. U-P-G (7+5=12)

Grosenick, Leigh E., ed., The Administration of the New Federalism: Objectives and Issues. Washington, DC: American Society for Public Adminisration, 1973. U-M (0+2=2)

Haider, Donald H., When Governments Come to Washington: Governors, Mayors, and Intergovernmental Lobbying. New York: Free Press, 1974. U-G (0+5=5)

Juster, F. Thomas, ed., The Economic and Political Impact of General Revenue Sharing. Washington, DC: National Science Foundation/Research Applied to National Needs, April, 1976. U-M (0+3=3)

Key, V. O., Jr., The Administration of Federal Grants to the States. Chicago: Public Administration Service, 1937. G-U (0+2=2)

Leach, Richard H., American Federalism. New York: W. W. Norton & Co., 1970. G-U (0+4=4)

Lilienthal, David E., TVA: Democracy on the March. New York: Harper & Brothers, 1953. U-G (2+1=3)

Maass, Arthur, ed., Area and Power: A Theory of Local Government. Glencoe, IL: Free Press, 1959. B-U (0+3=3)

MacMahon, Arthur W., John D. Millett and Gladys Ogden, The Administration of Federal Work Relief. Chicago: Public Administration Service, 1941. O-M-U (3+0=3)

MacMahon, Arthur, W., ed., Federalism: Mature and Emergent. New York: Russell & Russell, 1955. M-U-B (3+2=5)

Martin, Roscoe C., The Cities and the Federal System. New York: Atherton Press, 1965. U-G-P-M (4+4=8)

May, R. J., Federalism and Fiscal Adjustment. New York: Oxford University Press, 1969. F-U (2+1=3)

Nathan, Richard P., Allen D. Manuel, Suzannah E. Calkings and associates, Monitoring Revenue Sharing. Washington, DC: The Brookings Institution, 1975. U-F-M-G (0+7=7)

Nathan, Richard P., Charles F. Adams, and associates, Revenue Sharing: The Second Round. Washington, DC: The Brookings Institution, 1977. U-F (0+3=3)

Pressman, Jeffrey L., Federal Programs and City Politics: The Dynamics of the Aid Process in Oakland. Berkeley: University of California Press, 1975. U (0+5=5)

Reagan, Michael D., and John G. Sanzone, The New Federalism. New York: Oxford University Press, 1972. Subsequent ed. P-U-M-G (0+8=8)

Reuss, Henry S., Revenue-Sharing. New York: Praeger Publishers, 1970. U-P (2+3=5)

Riker, William H., Federalism: Origin, Operation and Significance. Boston: Little, Brown & Co., 1964. U-G (2+3=5)

Sanford, Terry, Storm Over the States. New York: McGraw-Hill, 1967. U-P (3+4=7)

Sharkansky, Ira, The Maligned States: Policy Accomplishments, Problems, and Opportunities. New York: McGraw-Hill, 1972. Subsequent ed. G (0+2=2)

Thompson, Richard E., Revenue Sharing: A New Era in Federalism. Washington, DC: Revenue Sharing Advisory Service, 1973. U-F-U (0+3=3)

Wagner, Richard E., The Fiscal Organization of American Federalism. Chicago: Markham Publishing Company, 1971. F (0+2=2)

Wheare, K. C., Federal Government. New York: Oxford University Press, 1946. U (2+2=4)

Wood, Robert C., 1400 Governments: The Political Economy of the New York Metropolitan Region. Cambridge: Harvard University Press, 1962. U-P (2+1=3)

Wright, Deil S., Federal Grants-in-Aid: Perspectives and Alternatives. Washington, DC: American Enterprise Institute for Public Policy Research, 1968. U-M (0+4=4)

Wright, Deil S., Understanding Intergovernmental Relations. North Scituate, MA: Duxbury Press, 1978. G-U (0+3=3)

State and Local Government

Adrian, Charles R., and Charles Press, Governing Urban America. New York: McGraw Hill, 1968. U-F-M (2+3=5)

Adrian, Charles R., State and Local Governments. New York: McGraw-Hill Book Company, 1960. Subsequent eds. M (0+2=2)

Allen, Ivan, Jr., Mayor: Notes on the Sixties. New York: Simon and Schuster, 1971. U (0+2=2)

Altshuler, Alan A., The City Planning Process. Ithaca, NY: Cornell University Press, 1965. U-O-P-G (3+2=5)

Banfield, Edward C., and James Q. Wilson, City Politics. Cambridge: Harvard University Press, 1963. U-B-M (2+4=6)

Banfield, Edward C., Political Influence. New York: Free Press, 1962. U-P (2+3=5)

Banovetz, James M. ed., Managing the Modern City. Washington, DC: International City Management Association, 1971. M-F-U (0+4=4)

Berkley, George E., The Democratic Policeman. Boston: Beacon Press, 1969. U-G (0+2=2)

Beyle, Thad, and J. Oliver Williams, eds., The American Governor in Behavioral Perspective. New York: Harper & Row, 1972. U (0+2=2)

Bollens, John C., John R. Bayes and Kathryn L. Utter, American County Government. Beverly Hills, CA: Sage Publications, 1969. M-U (0+2=2)

Bollens, John C., and John C. Ries, The City Manager Profession: Myths and Realities. Chicago: Public Administration Service, 1969. U (0+2=2)

Bollens, John C., and Henry J. Schmandt, The Metropolis: Its People, Politics and Economic Life. New York: Harper & Row, 1965. Subsequent eds. U (0+2=2)

Brown, F. Gerald, and Thomas P. Murphy, eds., Emerging Patterns in Urban Administration. Lexington, MA: Lexington Books, 1970. U-O (0+2=2)

Campbell, Alan K., Metropolitan America. New York: The Free Press, 1967. U-P-F (2+2=4)

Campbell, Alan K., ed., The States and the Urban Crisis. Englewood Cliffs, NJ: Prentice-Hall, 1970. U (2+2=4)

Cole, Richard L., Citizen Participation and the Urban Policy Process. Lexington, MA: D. C. Heath & Co., 1974. G (0+2=2)

Committee for Economic Development, A Fiscal Program for a Balanced Federalism. New York: Committee for Economic Development, 1967. G-U (3+0=3)

Committee for Economic Development, Modernizing Local Government. New York: Committee for Economic Development, 1966. U-P-M (2+1=3)

Committee for Economic Development, Modernizing State Government. New York: Committee for Economic Development, 1967. G-P-U-M (3+1=4)

Committee for Economic Development, Reshaping Metropolitan Government. New York: Committee for Economic Development, 1970. U-M (2+1=3)

Costikyan, Edward N., and Maxwell Lehman, Restructuring the Government of New York City: Report of the Scott Commission Task Force on Jurisdiction and Structure. New York: Praeger, 1972. U (0+2=2)

Devlin, Thomas C., Municipal Reform in the United States. New York: Putnam, 1896. M (0+2=2)

Eisenberg, Terry, Robert H. Fosen and Albert S. Glickman, Police-Community Action: A Program for Change in Police-Community Behavior Patterns. New York: Praeger, 1973. U (0+2=2)

Fantini, Mario, and Marilyn Gittell, Decentralization: Achieving Reform. New York: Praeger, 1973. U-G-B (0+3=3)

Fowler, Floyd J., Citizen Attitudes Toward Local Government Services and Taxes. Cambridge, MA: Ballinger Publishing Co., 1974. U (0+3=3)

Fox, Douglas M., The Politics of City and State Bureaucracy. Pacific Palisades, CA: Goodyear Publishing Co., 1974. U (0+3=3)

Frederickson, H. George, ed., Neighborhood Control in the 1970's. New York: Chandler, 1973. G-U (0+2=2)

Gerwin, Donald, Budgeting Public Funds: The Decision Process
in a Urban School District. Madison: University of Wisconsin Press, 1969. U-O-F-P (2+2=4)

Gittell, Marilyn, et al., School Boards and School Policy. New
York: Praeger, 1973. U-B (0+2=2)

Gleason, Bill, Daley of Chicago. New York: Simon and
Schuster, 1970. U-M (0+3=3)

Glendening, Parris N., and Mavis Mann Reeves, Controversies
of State and Local Political Systems. Boston: Allyn and
Bacon, 1972. U (0+2=2)

Grant, Daniel R., and H. C. Nixon, State and Local Government in America. Boston: Allyn and Bacon, 1963. Subsequent eds. U (0+2=2)

Greenstone, J. David, and Paul E. Peterson, Race and Authority in Urban Politics: Community Participation and the
War on Poverty. New York: Basic Books, 1973. U
(0+2=2)

Greer, Ann L., The Mayor's Mandate: Municipal Statecraft and
Political Trust. Cambridge, MA: Schenkman Publishing
Co., 1974. U (0+2=2)

Hawley, Willis D., and David Rogers, eds., Improving the Quality of Urban Management. Beverly Hills, CA: Sage Publications, 1974. Subsequent abridged ed. M-U (0+6=6)

Heller, Walter W., and Richard Ruggles, Revenue Sharing and
the City. Baltimore: Johns Hopkins University Press,
1968. U-F (2+1=3)

Hofferbert, Richard I., and Ira Sharkansky, eds., State and
Urban Politics. Boston: Little, Brown & Co., 1971. F-U
(0+2=2)

Jacob, Herbert, and Kenneth N. Vines, eds., Politics in the
American States. Boston: Little, Brown & Company,
1965. Subsequent eds. P-U-F (4+3=7)

Kotler, Milton, Neighborhood Government: The Local Foundations of Political Life. Indianapolis: Bobbs-Merrill, 1969. G-U (0+2=2)

Kotter, John P., and Paul R. Lawrence, Mayors in Action: Five Approaches to Urban Governance. New York: Wiley-Interscience, 1974. U-P (0+5=5)

Levine, Charles H., Racial Conflict and the American Mayor. Lexington, MA: Lexington Books, 1974. U (0+3=3)

Lindsay, John V., The City. New York: W. W. Norton, 1969. U (0+2=2)

Long, Norton E., The Unwalled City. New York: Basic Books, 1972. U (0+2=2)

Loveridge, Ronald D., City Managers in Legislative Politics. Indianapolis: Bobbs-Merrill, 1971. U (0+3=3)

Martin, Roscoe C., Metropolis in Transition: Local Government Adaptation to Changing Urban Needs. Washington, DC: Government Printing Office, 1963. U (0+2=2)

Mogulof, Melvin B., Governing Metropolitan Areas: A Critical Review of Councils of Government and the Federal Role. Washington, DC: The Urban Institute, 1971. U-G (0+4=4)

Nordlinger, Eric A., Decentralizing the City: A Study of Boston's Little City Halls. Cambridge, MA: MIT Press, 1972. U (0+2=2)

Rakove, Milton, Don't Make No Waves--Don't Back No Losers: An Insider's Analysis of the Daley Machine. Bloomington: University of Indiana Press, 1974. U (0+2=2)

Ransone, Coleman B., Jr., The Office of Governor in the United States. University, AL: University of Alabama Press, 1956. U (0+2=2)

Rogers, David, 110 Livingston Street: Politics and Bureaucracy in the New York School System. New York: Random House, 1968. U-B (0+2=2)

Rogers, David, The Management of Big Cities: Interest Groups and Social Change Strategies. Beverly Hills, CA: Sage Publications, 1971. U (0+2=2)

Royko, Mike, Boss: Richard J. Daley of Chicago. New York: E. P. Dutton, 1971. U-M (0+4=4)

Sayre, Wallace, and Herbert Kaufman, Governing New York City. New York: Russell Sage Foundation, 1960. U-P-M (3+2=5)

Shalala, Donna E., Neighborhood Government: Issues and Proposals. New York: American Jewish Committee, 1971. U (0+2=2)

Sharkansky, Ira, Regionalism in American Politics. Indianapolis: Bobbs-Merrill, 1970. U (0+2=2)

Steggert, Frank X., Community Action Groups and City Governments. Cambridge, MA: Ballinger, 1975. U (0+2=2)

Stillman, Richard J., The Rise of the City Manager: A Public Professional in Local Government. Albuquerque: University of New Mexico Press, 1974. U (0+2=2)

Stokes, Carl B., Promises of Power: A Political Autobiography. New York: Simon and Schuster, 1973. U (0+2=2)

Talbot, Allan R., The Mayor's Game: Richard Lee of New Haven and the Politics of Change. New York: Praeger, 1967. U (0+2=2)

Teaford, Jon C., The Municipal Revolution in America; Origins of Modern Urban Government, 1650-1825. Chicago: University of Chicago Press, 1975. U-M (0+2=2)

Wilson, James Q., The Amateur Democrat: Club Politics in Three Cities. Chicago: University of Chicago Press, 1962. U-B (3+0=3)

Wilson, James Q., ed., City Politics and Public Policy. New York: John Wiley & Sons, 1968. U-P-G (5+2=7)

Wilson, James Q., ed., Urban Renewal. Cambridge: MIT Press, 1966. U-P (2+2=4)

Wirt, Frederick M., Power in the City: Decision Making in San Francisco. Berkeley: University of California Press, 1974. U (0+2=2)

Yates, Douglas, Neighborhood Democracy: The Politics and Impacts of Decentralization. Lexington, MA: Lexington Books, 1973. U (0+2=2)

Yin, Robert K., and Douglas Yates, Street-Level Governments: Assessing Decentralization and Urban Services. Lexington, MA: Lexington Books, 1975. U (0+3=3)

Zimmerman, Joseph F., The Federated City: Community Control in Large Cities. New York: St. Martin's Press, 1972. U-G (0+3=3)

Zink, Harold, City Bosses in the United States. Durham, NC: Duke University Press, 1930. B-U (0+2=2)

Urban Social Systems

Agger, Robert, Daniel Goldrich and Bert Swandon, The Rulers and the Ruled. New York: John Wiley & Sons, 1964. U-P (3+0=3)

Alford, Robert F., Bureaucracy and Participation: Political Cultures in Four Wisconsin Cities. Chicago: Rand McNally, 1969. U-O-M-G (2+2=4)

Altshuler, Alan A., Community Control: The Black Demand for Participation in Large American Cities. New York: Pegasus, 1970. U-B (2+3=5)

Bailey, Robert, Jr., Radicals in Urban Politics: The Alinsky Approach. Chicago: University of Chicago Press, 1974. U (0+2=2)

Banfield, Edward C., The Unheavenly City Revisited. Boston: Little, Brown & Co., 1974. G-U (0+3=3)

Clark, Terry N., ed., Community Structure and Decision-Making. San Francisco: Chandler Publishing Company, 1968. B-U (2+1=3)

Crain, Robert L., Elihu Katz and Donald B. Rosenthal, The Politics of Community Conflict: The Fluoridation Decision. Indianapolis: The Bobbs Merrill Company, 1969. P-U (2+1=3)

Downs, Anthony, Opening Up the Suburbs: An Urban Strategy for America. New Haven: Yale University Press, 1974. U (0+2=2)

Downs, Anthony, Urban Problems and Prospects. Chicago: Markham, 1970. U-F (0+2=2)

Elazar, Daniel J., Cities of the Prairie: The Metropolitan Frontier and American Politics. New York: Basic Books, 1970. U-M (0+2=2)

Ginzberg, Eli, Manpower Strategy for the Metropolis. New York: Columbia University Press, 1968. U-M-T (3+0=3)

Greenberg, Stanley B., Politics and Poverty: Modernization Response in Five Poor Neighborhoods. New York: John Wiley & Sons, 1974. U (0+2=2)

Harrison, Bennett. Public Employment and Urban Poverty. Washington, DC: The Urban Institute, 1971. U-M (0+2=2)

Haskell, Mark A., The New Careers Concept: Potential for Public Employment of the Poor. New York: Praeger, 1969. U-M (0+2=2)

Hunter, Floyd, Community Power Structure. Chapel Hill: University of North Carolina Press, 1953. U-O (2+1=3)

Lewin, David, et al., The Urban Labor Market: Institutions, Information, Linkages. New York: Praeger, 1974. U (0+2=2)

Marris, Peter, and Martin Rein, Dilemmas of Social Reform. New York: Atherton Press, 1967. U (2+1=3)

Murphy, Thomas P., and John Rehfuss, Urban Politics in the Suburban Era. Homewood, IL: Dorsey Press, 1976. U (0+3=3)

O'Brien, David J., Neighborhood Organization and Interest Group Process. Princeton, NJ: Princeton University Press, 1975. U (0+2=2)

Schmandt, Henry J., and Warner Bloomberg, The Quality of Urban Life. Beverly Hills, CA: Sage Publications, 1969. U (2+1=3)

Silberman, Charles, Crisis in Black and White. New York: Random House, 1964. M-P-U (3+0=3)

COMPARATIVE PUBLIC ADMINISTRATION

Administration and Planning in Developing Countries

Adu, A. L., The Civil Service in New African States. New York: Frederick A. Praeger, 1965. C (4+1=5)

Caiden, Naomi, and Aaron Wildavsky, Planning and Budgeting in Poor Countries. New York: John Wiley & Sons, 1974. B-F-G-C (0+6=6)

Daland, Robert T., Brazilian Planning. Chapel Hill: University of North Carolina Press, 1967. O-C (3+0=3)

Gant, George F., Development Administration: Concepts, Goals, Methods. Madison: University of Wisconsin Press, 1979. G-C (0+2=2)

Goodnow, H. F., The Civil Service of Pakistan. New Haven: Yale University Press, 1964. C-O-B (4+1=5)

Gross, Bertram M., ed., Action Under Planning. New York: McGraw-Hill, 1967. T-C-B (2+2=4)

Heady, Ferrel, and Sybil L. Stokes, eds., Papers in Comparative Public Administration. Ann Arbor: University of Michigan Press, 1962. C-M-O-B (5+3=8)

Heady, Ferrel, Public Administration: A Comparative Perspective. New York: Marcel Dekker, 1966. Subsequent eds. O-G-M-B-C (4+6=10)

Hirschman, Albert O., Development Projects Observed. Washington, DC: The Brookings Institution, 1967. P-B (0+2=2)

Hsueh, S. S., ed., Public Administration in South and East Asia. Brussels: International Institute of Administrative Sciences, 1962. C (2+1=3)

Kingsburg, Joseph B., and Tahir Aktan, The Public Service in Turkey. Brussels: International Institute for Administrative Sciences, 1955. C-B (2+1=3)

Kriesberg, M., ed., Public Administration in Developing Countries. Washington, DC: The Brookings Institution, 1965. C-O (2+1=3)

Mason, Edward, Economic Planning in Underdeveloped Areas. New York: Fordham University Press, 1958. C-M-B (3+0=3)

Matthews, A. T. J., Emergent Turkish Administrators. Ankara: University of Ankara, 1955. C-B (2+1=3)

Meyer, Paul, Administrative Organization: A Comparative Study of the Organization of Public Administration. London: Stevens, 1957. C-O-B (3+1=4)

Raphaeli, Nimrod, ed., Readings in Comparative Public Administration. Boston: Allyn & Bacon, Inc., 1967. G-O-C-M (4+3=7)

Sharp, W. A., Field Administration in the United Nations System. New York: Frederick A. Praeger, 1961. M-U-C-B (4+0=4)

Swerdlow, Irving, ed,. Development Administration. Syracuse: Syracuse University Press, 1963. C-M-B (5+2=7)

Thurber, Clarence E., and Lawrence S. Graham, eds., Development Administration in Latin America. Durham, NC: Duke University Press, 1973. C (0+2=2)

Waterston, Albert, Development Planning: Lessons of Experience. Baltimore: Johns Hopkins Press, 1965. B-F-C (0+3=3)

Waterston, Albert, Planning in Pakistan. Baltimore: Johns Hopkins University Press, 1963. C-F (2+1=3)

Weidner, Edward W., Technical Assistance in Public Administration Overseas. Chicago: Public Administrative Service, 1964. G-C-B (5+2=7)

Wickwar, W. Hardy, Modernization of Administration in the Near East. London: Constable & Company, 1963. C-B (3+0=3)

Younger, Kenneth, The Public Service in New States. New York: Oxford University Press, 1960. O-M-C-B (5+1=6)

Developing Political and Social Systems

Almond, Gabriel A., and Sidney Verba, The Civic Culture. Princeton, NJ: Princeton University Press, 1963. O-P-F-C (4+2=6)

Almond, Gabriel, and James Coleman, The Politics of the Developing Areas. Princeton, NJ: Princeton University Press, 1960. C-M-B (5+2=7)

Apter, David, Ghana in Transition. New York: Atheneum Publishers, 1963. C-M (2+1=3)

Apter, David, The Politics of Modernization. Chicago: University of Chicago Press, 1965. C (2+2=4)

Berger, Morroe, Bureaucracy and Society in Modern Egypt. Princeton, NJ: Princeton University Press, 1957. C-O-B (3+2=5)

Braibanti, Ralph, and Joseph Spengler, Administrative and Economic Development in India. Durham, NC: Duke University Press, 1963. C-O-B (4+1=5)

Braibanti, Ralph, ed., Asian Bureaucratic Systems Emergent from the British Imperial Tradition. Durham, NC: Duke University Press, 1966. C-B (3+2=5)

Braibanti, Ralph, ed., Political and Administrative Development. Durham, NC: Duke University Press, 1969. C (0+3=3)

Braibanti, Ralph, Research on the Bureaucracy of Pakistan. Durham, NC: Duke University Press, 1966. B-C (2+2=4)

Braibanti, Ralph, and Joseph J. Spengler, eds., Tradition, Values and Socio-Economic Development. Durham, NC: Duke University Press, 1961. C (0+2=2)

Cox, Robert W., and Harold K. Jacobson, The Anatomy of Influence: Decision Making in International Organizations. New Haven: Yale University Press, 1973. B-C (0+2=2)

Eisenstadt, Shmuel N., Modernization: Protest and Change. Englewood Cliffs, NJ: Prentice-Hall, 1966. G-P-B-C (3+1=4)

Eisenstadt, Shmuel N., The Political Systems of Empires. New York: The Free Press, 1963. G-C (0+2=2)

Fallers, Lloyd A., Bantu Bureaucracy. Chicago: University of Chicago Press, 1965. C-B (2+1=3)

Fortes, Meyer, and E. E. Evans-Pritchard, eds., African Political Systems. New York: Oxford University Press, 1958. B-M (3+0=3)

Frank, Andre Gunder, Latin-America: Underdevelopment or Revolution. New York: Monthly Review Press, 1970. C (0+2=2)

Hagan, Everett, On the Theory of Social Change. Homewood, IL: The Dorsey Press, 1962. M-C-B (4+0=4)

Heaphey, James J., ed., Spatial Dimensions of Development Administration. Durham, NC: Duke University Press, 1971. C (0+2=2)

Hirschman, Albert O., Journeys Toward Progress: Studies of Economic Policymaking in Latin America. New York: Twentieth Century Fund, 1963. C-P-B-M (5+0=5)

Hirschman, Albert O., The Strategy of Economic Development. New Haven: Yale University Press, 1958. C-M-B (3+0=3)

Huntington, Samuel P., Political Order in Changing Societies. New Haven: Yale University Press, 1968. C-B (0+2=2)

Janowitz, Morris, The Military in the Political Development of New Nations. Chicago: University of Chicago Press, 1964. C-T-B (3+1=4)

Johnson, John, The Role of the Military in Underdeveloped Countries. Princeton, NJ: Princeton University Press, 1962. C-B (3+1=4)

La Palombara, Joseph G., ed., Bureaucracy and Political Development. Princeton, NJ: Princeton University Press, 1963. G-O-B-C (4+2=6)

La Palombara, Joseph, and Myron Wiener, eds., Political Parties and Political Development. Princeton, NJ: Princeton University Press, 1966. B-C (0+2=2)

Leibenstein, Harvey, Economic Backwardness and Economic Growth. New York: John Wiley & Sons, 1957. C-O-M (3+0=3)

Lerner, Daniel, The Passing of Traditional Society. New York: The Free Press, 1958. C (3+1=4)

McClelland, David, The Achieving Society. Princeton: D. Van Nostrand Company, 1961. C-O-T-M-P-G (8+2=10)

Montgomery, John D., and William J. Siffen, eds., Approaches to Development. New York: McGraw-Hill, 1966. M-C-B (4+2=6)

Price, Robert M., Society and Bureaucracy in Contemporary Ghana. Berkeley: University of California Press, 1975. C (0+2=2)

Pye, Lucian W., Aspects of Political Development. Boston: Little, Brown & Company, 1966. O-P-B-C (3+2=5)

Pye, Lucian W., and Sydney Verba, Political Culture and Political Development. Princeton, NJ: Princeton University Press, 1965. C (2+1=3)

Riggs, Fred W., Administration in Developing Countries: The Theory of Prismatic Society. Boston: Houghton Mifflin Company, 1965. G-O-C-B-M (6+4=10)

Riggs, Fred W., Administrative Reform and Political Responsiveness: A Theory of Dynamic Balancing. Beverly Hills, CA: Sage Publications, 1971. C (0+2=2)

Riggs, Fred W., The Ecology of Public Administration. New York: Asia Publishing House, 1961. B-O-C-G (7+2=9)

Riggs, Fred W., ed., Frontiers of Development Administration. Durham, NC: Duke University Press, 1970. C (0+3=3)

Riggs, Fred W., ed. Thailand: The Modernization of a Bureaucratic Polity. Honolulu: East-West Center Press, 1965. C-B (3+2=5)

Rogers, Everett M., Diffusion of Innovations. New York: The Free Press, 1962. M-C-O (2+2=4)

Russett, Bruce M., et al., World Handbook of Political and Social Indicators. New Haven: Yale University Press, 1964. C-U (2+1=3)

Scott, James C., Comparative Political Corruption. Englewood Cliffs, NJ: Prentice-Hall, 1972. B-C (0+2=2)

Siffin, William J., The Thai Bureaucracy. Honolulu: East-West Center Press, 1966. C (2+1=3)

Siffin, William J., ed., Toward the Comparative Study of Public Administration. Bloomington, IN: Department of Government, Indiana University, 1957. O-B-C-M (4+3=7)

Steiner, Kurt, Local Government in Japan. Stanford, CA: Stanford University Press, 1965. U-C (3+0=3)

Tilman, Robert O., Bureaucratic Transition in Malaya. Durham, NC: Duke University Press, 1964. C-B (3+1=4)

Uphoff, Norman T., and Warren F. Ilchman, eds., The Political Economy of Development: Theoretical and Empirical Contributions. Berkeley: University of California Press, 1972. C (0+2=2)

Waldo, Dwight, ed., <u>Temporal Dimensions of Development Administration</u>. Durham, NC: Duke University Press, 1970. C (0+2=2)

Ward, Robert E., and D. A. Rustow, <u>Political Modernization in Japan and Turkey</u>. Princeton, NJ: Princeton University Press, 1964. C-B (3+1=4)

Weiner, Myron, <u>Politics of Scarcity</u>. Chicago: University of Chicago Press, 1962. C-M (3+0=3)

Wraith, Ronald, and E. Simpkins, <u>Corruption in Developing Countries</u>. London: Allen & Unwin, 1963. C-B (3+2=5)

PUBLIC PERSONNEL ADMINISTRATION

Public Personnel Systems

Aronson, Sidney H., Status and Kinship in the Higher Civil Service: Standards of Selection in the Administrations of John Adams, Thomas Jefferson and Andrew Jackson. Cambridge: Harvard University Press, 1964. M-O (2+2=4)

Bakke, E. Wright., The Mission of Manpower Policy. Kalamazoo, MI: The W. E. Upjohn Institute for Employment Research, 1969. U-M-G (2+2=4)

Beach, Dale, ed., Managing People at Work: Readings in Personnel. New York: Macmillan Publishing Company, 1975. G-M (0+2=2)

Bendix, Reinhard. Higher Civil Servants in American Society. Boulder: University of Colorado Press, 1949. M-O-B (2+1=3)

Cayer, N. Joseph, Public Personnel Administration in the United States. New York: St. Martin's Press, 1975. G (0+2=2)

Chapman, Brian, The Profession of Government: The Public Service in Europe. Westport, CT: Greenwood Press, 1959. G-O-M-C (4+3=7)

Corson, John J., and Paul R. Shale, Men Near the Top. Baltimore: Johns Hopkins University Press, 1966. G-O-M (4+4=8)

Crouch, Winston W., ed., Local Government Personnel Administration. Washington, DC: International City Management Association, 1976. M (0+3=3)

278

Dale, H. E., The Higher Civil Service of Great Britain. New
York: Oxford University Press, 1941. M-B (0+2=2)

Dogon, M., ed., The Mandarins of Western Europe: The Political Role of Top Civil Servants. New York: John Wiley &
Sons, 1975. C-B (0+2=2)

Donovan, J. J., ed., Recruitment and Selection in the Public
Service. Chicago: Public Personnel Association, 1968.
G-M (0+2=2)

Fear, Richard A., The Evaluation Interview. New York:
McGraw-Hill Book Company, 1958. Subsequent eds. M
(0+2=2)

Fish, Carl Russell, The Civil Service and the Patronage.
Cambridge: Harvard University Press, 1904. G-M (0+3=3)

Foulke, William Dudley, Fighting the Spoilsmen: Reminiscences
of the Civil Service Reform Movement. New York and
London: G. P. Putnam's Sons, 1919. G-B (0+2=2)

French, Wendell, The Personnel Management Process. Boston:
Houghton Mifflin, 1964. M-T (3+2=5)

Friedrich, Carl J., et al., Problems of the American Public
Service. New York: McGraw-Hill, 1935. M (0+2=2)

Golembiewski, Robert T., and Michael Cohen, eds., People in
the Public Service: A Reader in Public Personnel Administration. Itasca, IL: F. E. Peacock Publishers, 1970.
Subsequent eds. G-M (0+5=5)

Gordon, Robert A., and J. E. Howell, Higher Education for
Business. New York: Columbia University Press, 1959. M
(3+0=3)

Glueck, William F., Personnel: A Diagnostic Approach.
Homewood, IL: Business Publications, 1974. M-G (0+2=2)

Hammer, U. Clay, Contemporary Problems in Personnel. Chicago: St. Claire Press, 1974. M-G (0+2=2)

Harvey, Donald R., The Civil Service Commission. New York: Praeger Publishers, 1970. G-M (0+4=4)

Heclo, Hugh, A Government of Strangers. Washington, DC: The Brookings Institution, 1977. M-P-G (0+7=7)

Hoogenboom, Ari, Outlawing the Spoils: A History of the Civil Service Reform Movement, 1865-1883. Urbana: University of Illinois Press, 1961. M (0+2=2)

House, Robert J., Management Development. Ann Arbor: Graduate School of Business Administration, University of Michigan, 1967. M-O-G (2+1=3)

Huntington, Samuel P., The Soldier and the State. New York: Vintage Books, 1957. M-P (3+0=3)

Janowitz, Morris, The Professional Soldier. New York: The Free Press, 1960. M-B-P-O (6+0=6)

Jongeward, Dorothy, and Dru Scott, Affirmative Action for Women: A Practical Guide. Reading, MA: Addison-Wesley Publishing Company, 1974. M (0+2=2)

Kammerer, Gladys M., Impact of War on Federal Personnel Administration, 1939-1945. Lexington: University of Kentucky Press, 1951. M (0+2=2)

Kilpatrick, Franklin P., Milton C. Cummings, and M. Kent Jennings, The Image of the Federal Service. Washington, DC: The Brookings Institution, 1964. M-O-G (2+3=5)

Kilpatrick, Franklin P., et al., Source Book of a Study of Occupational Values and the Image of the Federal Service. Washington, DC: The Brookings Institution, 1964. O-P (2+1=3)

Kranz, Harry, The Participatory Bureaucracy: Women and Minorities in a More Representative Public Service. Lexington, MA: D. C. Heath & Co., 1976. M-G (0+2=2)

Krislov, Samuel, The Negro in Federal Employment. The Quest for Equal Opportunity. Minneapolis: University of Minnesota Press, 1967. G-M (0+3=3)

Krislov, Samuel, Representative Bureaucracy. Englewood Cliffs, NJ: Prentice Hall, 1974. C-M-O-G (0+7=7)

Lopez, Felix M., Jr., Evaluating Employee Performance. Chicago: Public Personnel Association, 1968. G-M (0+2=2)

Macy, John W., Jr., Public Service: The Human Side of Government. New York: Harper & Row, 1971. G-M (0+4=4)

Mann, Dean E., and J. W. Doig, The Assistant Secretaries: Problems and Processes of Appointment. Washington, DC: The Brookings Institution, 1965. M-P-G (2+2=4)

Megginson, Leon C., Personnel: A Behavioral Approach to Administration. Homewood, IL: Irwin Press, 1967. M-G (2+1=3)

Mosher, Frederick C., Democracy and the Public Service. New York: Oxford University Press, 1968. M-O-P-U-C-G (6+15=21)

Mosher, William E., and J. Donald Kingsley, Public Personnel Administration. New York: Harper & Brothers, 1936. Subsequent eds. M (0+2=2)

Nigro, Felix A., and Lloyd G. Nigro, The New Public Personnel Administration. Itasca, IL: F. E. Peacock Publishers, 1976. Subsequent ed. M-G (0+5=5)

Nigro, Felix A., Public Personnel Administration. New York: Holt Publishers, 1959. M (3+0=3)

Odiorne, George S., Personnel Administration by Objectives. Homewood, IL: Richard D. Irwin, 1971. M (0+2=2)

Odiorne, George S., Personnel Policy: Issues and Practices. Columbus, OH: Charles E. Merrill Publishing Company, 1963. M-G (2+1=3)

Patten, Thomas H., Jr., Manpower Planning and the Development of Human Resources. New York: John Wiley & Sons, 1971. M (0+2=2)

Pfiffner, John M., and Marshall Fels, The Supervision of Personnel: Human Relations in the Management of Men. Englewood Cliffs, NJ: Prentice-Hall, 1951. Subsequent eds. M (3+1=4)

Pigors, Paul, and Charles A. Myers, Personnel Administration. New York: McGraw-Hill, 1947. Subsequent eds. M-T (3+2=5)

Powell, Norman J., Personnel Administration in Government. Englewood Cliffs, NJ: Prentice-Hall, 1956. B-M (0+2=2)

Rosenbloom, David H., Federal Service and the Constitution: The Development of the Public Employment Relationship. Ithaca, NY: Cornell University Press, 1971. G-M (0+3=3)

Sadacca, Robert, The Validity and Discriminatory Impact of the Federal Service Entrance Examination. Washington, DC: The Urban Institute, September, 1971. M (0+2=2)

Sayre, Wallace S., ed., The Federal Government Service. Englewood Cliffs, NJ: Prentice-Hall, 1954. Subsequent eds. G-O-M (0+3=3)

Shafritz, Jay M., ed., A New World: Readings on Modern Public Personnel Management. Chicago: International Personnel Management Association, 1975. G-M (0+6=6)

Shafritz, Jay M., Position Classification: A Behavioral Analysis for the Public Service. New York: Praeger, 1973. G-M (0+4=4)

Siegel, Gilbert B., ed., Human Resource Management in Public Organizations. Los Angeles: University Publishers, 1972. M-G (0+4=4)

Smith, Darrell Hevenor, The United States Civil Service Commission: Its History, Activities and Organization. Baltimore: Johns Hopkins University Press, 1928. G-M (0+2=2)

Stahl, O. Glenn, The Personnel Job of Government Managers. Chicago: International Personnel Management Association, 1971. M-G (0+4=4)

Stahl, O. Glenn, Public Personnel Administration. New York: Harper & Row, 1936. Subsequent eds. M-C-G (2+11=13)

Stanley, David T., The Higher Civil Service. Washington, DC: The Brookings Institution, 1964. M-O-P-G-C (3+4=7)

Stanley, David T., et al., Men Who Govern: A Biographical Profile of Federal Political Executives. Washington, DC: The Brookings Institution, 1967. M-P (2+2=4)

Stewart, Frank Mann, The National Civil Service Reform League: History, Activities and Problems. Austin: University of Texas Press, 1929. G-M (0+2=2)

Strauss, George, and Leonard R. Sayles, Personnel: The Human Problems of Management. Englewood Cliffs, NJ: Prentice-Hall, 1960. Subsequent eds. M-O-T-G (4+2=6)

Thompson, Frank J., Personnel Policy in the City: The Politics of Jobs in Oakland. Berkeley: University of California Press, 1977. M-G (0+6=6)

Tilove, Robert, Public Employee Pension Funds: A Twentieth Century Fund Report. New York: Columbia University Press, 1976. M (0+2=2)

Tolchin, Martin, and Susan Tolchin, To the Victor: Political Patronage From the Clubhouse to the White House. New York: Random House, 1971. M (0+2=2)

Van Riper, Paul P., History of the United States Civil Service. Evanston, IL: Row, Peterson and Company, 1958. O-M-C-G (2+7=9)

Vaughn, Robert G., The Spoiled System. New York: Charterhouse, 1972. M-G (0+5=5)

Warner, W. Lloyd, et al., The American Federal Executive. New Haven: Yale University Press, 1963. G-O-P-M (6+2=8)

Warren, Malcolm W., Training for Results. Reading, MA: Addison-Wesley Publishing Company, 1969. M-G (0+2=2)

Yoder, Dale, Personnel Management and Industrial Relations. Englewood Cliffs, NJ: Prentice-Hall, 1938.   Subsequent eds. G-M-T (3+0=3)

Labor Relations in Public Employment

Chickering, A. Lawrence, ed., Public Employee Unions; A Study of the Crisis in Public Sector Labor Relations. Lexington, MA: D. C. Heath & Company, 1976. G-M (0+3=3)

Flynn, Ralph J., Public Work, Public Workers. Washington, DC: New Republic, 1975. U (0+2=2)

Gershenfeld, Walter J., Joseph Lowenberg, and Bernard Ingster, eds., Scope of Public-Sector Bargaining. Lexington, MA: Lexington Books, 1977. M (0+2=2)

Heisel, W. D., and J. D. Hallihan, Questions and Answers on Public Employee Negotiation. Chicago: Public Personnel Association, 1967. M (0+2=2)

Horton, Raymond D., Municipal Labor Relations in New York City: Lessons of the Lindsey-Wagner Years. New York: Praeger, 1973. M-G (0+2=2)

Juris, Harvey A., and Peter Feuille, Police Unionism: Power and Impact in Public Sector Bargaining. Lexington, MA: Lexington Books, 1973. U-M (0+2=2)

Nesbitt, Murray B., Labor Relations in the Federal Government Service. Washington, DC: The Bureau of National Affairs, 1976. M (0+4=4)

Nigro, Felix A., Management-Employee Relations in the Public Service. Chicago: Public Personnel Association, 1969. G-M (0+4=4)

Pops, Gerald M., Emergence of the Public Sector Arbitrator. Lexington, MA: D. C. Heath & Company, 1976. M (0+2=2)

Reynolds, Lloyd G., Labor Economics and Labor Relations.
    Englewood Cliffs, NJ: Prentice-Hall, 1949.   Subsequent
    eds. M-G (2+2=4)

Richardson, Reed C., Collective Bargaining by Objectives.
    Englewood Cliffs, NJ: Prentice-Hall, 1977. M (0+2=2)

Schick, Richard P., and Jean J. Couturier, The Public Interest
    in Government Labor Relations.   Cambridge, MA: Bal-
    linger Publishing Company, 1977. M (0+2=2)

Stagner, Ross, and Hjalmar Rosen, Psychology of Union-Man-
    agement Relations.   Belmont: Wadsworth Co., 1965.
    M-T-G (2+2=4)

Stanley, David T., Managing Local Government Under Union
    Pressure.   Washington, DC: The Brookings Institution,
    1972. G-M (0+4=4)

Stieber, Jack, Public Employee Unionism; Structure, Growth,
    Policy. Washington, DC: The Brookings Institution, 1973.
    G-M (0+6=6)

Wellington, Harry H., and Ralph K. Winter, Jr., The Unions and
    the Cities.   Washington, DC: The Brookings Institution,
    1971. U-G-M (0+3=3)

Weitzman, Joan, The Scope of Bargaining in Public Employ-
    ment. New York: Praeger, 1975. U (0+2=2)

Zagoria, Sam, ed., Public Workers and Public Unions.   Engle-
    wood Cliffs, NJ: Prentice-Hall, 1972. M-G (0+4=4)

BUDGETING AND FINANCE

Public Finance

Anderson, James E., ed., Politics and Economic Policy-Making. Reading, MA: Addison-Wesley, 1970. F (2+1=3)

Anderson, William H., Financing Modern Governments: The Political Economy of the Public Sector. Boston: Houghton Mifflin Co., 1973. G-F (0+2=2)

Aronson, J. Richard, and Eli Swartz, eds., Management Policies in Local Government Finance. Washington, DC: International City Management Association, 1975. F-M (0+4=4)

Bahl, Roy, and Walter Vogt, Fiscal Centralization and Tax Burdens: State and Regional Finance of City Services. Cambridge, MA: Ballinger Publishing Co., 1975. U-F (0+2=2)

Bator, Francis, The Question of Government Spending. New York: Harper & Row, 1960. P-B-F (5+1=6)

Benson, Georges, et al., eds., The American Property Tax: Its History, Administration and Economic Impact. Clairmont, CA: Institute for Studies in Federalism, Clairmont College, 1965. F (0+2=2)

Blinder, Alan S., et al., The Economics of Public Finance. Washington, DC: The Brookings Institution, 1974. F (0+2=2)

Buchanan, James M., Public Finance in Democratic Process. Chapel Hill: University of North Carolina Press, 1962. P-F-G (2+1=3)

Buchanan, James M., and Marilyn R. Flowers, The Public Finances: An Introductory Textbook. Homewood, IL: Richard D. Irwin, 1960. Subsequent eds. F (0+4=4)

Burkhead, Jesse, and Jerry Minar, Public Expenditure. New York: Aldine-Atherton, 1971. F (0+4=4)

Crecine, John P., ed., Financing the Metropolis: Public Policy in Urban Economics. Beverly Hills, CA: Sage Publications, 1970. F-U (0+3=3)

Due, John F., Government Finance. Homewood, IL: Richard D. Irwin, 1954. Subsequent eds., F (2+2=4)

Ecker-Racz, L. Laszio, It's Your Business: Local and State Finance. New York: National Municipal League, 1976. F (0+2=2)

Ecker-Racz, L. Laszio, The Politics and Economics of State-Local Finance. Englewood Cliffs, NJ: Prentice-Hall, 1970. U-F (2+5=7)

Eckstein, Otto, Public Finance. Englewood Cliffs, NJ: Prentice-Hall, 1964. Subsequent eds. F-T-G (3+4=7)

Gross, Malvern J., Jr., Financial and Accounting Guide for Nonprofit Organizations. New York: Ronald Press, 1972. Subsequent eds. T-F (0+2=2)

Groves, Harold M., Financing Government. New York: Holt, Rinehart & Winston, 1939. Subsequent eds. F (2+3=5)

Haveman, Robert H., The Economics of the Public Sector. New York: John Wiley & Sons, 1970. Subsequent eds. F-G (0+3=3)

Hay, Leon B., and R. M. Mikesell, Governmental Accounting. Homewood, IL: Richard D. Irwin, 1974. T-F (0+2=2)

Heller, Walter W., New Dimensions of Political Economy. New York: W. W. Norton Company, 1967. F-P-U-G-B (6+6=12)

Hirsch, Werner Z., The Economics of State and Local Government. New York: McGraw-Hill, 1970. P-F (0+2=2)

Keynes, John Maynard, The General Theory of Employment, Interest and Money. New York: Harcourt, Brace & World, 1936. M-F-B (2+1=3)

Kirst, Michael W., Government Without Passing Laws. Chapel Hill: University of North Carolina Press, 1969. F-P-G (2+2=4)

Lewis, Wilfred, Jr., Federal Fiscal Policy in the Postwar Recessions. Washington, DC: The Brookings Institution, 1962. F (4+0=4)

Manley, John F., The Politics of Finance. Boston: Little, Brown & Company, 1970. F-G (2+2=4)

Maxwell, James A., Financing State and Local Governments. Washington, DC: The Brookings Institution, 1965. Subsequent eds. G-U-F (4+5=9)

Meltsner, Arnold J. The Politics of City Revenue. Berkeley and Los Angeles: University of California Press, 1971. U-G-F (0+5=5)

Moak, Lennox L., Administration of Local Governmental Debt. Chicago: Municipal Finance Officers Association, 1970. F (0+2=2)

Moak, Lennox L., and Albert M. Hillhouse, Concepts and Practices in Local Government Finance. Chicago: Municipal Finance Officers Association, 1975. F-M 0+4=4)

Mosher, Frederick C., and Orville F. Poland, The Costs of American Governments. New York: Dodd, Mead and Company, 1964. U-F (3+0=3)

Musgrave, Richard A., ed., Essays in Fiscal Federalism. Washington, DC: The Brookings Institution, 1965. U-F (3+0=3)

Musgrave, Richard A., and Peggy B. Musgrave, Public Finance in Theory and Practice. New York: McGraw-Hill, 1973. Subsequent eds. P-F-M (0+6=6)

Musgrave, Richard A., The Theory of Public Finance. New York: McGraw-Hill, 1959. F-B-G (4+1=5)

Mushkin, Selma, ed., Public Prices for Public Products. Washington, DC: The Urban Institute, 1972. F-M (0+2=2)

Netzer, Dick, Economics of the Property Tax. Washington, DC: The Brookings Institution, 1966. P-F (2+1=3)

Okun, Arthur M., The Political Economy of Prosperity. Washington, DC: The Brookings Institution, 1970. F (3+0=3)

Oldman, Oliver, and Ferdinand P. Schoettle, State and Local Taxes and Finance: Text, Problems and Cases. Mineola, NY: Foundation Press, 1974. G-F (0+2=2)

Pechman, Joseph A., Federal Tax Policy. Washington, DC: The Brookings Institution, 1966. Subsequent eds. F-G (2+8=10)

Peterson, George E., ed., Property Tax Reform. Washington, DC: The Urban Institute, 1973. F (0+2=2)

Samuelson, Paul A., Economics. New York: McGraw-Hill, 1948. Subsequent eds. F-M (0+2=2)

Scott, Claudia D., Forecasting Local Government Spending. Washington, DC: The Urban Institute, 1972. U-F (0+4=4)

Sharkansky, Ira, The Politics of Taxing and Spending. Indianapolis: Bobbs-Merrill Company, 1969. F-U-P-G (6+8=14)

Shoup, Carl S., Public Finance. Chicago: Aldine Publishing Company, 1969. F (2+1=3)

Steiss, Alan Walter, Local Government Finance. Lexington, MA: D. C. Heath/Lexington Books, 1975. F (0+2=2)

Wallace, Robert A., Congressional Control of Federal Spending. Detroit: Wayne State University Press, 1960. F-G (2+1=3)

The Budgetary Process

Anton, Thomas J., The Politics of State Expenditures in Illinois. Urbana: University of Illinois Press, 1966. F-P-U-G (2+6=8)

Argyris, Chris, The Impact of Budgets on People. New York: Controllership Foundation, 1950. F (0+2=2)

Bahl, Roy, Metropolitan City Expenditures. Lexington: University of Kentucky Press, 1968. F (0+2=2)

Balutis, Alan P., and Daron K. Butler, The Political Purse-strings: The Role of the Legislature in the Budgetary Process. New York: Halstead Press, 1975. F (0+2=2)

Blechmon, Barry E., Edward M. Gramlick, and Robert W. Hartman, Setting National Priorities: The 1976 Budget. Washington, DC: The Brookings Institution, 1976. F-M (0+2=2)

Brundage, Percival Flack, The Bureau of the Budget. New York: Praeger, 1970. F (0+3=3)

Buck, Arthur Eugene, The Budget in Government of Today. New York: Macmillan Publishing Co., 1934. F (0+2=2)

Buck, Arthur Eugene, Public Budgeting. New York: Harper & Row, 1929. F (0+2=2)

Burkhead, Jesse, Government Budgeting. New York: John Wiley & Sons, 1956. F-G-M-T (5+8=13)

Burkhead, Jesse, and Paul Bringewatt, Municipal Budgeting: A Primer for the Elected Official. Syracuse, NY: Syracuse University Press, 1974. F (0+2=2)

Chartrand, Robert, Kenneth Janda, and Michael Hugo, eds., Information Support, Program Budgeting and the Congress. New York: Spartan, 1968. F (0+2=2)

Cheek, Logan M., Zero Base Budgeting Comes of Age. New York: American Management Association, 1977. M-F (0+3=3)

Committee for Economic Development, Budgeting for National Objectives. New York: The Committee for Economic Development, 1966. F-P-M (3+0=3)

Crecine, John P., Governmental Problem Solving: A Computer Simulation of Municipal Budgeting. Chicago: Rand McNally, 1969. P-T-F (2+5=7)

Davies, James W., Jr., ed., Politics, Programs and Budgets. Englewood Cliffs, NJ: Prentice-Hall, 1969. F-U-G (3+4=7)

Doubleday, D. Jay, Legislative Review of the Budget in California. Berkeley: Institute of Governmental Studies, University of California, 1967. F (0+2=2)

Fenno, Richard F., The Power of the Purse: Appropriation Politics in Congress. Boston: Little, Brown & Company, 1966. F-P-G (4+9=13)

Fisher, Louis, Presidential Spending Power. Princeton, NJ: Princeton University Press, 1975. F-U (0+4=4)

Golembiewski, Robert T., and Jack Rabin, eds., Public Budgeting and Finance. Itasca, IL: F. E. Peacock Publishers, 1968. Subsequent eds. F-O-G-U (6+2=8)

Heclo, Hugh, and Aaron Wildavsky, The Private Government of Public Money: Community and Policy Inside British Politics. Berkeley: University of California Press, 1974. Subsequent ed. C-F (0+2=2)

Hofstede, Geert H., The Game of Budget Control: How to Live With Budgetary Standards and Yet Be Motivated By Them. New York: Humanities Press, 1968. F-T (0+2=2)

Horn, John Stephen, Unused Power: The Work of the Senate Committee on Appropriations. Washington, DC: The Brookings Institution, 1970. G-F-P (0+4=4)

Hovey, Harold A., The Planning-Programming-Budgeting Approach to Government Decision-Making. New York: Frederick A. Praeger, 1968. F-T-P (2+1=3)

Howard, S. Kenneth, Changing State Budgeting. Lexington, KY: Council of State Governments, 1973. G-F (0+6=6)

Howard, Kenneth S., and Gloria A. Grizzle, Whatever Happened to State Budgeting? Lexington, KY: Council of State Governments, 1972. F (0+2=2)

Ippolito, Dennis S., The Budget and National Politics. New York: W. H. Freeman & Co., 1978. G (0+2=2)

Lee, Robert D., and Ronald W. Johnson, Public Budgeting Systems. Baltimore: University Park Press, 1973. Subsequent eds. G-F-M (0+7=7)

LeLoup, Lance, Budgetary Politics: Dollars, Deficits, Decisions. Brunswick, NJ: King's Court Communications, 1977. F-P-G (0+6=6)

Levy, Frank S., Arnold J. Meltsner, and Aaron Wildavsky, Urban Outcomes: Schools, Streets and Libraries. Berkeley: University of California Press, 1974. P-B-F-U (0+5=5)

Lewis, Wilfred, Jr., ed., Budget Concepts for Economic Analysis. Washington, DC: The Brookings Institution, 1968. F-G (3+0=3)

Lord, Guy, The French Budgetary Process. Berkeley: University of California Press, 1973. F (0+2=2)

Lyden, Fremont J., and Ernest G. Miller, eds., Public Budgeting: Program Planning and Implementation. Englewood Cliffs, NJ: Prentice-Hall, 1968. Subsequent eds. G-U-P-M-F-T (7+13=20)

McKean, Roland N., Public Spending. New York: McGraw-Hill, 1968. F-G (0+2=2)

Merewitz, Leonard, and Stephen H. Sosnick, The Budget's New Clothes. Chicago: Markham Publishing Company, 1971. G-F-B-M (0+10=10)

Moak, Lennox L., and Kathryn W. Killian, A Manual of Techniques for the Preparation, Consideration, Adoption, and Administration of Operating Budgets. Chicago: Municipal Finance Officers Association, 1963. F-M (0+2=2)

Mosher, Frederick C., Program Budgeting: Theory and Practice. Chicago: Public Administration Service, 1954. T-F-G (0+3=3)

Mowitz, Robert J., The Design and Implementation of Pennsylvania's Planning, Programming, Budgeting System. University Park, PA: Institute of Public Administration, Pennsylvania State University, 1970. G-T-M (0+3=3)

Nienaber, Jeanne, and Aaron Wildavsky, The Budgeting and Evaluation of Federal Recreation Programs. New York: Basic Books, 1973. F (0+2=2)

Novick, David, ed., Current Practice in Program Budgeting (PPBS): Analysis and Case Studies Covering Government and Business. New York: Crane, Russak, 1973. G-F-M (0+3=3)

Novick, David, Origin and History of Program Budgeting. Santa Monica, CA: The Rand Corporation, 1966. F (0+2=2)

Novick, David, ed., Program Budgeting. Cambridge: Harvard University Press, 1965. G-U-M-P-F-T-B (9+8=17)

Ott, David J., and F. Attiat Ott, Federal Budget Policy. Washington, DC: The Brookings Institution, 1965. Subsequent eds. F-G (4+7=11)

Pechman, Joseph, ed., Setting National Priorities: The 1978 Budget. Washington, DC: The Brookings Institution, 1977. Issued Annually. F (0+2=2)

Proxmire, William. Uncle Sam: The Last of the Bigtime Spenders. New York: Simon & Schuster, 1972. G-F (0+2=2)

Pyhrr, Peter A., Zero Base Budgeting. New York: John Wiley & Sons, 1973. M-G-F (0+9=9)

Sarant, Peter C., Zero-Base Budgeting in the Public Sector: A Pragmatic Approach. Reading, MA: Addison-Wesley Publishing Company, 1978. F (0+2=2)

Schick, Allen, Budget Innovation in the States. Washington,
DC: The Brookings Institution, 1971. G-F-B-M (0+11=11)

Schultze, Charles L., The Politics and Economics of Public
Spending. Washington, DC: The Brookings Institution,
1968. G-F-P-M-B (7+7=14)

Smithies, Arthur, The Budgetary Process in the United States.
New York: McGraw-Hill, 1955. F-M (4+2=6)

Stedry, Andrew C., Budget Control and Cost Behavior. Englewood Cliffs, NJ: Prentice-Hall, 1960. F (0+2=2)

Steiss, Allan W., Public Budgeting and Management. Lexington,
MA: D. C. Heath and Company, 1972. F (0+3=3)

Wanat, John, Introduction to Budgeting. North Scituate, MA:
Duxbury Press, 1978. F-G (0+3=3)

Wildavsky, Aaron, Budgeting: A Comparative Theory of Budgetary Process. Boston: Little, Brown & Co., 1975.
M-B-F-G (0+5=5)

Wildavsky, Aaron, The Politics of the Budgetary Process.
Boston: Little, Brown & Company, 1964.
G-O-U-P-B-M-F-T (15+21=36)

Index